Lucas Malet, Dissident Pilgrim

Popular novelist, female aesthete, Victorian radical, and proto-modernist, Lucas Malet (Mary St. Leger Harrison, 1852–1931) was one of the most successful writers of her day, yet few of her remarkable novels remain in print. Malet was a daughter of the 'broad church' priest and well-known Victorian author Charles Kingsley; her sister, Rose; her uncle, Henry Kingsley; and her cousin Mary Henrietta Kingsley were also published authors. Malet was part of a creative dynasty from which she drew inspiration but against which she rebelled, both in her personal life and in her published work. This collection brings together for the first time a selection of scholarly essays on Malet's life and writing, foregrounding her contributions to nineteenth- and twentieth-century discourses surrounding disability; psychology; religion; sexuality; the New Woman; and decadent, aesthetic, and modernist cultural movements. The essays contained in this volume explore Malet's authorial experience—from both within the mainstream of the British literary tradition and, curiously, from outside it—supplementing and nuancing current debates about *fin-de-siècle* women's writing. The collection asks the questions "who was Lucas Malet?" and "how—despite its popularity—did her courageous, unique, and fascinating writing disappear from view for so long?"

Jane Ford is a Lecturer in English Studies at Teesside University. She is a specialist in the literature and culture of the *fin de siècle*, and she is currently completing a monograph which examines the complex network of metaphors that emerged around late nineteenth-century conceptions of economic self-interest and exploitation. She is co-editor of *Economies of Desire at the Victorian Fin de Siècle: Libidinal Lives* (Routledge, 2016) and has published essays on Vernon Lee, Lucas Malet, and Bertram Mitford.

Alexandra Gray is a Visiting Lecturer in English Literature at the University of Portsmouth. Alexandra's research interests include the New Woman, *fin-de-siècle* literature and culture, art history and criticism, and medical and psychiatric history. She recently published her first monograph, *Self-Harm in New Woman Writing* (Edinburgh University Press, 2017), and has also written on the work of the Irish New Woman, George Egerton, hyperhidrosis in fiction, and the orphan figure in Victorian literature and culture. She is a co-editor of "The Gateless Barrier," an online impact project for the purposes of feminist literary recovery, featuring research on Lucas Malet's life and work.

Among the Victorians and Modernists

Edited by Dennis Denisoff

This series publishes monographs and essay collections on literature, art, and culture in the context of the diverse aesthetic, political, social, technological, and scientific innovations that arose among the Victorians and Modernists. Viable topics include, but are not limited to, artistic and cultural debates and movements; influential figures and communities; and agitations and developments regarding subjects such as animals, commodification, decadence, degeneracy, democracy, desire, ecology, gender, nationalism, the paranormal, performance, public art, sex, socialism, spiritualities, transnationalism, and the urban. Studies that address continuities between the Victorians and Modernists are welcome. Work on recent responses to the periods such as Neo-Victorian novels, graphic novels, and film will also be considered.

10 **Edwardian Culture**
Beyond the Garden Party
Samuel Shaw, Sarah Shaw and Naomi Carle

11 **The Female Fantastic**
Gendering the Supernatural in the 1890s and 1920s
Edited by Elizabeth McCormick, Jennifer Mitchell, and Rebecca Soares

12 **Art, Race, and Fantastic Color Change in the Victorian Novel**
Jessica Durgan

13 **Philanthropy and Early Twentieth-Century British Literature**
Milena Radeva-Costello

14 **Lucas Malet, Dissident Pilgrim**
Critical Essays
Edited by Jane Ford and Alexandra Gray

For more information about this series, please visit: https://www.routledge.com/Among-the-Victorians-and-Modernists/book-series/ASHSER4035

Lucas Malet, Dissident Pilgrim

Critical Essays

Edited by
Jane Ford and
Alexandra Gray

New York London

First published 2019
by Routledge
52 Vanderbilt Avenue, New York, NY 10017

and by Routledge
2 Park Square, Milton Park, Abingdon, Oxon, OX14 4RN

First issued in paperback 2020

Routledge is an imprint of the Taylor & Francis Group, an informa business

Library of Congress Cataloging-in-Publication Data
Names: Ford, Jane, 1983– editor. | Gray, Alexandra (Senior Lecturer in English literature), editor.
Title: Lucas Malet, dissident pilgrim : critical essays / edited by Jane Ford and Alexandra Gray.
Description: New York, NY : Routledge, 2019. |
Series: Among the Victorians and modernists ; 14 | Includes bibliographical references and index. | Description based on print version record and CIP data provided by publisher; resource not viewed.
Identifiers: LCCN 2018048148 (print) | LCCN 2018058950 (ebook)
Subjects: LCSH: Malet, Lucas, 1852–1931—Criticism and interpretation.
Classification: LCC PR4759.H42 (ebook) | LCC PR4759.H42 Z748 2019 (print) | DDC 823/.8—dc23
LC record available at https://lccn.loc.gov/2018048148

ISBN 13: 978-0-367-66193-9 (pbk)
ISBN 13: 978-0-367-14615-3 (hbk)

Typeset in Sabon
by codeMantra

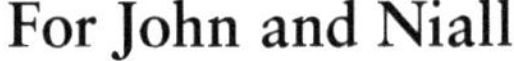
For John and Niall

Contents

Notes on Contributors

Louise Benson James is a doctoral candidate and teaching assistant at the University of Bristol. Her thesis, "Hysteria and the Gothic in Women's Fiction," examines the intersections of medical hysteria and gothic language in fiction by women and medical texts in the long nineteenth century. Her research explores the troubled distinction between metaphor and materiality in narratives of the body, and psychosomatic symptomologies, Victorian medical treatments and technologies, and constructions of masculinity and femininity through language and pathology. She is the co-editor of the *Postgraduate Journal of Medical Humanities* and coordinates the University of Bristol seminar series "Literary and Visual Landscapes."

Catherine Delyfer is currently Professor of English at the University of Toulouse, France. Her publications focus on *fin-de-siècle* culture and neglected late-Victorian female writers. She is the author of a monograph on Lucas Malet's pictorial poetics, *Art and Womanhood in Fin-de-Siècle Writing: the Fiction of Lucas Malet, 1880–1931* (Pickering and Chatto, 2011); a contributor to *The History of British Women's Writing, 1880–1920* (Holly Laird ed., Palgrave Macmillan, 2016); and the editor of two recent collections of essays, *Aesthetic Lives* (Rivendale Press, 2013, co-edited with B. Coste) and *Reconnecting Aestheticism and Modernism: Continuities, Revisions, Speculation* (Routledge, 2017, co-edited with B. Coste and C. Reynier).

Jill R. Ehnenn is Professor of English at Appalachian State University, where she teaches Victorian Studies. She also teaches LGBT Studies and Queer Theory in the Gender, Women's, and Sexuality Studies Program. She is the author of *Women's Literary Collaboration, Queerness and Late-Victorian Culture* (Ashgate, 2008) and of various articles on nineteenth-century female writers, including Michael Field, Vernon Lee, Elizabeth Siddal, and Dorothy Worthsworth. Her work on contemporary topics includes queering Harry Potter and reading the lesbian romance novel. Her current book project is titled *Michael Field's Revisionary Poetics* (Forthcoming, Edinburgh University Press).

Jane Ford is a Lecturer in English Studies at Teesside University. She is a specialist in the literature and culture of the *fin de siècle*, and she is currently completing a monograph which examines the complex network of metaphors that emerged around late nineteenth-century conceptions of economic self-interest and exploitation. She is co-editor of *Economies of Desire at the Victorian Fin de Siècle: Libidinal Lives* (Routledge, 2016) and has published essays on Vernon Lee, Lucas Malet, and Bertram Mitford.

Alexandra Gray is a Visiting Lecturer in English Literature at the University of Portsmouth. Alexandra's research interests include the New Woman, *fin-de-siècle* literature and culture, art history and criticism, and medical and psychiatric history. She has recently published her first monograph, *Self-Harm in New Woman Writing* (Edinburgh University Press, 2017), and has also written on the work of the Irish New Woman, George Egerton, hyperhidrosis in fiction, and the orphan figure in Victorian literature and culture. She is a co-editor of "The Gateless Barrier," an online impact project for the purposes of feminist literary recovery, featuring research on Lucas Malet's life and work.

Alani Hicks-Bartlett received a Joint PhD from the University of California, Berkeley, in Romance Languages and Literatures, and Medieval Studies, with a Designated Emphasis in Women, Gender and Sexuality Studies, in 2016. She is also a doctoral candidate in Modern Languages and Literatures at Middlebury College, where her research focuses on metaphors of artistic failure, dis/ability, and the corporeal fragmentation of women in late nineteenth-century literature. In recent years, she has received fellowships and grants to pursue work in digital humanities; a Middlebury Director Prize for Academic Excellence; a Ford Foundation Predoctoral Fellowship; and various language, poetry, and teaching awards.

Holly A. Laird is Frances W. O'Hornett Professor of English in the Henry Kendall College of Arts & Sciences at The University of Tulsa. She has published extensively on Victorian and modern literature, culture, and theory, especially turn-of-the-twentieth-century writing and transatlantic modernism. She is especially interested in women writers—having edited *Tulsa Studies in Women's Literature* from 1988 to 2005 and volume seven of *The History of British Women's Writing, 1880–1920* in 2016. Laird has a long-standing fascination with the lyric, which has led her to a book on D.H. Lawrence's poetic sequences and a second book on co-authored verse, fiction, and autobiographies, *Women Co-Authors*, as well as various articles on Michael Field, Elizabeth Barrett Browning, Edith Sitwell, and *fin-de-siècle* poetry, among other topics.

Patricia Lorimer Lundberg is Professor Emerita at Indiana University Northwest, having served on the faculty as Professor of English and Women's Studies for a number of years. She was a founding Executive Director of the Center for Regional Excellence and the Center for Cultural Discovery and Learning. Her doctorate is from Loyola University Chicago, where she also earned a BA Summa Cum Laude and a Masters in English. Her essays and literary biography of Lucas Malet, *An Inward Necessity: The Writer's Life of Lucas Malet*, (2003) are the culmination of decades of research on Malet. Between 2007–2018, she served as Executive Director of Humanities West in San Francisco and currently serves on the Boards of Directors of the Lundberg Institute and Ars Minerva.

Crescent Rainwater is a doctoral candidate and a Graduate Teaching Fellow at the University of California, Los Angeles. She is writing a thesis entitled "Twentieth-Century Victorians: Lucas Malet, Netta Syrett, Dorothy Richardson, and Fin-de-Siècle Culture in the Development of the English Novel." She is particularly interested in the way that English women novelists at the turn of the twentieth century were influenced by British aestheticism in their development of liberating narratives for their women protagonists. She has a biographical entry on Netta Syrett in *Companion to Victorian Popular Fiction* (McFarland, 2018). She was the recipient of the Grace M. Hunt English Reading Room Fellowship for Archival Research in summer 2016. She holds an MA in Gender, Sexuality, and Culture from University College Dublin.

Ruth Robbins is Professor of English and Director of Research for Cultural Studies at Leeds Beckett University. She is the author of *Literary Feminisms* (2000); *Pater to Forster* (2003); *Subjectivity* (2005); *Oscar Wilde* (2011); and, with Emma Liggins and Andrew Maunder, *The British Short Story* (2010).

Talia Schaffer is a Professor of English at Queens College, City University of New York (CUNY), and the Graduate Center, CUNY. She is the author of *Romance's Rival: Familiar Marriage in Victorian Fiction* (2016); *Novel Craft: Victorian Domestic Handicraft and Nineteenth-Century Fiction* (2011); and *The Forgotten Female Aesthetes; Literary Culture in Late-Victorian England* (2001). She has also co-edited and edited several special issues, scholarly editions, and collections. Her articles focus on Victorian familial, domestic, and marital norms, with special attention to women's writing and disability studies. Schaffer's current project, "Critical Care," explores 'ethics of care' as a way to read social relations in Victorian fiction.

Clare Walker Gore currently holds a Junior Research Fellowship at Trinity College, Cambridge, having studied for her BA, MPhil, and

PhD degrees at Selwyn College, Cambridge. She has published several articles on nineteenth-century topics, including "The Additional Attraction of Affliction: Disability, Sex and Genre Trouble in *Barchester Towers*" (*Victorian Literature and Culture,* 2017), "Noble Lives: Writing Masculinity and Disability in the Late Nineteenth Century" (*Nineteenth-Century Contexts*, 2014), and "'Setting Novels at Defiance': Novel Reading and Novelistic Form in Charlotte M. Yonge's *The Heir of Redclyffe*" (*Nineteenth-Century Gender* Studies, 2014). She has also edited a new edition of Dinah Mulock Craik's out-of-print novel *A Noble Life* (Victorian Secrets, 2016) and contributed chapters to several book collections, including *Queer Victorian Families: Curious Relations in Literature* (Routledge, 2015) and *The Variable Body in History* (Peter Lang, 2016). She was named one of the BBC/Arts and Humanities Research Council (AHRC) "New Generation Thinkers" for 2015/2016.

Acknowledgements

We would like to thank the *Journal of Literary & Cultural Disability Studies* for permission to reprint a revised version of Jill Ehnenn's essay "Reorienting the Bildungsroman: Progress Narratives, Queerness, and Disability in *The History of Sir Richard Calmady* and *Jude the Obscure*" in this volume (2017 11.2: 151–68). We also thank *The Henry James Review* for their permission to reprint a revised version of Talia Schaffer's essay "Some Chapter of Some Other Story: Henry James, Lucas Malet, and the Real Past of *The Sense of the Past*" (1996 17.2: 109–28). This research has been incredibly important in establishing Malet's influence and centrality within the *fin-de-siècle* literary landscape, and we are delighted to be able to bring together these path-breaking essays with exciting new scholarship to make the strongest case for her recovery. Thanks to L. Tom Perry Special Collections at Brigham Young University for granting permission to reproduce the transcript of "In Memoriam: Ernest D. Chesterfield" in the Appendix. We are also grateful to University College London Special Collections, Archives & Records for their helpful response to our enquiries about Malet's time at the Slade. Thanks are particularly due to Patricia Lorimer Lundberg for kindly agreeing to write the foreword for this volume. In a very real sense, Lundberg's detailed and meticulously researched biography has made our own critical reappraisals of Malet's work possible.

This volume is part of a broader set of initiatives to draw attention to the work of marginalised women writers of the late nineteenth and early twentieth centuries. Focusing initially on Malet, we facilitated a series of public reading groups—a venture that has been made possible by means of a crowdfunding campaign. After an unsuccessful funding application, we were touched that so many people saw the value of this initiative (especially in the current climate, when so many worthy causes compete for our investment). Many thanks, then, to all who supported the campaign and to the members of the public who shared our fascination with Malet's writing at an initial reading group in November 2017. Thanks to University Centre Shrewsbury for hosting and promoting this event.

Finally, we would like to thank our lovely contributors for their enthusiasm for this volume as well as John Redmond and Matthew Bradley for their comments. *Lucas Malet, Dissident Pilgrim* is dedicated to our partners, John Redmond and Niall Gray, who freed up our time to work on the collection and supported us (in innumerable ways) throughout the process.

Brief Chronology of Lucas Malet's Life and Works

1852 Mary St. Leger Kingsley is born on 4 June 1852 at Eversley Rectory in Hampshire, third child of Charles and Frances Kingsley (née Grenfell).

1872 Mary Kingsley is enrolled at Slade School of Fine Art. Her name only appears in the 1872–3 fees book, suggesting that she entered and left in the same academic year. Though she would not continue on this trajectory, her writing exhibits a sustained interest in the visual arts.

1875 Charles Kingsley dies on 23 January at the age of 55.

1876 18 July Mary Kingsley marries Rev. William Harrison (the late Charles Kingsley's curate) at St. Mary's Church in Byfleet, Surrey. The marriage would prove unhappy.

1882 *Mrs. Lorimer: A Sketch in Black and White*, Mary Harrison's first novel, published under the pseudonym Lucas Malet. *Mrs. Lorimer* dramatises the difficulties faced by a woman of artistic talent whose passions are checked at every turn.

1883 After a living becomes available, Harrison and "Lucas Malet" move to Clovelly Rectory in Devon. The Devon landscape would feature heavily in the *Wages of Sin* (1891).

1885 *Colonel Enderby's Wife,* a novel about an unhappy marriage in which the role of the self-sacrificing wife and the tyrant husband are reversed as the husband suffers his wife's cruelty.

1887 *Little Peter: A Christmas Morality for Children of Any Age,* a children's fable with a warning against the ill-treatment of others; the short story anticipates modernism's self-awareness and preoccupation with the concerns of genre.

1888 *A Counsel of Perfection*, a novel about a dutiful daughter whose life is consumed by her father's selfish scholarly ambitions.

1891 *The Wages of Sin*, a novel about an aspiring female artist who falls in love with a famous painter only to find he has an illegitimate family. It explores the heroine's aesthetic and sexual awakening. In January Malet leaves her home at Clovelly to begin a tour of the Continent that includes Naples; Rome; Perugia; and Vevey, Switzerland. The trip is justified on therapeutic grounds, but in reality, this departure represents a separation from Harrison. Later in the year Malet travels to Bournemouth and there meets Vernon Lee. Frances Kingsley dies on 11 December, naming Malet's sister, Rose Kingsley, as literary executor.

1894 With Rose, Malet travels to Ceylon (now Sri Lanka), Karachi, and Bombay (now Mumbai). Malet would draw on this experience in her 1916 novel *Damaris*, which is set in "Bhutpur."

1896 *The Carissima: A Modern Grotesque*, a gothic novella that explores the mental disintegration of its Byronic hero as a metaphor for the threat to society posed by the 'modern' woman.

1897 William Harrison dies on 27 April of tuberculosis. Though Malet had not seen Harrison for some time, she is present at his death, along with Rose Kingsley and their cousin Mary Henrietta Kingsley—the latter an accomplished nurse.

1898 In May, Malet's younger brother dies in Queensland, Australia. His management of his Australian property was haphazard, and it is believed that he committed suicide.

1899 Malet travels to New York to undertake research for *The Gateless Barrier* and visit her brother Maurice. She spends only six days in America.

1900 *The Gateless Barrier,* a gothic romance in which a female ghost haunts the home of an ailing decadent villain.

1901 *The History of Sir Richard Calmady: A Romance*, Malet's best-known and most controversial novel, detailing the (sexual) life of a disabled aristocrat; the novel received both critical acclaim and censure.

1902 It is likely that Malet is received into the Catholic Church in 1902, although there is some evidence to suggest that she may have converted to the faith alongside her second cousin and adopted daughter, Lilian Vallings, in 1906.

1905 Malet informally adopts Lilian Vallings, later a professional opera singer performing under the name Gabrielle Vallings. "The Threatened Re-Subjection of Woman," a response to American President Roosevelt's 1904 congressional address. Malet argued that increased freedoms were problematic for all but a few middle-class women because most women were more fit for motherhood than for work; the essay was widely misunderstood as anti-feminist.

1906 *The Far Horizon*, a novel of Catholic conversion about the life and death of an ascetic, celibate hero who questions the meaninglessness of his bourgeois circumstances.

1909 *The Score*, a volume which misleadingly contains the two apparently unrelated novella-length stories "Miserere Nobis" and "The Courage of Her Convictions." "Miserere Nobis" is a first-person confession narrative about a patricide. "The Courage of Her Convictions" features Poppy St. John, an actress who originally appeared in *The Far Horizon* and describes her ill-fated relationship with a violent politician.

1910 *The Wreck of the Golden Galleon*, a short story presented as an illustrated novel; the plot centres around the unreciprocated desires of an older woman for her younger lodger. In November, Maurice Kingsley, Malet's older brother, dies.

1911 *Adrian Savage,* a study of the fortunes of two fictional women whose lives intersect with that of the titular hero in France and England, respectively. In November Malet and Gabrielle Vallings travel to Paris for Valling's operatic training. Malet returns home by Christmas, but Vallings stays on to complete her training.

1916 *Damaris,* set in nineteenth-century India and the first of two novels about Damaris Verity and her relationships with both her father and his would-be mistress.

1919 *Deadham Hard: A Romance*, the second of Malet's novels about Damaris Verity; the plot follows Damaris's development as an author and a woman.

1920 *The Tall Villa*, a gothic tale about an abandoned wife who falls in love with the ghost of a man who committed suicide. There are striking similarities to *The Gateless Barrier*, although the gender of the earthbound lover and ghost are inverted.

1922 *Da Silva's Widow and Other Stories*, a collection of nine short stories on a variety of subjects. Two of these, "A Boy's Love" and "How they Met Again," introduce the cast of Malet's 1923 novel *The Survivors.*

1923 Early in 1923 Malet and Vallings move to Vevey in Switzerland. This move is largely determined by a need to reduce their cost of living and tax commitments. This is a period of real financial difficulty for Malet and Vallings. *The Survivors*, Malet's most formally experimental novel, is set during the First World War, and the events of the novel take place at a hospital for the care of injured soldiers.

1924 *The Dogs of Want: A Modern Comedy of Errors*, Malet's final novel, is a modernist romance depicting contrasting female types, one Victorian, the other 'modern,' who compete for the affections of the same man.

1925 Rose Kingsley dies of breast cancer on 17 August. Malet is present at her death.

1931 Malet dies at Tenby, South Wales, on 27 October from colon cancer. Her funeral is held at St. Teilo's Catholic Church. Her final resting place cannot be exactly determined, but it seems likely that she is buried in an unmarked grave at the old cemetery off Narberth Road in Tenby.

1932 *The Private Life of Mr Justice Syme*, posthumous sequel to *The Dogs of Want*, completed by Gabrielle Vallings. It follows the plight of two interlinked marriages of convenience.

Foreword

Patricia Lorimer Lundberg

In September 1983, I experienced my first semester in a PhD programme as a very nontraditional student. A research methods course required me to create a bibliography, and I found myself searching the university library for a research subject that would not bore me to tears. My attention wandered, and I headed for a table full of fire-sale books, a little work-avoidance browse that launched me on my academic trajectory for the next two decades. On that sale table, *Mrs. Lorimer* by Lucas Malet, published a century earlier in 1882, could be had for a dollar. I myself was Mrs Lorimer. Who, indeed, was Lucas Malet?

Little available research existed on Lucas Malet in the usual bibliographies and biographies. I learned soon enough that she had once been an acclaimed woman writer. But there was no full recounting of her prodigious literary output, and her books were scarce and expensive to collect. She seemed vaguely remembered as Polly, the younger daughter of Charles Kingsley. In 1983 there was no internet to consult—it took another decade for the gift of online searches, and even then, little was discoverable online about Lucas Malet. From 1984 until 2003, when I published her literary biography *"An Inward Necessity": The Writer's Life of Lucas Malet*, I compulsively spent my free time travelling to far-flung libraries and family archives to rediscover this fine writer who signed herself Mrs (Mary) St. Leger Harrison or MSLH. Later, as a cigar-smoking and gender-bending celebrity, she preferred Lucas Malet.

Then there are the challenges one faces when one's research subject burns their papers, dies in penury, and lies in an unmarked grave! Tragically, the family disposed of the first editions and most of the correspondence. In the case of Mary St. Leger Harrison/Lucas Malet, it is fortunate that she lived many years with her 'adoptive niece' Gabrielle Vallings, whose own niece, Angela Covey-Crump, remembered both women and gave me access to a huge batch of loose family papers mouldering away in the garage in Ely. It is also fortunate that in her penury Lucas Malet wrote a number of grant applications to the Royal Literary Fund (now archived in London), into which she poured both a record of her long publishing success and her later financial humiliation between 1917 and 1931, when she died in Tenby, Wales.

Lucas Malet wrote for more than fifty years while living an unconventional life. She became the most famous of the literary Kingsleys and yet the most quickly forgotten. She had a significant impact on British letters, especially with her *History of Sir Richard Calmady*, begun in 1887 and published finally in 1901, when she was touted as the literary lion of London. She embodies in one writer a wealth of narrative strategies: as I argued in *An Inward Necessity*, Malet "transgressed [Victorianism's] rigid borders and reached the pinnacle of literary acclaim as the winds of change swept her through literary waves of Gothic, Aestheticism, and Naturalism into the so-called Modernist age" (Lundberg 2003, 4).

As I read Malet's novels and researched their critical reception over the years, I became more and more confounded that she could have lost her rightful place among the literary giants of her time—George Eliot, George Meredith, Henry James, Thomas Hardy, Virginia Woolf. In this one novelist's oeuvre, we can study the development of the novel from the nineteenth to the twentieth centuries. She brought us a breathtaking breadth of perspective, a deep understanding of human nature, innovations in style, and daring and transgressive characters. Lucas Malet was rightly celebrated in her time for her groundbreaking works, and she deserves to be celebrated still.

My search for Lucas Malet traversed an era when focusing—and risking—one's research career on a lost woman writer met with little support, certainly not much in the universities where I spent five years of graduate school and seventeen years before leaving as a tenured professor. How many such efforts have floundered? It is a wonder that Lucas Malet and other deserving women writers have been rediscovered at all, given the decades of costly and dedicated effort such an endeavour consumes.

Nothing could cap my own life as an English professor better than to have helped, along with early Malet researchers Talia Schaffer, Patricia Srebrnik, Mary Ann Gillies, Sunie Fletcher, and others, to rediscover the writing life of Lucas Malet. These early Malet scholars and a gratifying number of others now working on lost women writers continue to deepen our understanding of the ways the literary reputations of these writers have been insidiously diminished, especially those women writers who themselves led lives considered transgressive for their time.

I have been delighted to learn that, finally, many Lucas Malet scholars now toil on her behalf, that students can learn about her work, and that a collection of academic essays about her has found favour at a prestigious press. These advances in literary history have been a long time coming.

Reading Malet "through the eyelashes"

An Introduction to Her Life and Work

Jane Ford and Alexandra Gray

In a 1901 *New York Times* article, William Livingstone Alden teasingly claims to have "skimmed an advance copy" of Lucas Malet's new book *The History of Sir Richard Calmady* (1901). He writes, "I fancy it is going to prove the best book [Malet] has yet written. It is, however, too important a book to be written about after skimming only" (1901, 9). And important it certainly was. The novel, which offered a candid treatment of the (sexual) life of a disabled aristocrat, was outsold only by Rudyard Kipling's *Kim* (O'Connell 2012, 109). A publishing sensation, the novel caused, in William Barry's words, "every table it is talked over [to be] turned to a battlefield," and Janet Hogarth prudishly declared that "[t]here are pages which, if read at all, can only be read through the eyelashes" (Barry 1901, 20; Hogarth 1902, 540). Noting Malet's debt to the French naturalists, Mary Elizabeth Wilson Sherwood remarked that "certain passages of it are quite as bad and immoral as anything that Zola has ever written" (Sherwood 1901, 854). American publishers evidently agreed, skittishly removing from their first edition a passage which appeared to describe a scene of genital stimulation. Today the book and its author, one of the most successful writers of her day, are virtually unknown.

Born Mary St. Leger Kingsley, Lucas Malet (1852–1931) was part of a formidable family of writers and explorers. Her father was the 'broad church' priest and popular Victorian author Charles Kingsley. Malet's uncles, Henry and George Kingsley, were published authors, and her sister Rose produced acclaimed nonfiction on topics such as European art and gardening; Malet's cousin (George's daughter) was the African travel writer Mary Henrietta Kingsley. In a career which spanned around fifty years, Malet published seventeen popular novels, two volumes of short fiction, and completed her father's novel *The Tutor's Story* (1916). Part of a prominent literary circle, Malet mixed with such noted figures as Vernon Lee, Henry James, and Thomas Hardy—the latter two, as Talia Schaffer demonstrates, almost certainly appropriated Malet's ideas (Schaffer Chapter 8, this volume). Deeply influenced by George Eliot—whom she praised as "immeasurably the greatest" of women writers—Malet aspired towards realism's spirit of psychological enquiry but was by no means wedded to its forms (Malet 1888a, 298). Instead, she wrote with facility across a number of genres. Frequently compared to Henry James, she wrote beautifully crafted aesthetic prose featuring arcane objects and gorgeous sartorial description, imperial narratives, and tales of gothic horror. In the twentieth century, Malet contributed to developments in modernist prose, producing frequently oblique dialogue, moments of temporal dislocation, and symbolic scenes of sapphic pleasure.

Though she is little known today, Malet was almost universally praised for her technical skill, wit, and life-like characterisation. In an 1899 edition of *The London Review*—a piece revealingly titled "Well-Known Women"—she was touted as "beyond doubt, one of the cleverest of living women novelists" (578). And even in 1916, when her popularity had waned M.P. Willcocks suggested that "[i]n the creation of atmosphere there is no living writer who surpasses Lucas Malet at her best" (98). Where she was criticised, it was invariably for her preoccupation with so-called morbid or indecent themes. In particular, after her identity had been revealed, many were shocked that such subversive content could originate from the pen of a daughter of Charles Kingsley. A locus of indignant feeling, Malet's 1891 novel *The Wages of Sin* offered daring representations of poverty, prostitution, and extramarital sex. In an incensed personal letter to Malet, James Baker complained, "anything 'spicy' is always caught at ... it is the opening up of a vile life which makes your book a success," and "it made me inexpressly sad" to know that "it was the daughter of Charles Kingsley that had written it" (qtd. in Lundberg 2003, 157–8). Similarly, in the aftermath of *Calmady's* publication, *The Nineteenth Century* carried a piece by the writer and Liberal M.P Herbert Paul on "Art and Eccentricity." Citing Ruskin's remarks on the grotesque in architecture—in particular Ruskin's belief that the "delight in the contemplation of bestial degradation [is ...] the most hopeless state into which the human mind can fall"—Paul preaches that "physical and mental disease ... [are] not a proper subject for artistic treatment" (Ruskin 1853, 121; Paul 1902, 257). Singling out *Calmady*, Paul remarks, "we have lately been introduced to a legless baronet"; "it is not the function of the artist to depict such monsters"; "[h]eroes should have the usual assortment of limbs" (254, 257).

Using the same architectural simile, a *Morning Oregonian* review of *The Carissima* (1896) remarked that in the "peculiar sinister effectiveness of the gargoyle of medieval architecture ... one finds the symbols for the element of effectiveness in 'The Carissima'" ("Review of New Books" 1896, 19). Evidently entertained that the person responsible for this "sinister" production is a daughter of Kingsley, the reviewer stoops to biographical speculation:

> to create these gargoyles and live in the room with them ... as this author must have done, was to pay the full price for her laurels... It

> would be interesting to know if Lucas Mallet [*sic*] is the daughter for whom Kingsley wrote the warning lines that begin:
> "Be good, dear child, and let who will, be clever."
>
> (19)

What such critical perspectives react to is Malet's candidness, the calibration of her authorial lens to subjects dark, base, or low—in other words, her naturalism. But Malet's writing only began to attract this kind of attention from the 1890s. In his 1887 *Pioneer* article "A Note on Paul Bourget," Havelock Ellis cites Malet as an example of the tendency towards *reserve* in English writing. In the piece, which compares Bourget's *Cruelle Énigme* to Malet's *Colonel Enderby's Wife*—novels both published that year—Ellis praises *Enderby* as a "careful and powerfully told story of an unhappy marriage" (Ellis 1932, 58). He regrets, however, that it is "raised on a conventionally moral, not, as with the French novelist, on a psychological basis; she calls the novel 'a moral dissecting room'" (59). The "moral dissecting room" is, of course, a nod to Eliotean realism and does not necessarily imply the elevation of moral, over psychological, examination, but certainly these novels are a little chaste. In a remark which may well have had a major impact on Malet's literary development, Ellis suggests that

> we are not likely to see in England, at present, any successful union of the French and English novel, because our great English novelists have not touched the facts of life with the same frankness and boldness, and their conception of normal life is unduly restricted.
>
> (59)

It is after Ellis's piece that Malet's novels take on their more subversive aspect, and by 1896 she openly aligns herself with naturalism:

> I am much more given … to reading French than English fiction, and any little knowledge I may have of style and method I have so learned … Balzac, Gautier, Flaubert, and De Maupassant—and among the living men, Bourget, an occasional Zola, Daudet … and (in translations) Turgenieff, Tolstoi, and Dostoieffsky are the writers who interest me most.
>
> (qtd. in Dolman 1896, 149)

Not coincidentally, "Turgenieff," "Tolstoi," and "Dostoieffsky" are the three Russian novelists named by Ellis in "A Note." If it was indeed Ellis that promoted a narrative realignment towards naturalist principals, then Malet was well aware of the kind of reaction she was likely to elicit. Indeed, Ellis's remarks prophetically reveal the tone of her later reviews: "the recent English novelists who have been touched by French influence constantly offend by their cruel and vulgar extravagance" (Ellis 1932, 59–60).

The History of Sir Richard Calmady, published five years after Ellis's "Note," would do little to abjure Malet's accused extravagance, preoccupied as the novel was with the power of the grotesque to provoke necessary social and political debate. According to Catherine Delyfer, Malet "made disability the very linchpin of her reflection on gender, ethics, beauty and art" (Delyfer 2001, 83) laying bare outdated assumptions about nonnormative bodies as a means to question nineteenth-century taxonomies of class and gender. Malet's foregrounding of alterity in *Calmady* has been central to important recoveries of disability in the period (Miller 2011; O'Connell 2012; Walker Gore 2014; Ehnenn 2017). However, tempting as it is to read Malet's most well-known novel as a provocative—and uncomplicatedly radical—politicisation of the disabled body, *Calmady* is just one example of a complex nexus of concerns about corporeality that surface across Malet's literary opus.

From the deformed rescuer in *Little Peter* (1888), the phantom dog in *The Carissima* (1896), and the monstrously fleshly Montague Rivers in *The Gateless Barrier* (1900), the grotesque features in Malet's works in a range of guises. Embodied monstrosity appears often in women whose moral obliquity is signposted by their insistent corporeality: the fallen woman (*Wages of Sin*); the scheming flirt (*The Carissima*); the incestuous adulterer (*Calmady*); the power-hungry woman of influence (*Damaris/Deadham Hard*); the ailing, demanding mother (*The Far Horizon*); and the vampiric matron (*The Survivors*). Exemplary of this is Miranda Povey, the fifty-year-old heroine of Malet's novella *The Wreck of the Golden Galleon* (1910), whose sexuality awakens too late to put her starving, ageing body to sexual or reproductive use. In an act of erotic transference, Malet's love-struck spinster worships the trinket given to her by the undeserving object of her affections: a small golden ship which, backlit by candles, she visually consumes from her bed. As she reclines gazing at the golden galleon, in a scene of quasi-religious yet sexually charged reverie, Miranda dreams of marriage to her young lodger, Willy Evans. We are told that

> her hands trembled as they lay crossed upon her bosom, though whether from the lowness of the temperature or from glad emotion it would be difficult to determine ... she became sensible of a rapture, both of soul and body, so exquisite as to be almost unendurable. She had no wish for it to cease, yet feared she could not support it and continue to live. She struggled to cry out, but her voice refused to come. And so she lay rigid, helpless, mute, transfixed by delicious anguish.
>
> (114–6)

Like other novelists publishing during the early years of the twentieth century—Victoria Cross, E.M. Forster, Henry James, and John Galsworthy are notable examples—Malet explores the possibilities of female sexuality, but if her narrativisation of thwarted desire is designed as a rallying call to women or a punishment for transgression, it misses the mark on both counts. Miss Povey's hunger for affection, her obsessive efforts at spiritual and bodily service to Willy Evans, and her erotic exhaustion from nights of passionate worship are more pathetic than emancipatory. Her "delicious anguish," naïve and misdirected, serves only to highlight her entombment in a body that can neither revel in sin nor be subject to the kinds of punishment meted out to transgressive women in the works of Malet's contemporaries.

While the female body regularly serves as a synecdoche for corruption and a vessel of moral and physical degeneration in Malet's novels, it is as often the site of corporeal *dis*embodiment, a troubling form of monstrosity that symbolises the dangers of women's suppression, and, equally, the threat of the modern. Although the grotesque emerges as both a cause of and a cure for the weakness of human desire in Malet's literary panorama, it also exemplifies her shifting position in relation to contemporary debates about class, gender, politics, art, religion, and sexuality.

This volume, then, makes the case that far from offering interest of a minor sort, Lucas Malet was an important and influential figure on the late nineteenth- and early twentieth-century literary landscape: a writer who generated great controversy, influenced her better-remembered contemporaries, and had fascinating and provocative things to say about the major issues of her day. Although it contains much that will be new to (the few) seasoned Maletians, this introduction has been designed as an orientation to Malet's life and gives a chronological account of key aspects of her biography while highlighting the distinctive features of her style, politics, and personal philosophy.

Early Life

Born on 4 June 1852, Lucas Malet was the third of the four children of Charles and Frances Kingsley. Holding the belief that man's duty is to "go out into the world and seek [his] fortune," while women are "taken care of at home" (Thorp 1975, 105) Charles Kingsley sent the boys, Maurice (1847–1910) and Grenville (1858–98), away to school. Themselves desperate for a good education, Malet and her sister Rose (1844–1925) felt the injustice of this arrangement. Tellingly, in adulthood, Rose strived to secure equal educational opportunities for women, setting up the Leamington High School for Girls in 1883.

Malet's relationship to Charles Kingsley's legacy was complex, marked by competing impulses to challenge the philosophies to which he subscribed and to reconcile her burgeoning literary persona with his influence on her life as a woman and a writer. Though she expressed affection for her father, publicly praising his "gentleness" and "kindly delicacy," his influence on young Mary St. Leger—or Pol/Polly as she was known amongst the family—was most certainly oppressive (Dolman 1896, 148). In an 1899 interview with Mary Angela Dickens, Malet reported that she was a lonely, sequestered child who was "absolutely forbidden" to read novels (Dickens 1899, 522). These feelings of isolation can only have been exacerbated by the fact that on two occasions (in 1869–70 and again for a lecture circuit in 1874) Kingsley selected Rose to join him on his American tour, while Malet was left at home to take care of their, by then, invalid mother.

Between 1872 and 1873 Malet, who had aspirations to become a professional painter, was enrolled at the Slade School of Art, where she studied alongside Evelyn De Morgan (then Pickering). Following Kingsley's death in 1876, Malet married William Harrison, Kingsley's curate and a man some twelve years her senior. As Patricia Lorimer Lundberg makes clear, Kingsley could not have forced Malet to marry Harrison, as some critics have suggested (Srebrnik 1994; Lundberg 2003, 55). The fees books at Slade indicate that Malet left in 1873, and therefore the decision to abandon her artistic studies would seem to have little to do with her marriage. As Catherine Delyfer shows, though Malet's career as an artist was cut short, her "engagement with the visual arts forms an intricate part of her writing" (Delyfer 2011, 4). Perhaps unsurprisingly, the marriage to Harrison was unhappy, and Malet suffered poor mental health and nervous relapses. In 1878, apparently after a hint from Max Müller, Malet began work on her debut novel, *Mrs. Lorimer: A Sketch in Black and White* (1882). The text explores the fate of an artistically gifted young widow who is only able to explore her talents once her sick husband has died, and her eyes have been opened to romantic desire. While the plot seems to dramatise Malet's own experience of widowhood and later artistic endeavours, it suggests that female creative powers alone cannot overcome strict Victorian social, moral, and economic mores, and the novel ends with Elizabeth Lorimer's self-induced illness and death.

Malet evidently felt that her literary career flew in the face of Kingsley's plans for her. In an interview with Frederick Dolman, she confessed, "I never wrote until some time after [my father's] death. I am not altogether sure he would have cared about my working. He held the old-fashioned and chivalrous notion that women should be treated *en princesse*" (Dolman 1896, 147). Though Malet offered contradictory accounts of her pseudonym—variously as a cover "to hide behind in case of failure" and to ensure that her "work might be judged on its merits"—it is certain that she intended to bypass Kingsley (Dolman 1896, 149; Whitelock 1901, 784). "Lucas Malet" was a deliberate allusion to the writer's *female* ancestors—her paternal grandmother, Mary Lucas, and her great-great-aunt Malet. "As these two women were exceptionally clever" Malet explains, "I thought it was from them that the wits of the family came" (Dolman 1896, 149).

Despite her success, Malet partly depended on an income from posthumous sales of Charles Kingsley's works and at various times in her life was forced to negotiate with publishers over new editions that could supplement the sales of her own novels. He cast a shadow over her career long after his death since she was forced to respond to accusations that her novels soiled his good name. Answering Baker's letter, in which he claimed it was "reverence for [Kingsley's] memory which intensified my sadness at your book" (qtd. in Lundberg 2003, 157–8), Malet wrote,

> ... a letter, such as you have elected to address to me, is I consider quite unpardonable—contrary to all the rules of courtesy ... Nor can I imagine what end you propose to gain by writing to me. That it will affect the circulation of the book in question, you must know, is impossible. That it will alter my opinion as to the worth of that book, or, in any degree influence my future writing, is, if you will consider the matter without prejudice, equally impossible.
>
> All, and more than all, which you are pleased to say to me was, I must remind you, said to my father about his novel "Yeast". "Yeast" has survived the dislike of its critics. It is conceivable that "The Wages of Sin" may do likewise.
>
> (qtd. in Lundberg 2003, 157–8)

Although highly defensive of her family's reputation, satirical representations of clergymen akin to her father and husband appeared often in Malet's fiction. In her debut novel, criticism of the brand of muscular Anglicanism with which Kingsley was associated is dramatised to comic effect by the "distressingly energetic" Mr Leeper (Malet 1882, 167). The aptly-named vicar, we are told, "believed that he possessed the original healthy mind in a healthy body" (167) and "belonged to that section of English Churchmen which, not contented with trying to rule the Church, has a strong desire to rule the world as well" (167–8). Like her ungenerous depiction of Dr. Casteen, a rector and well-known author to whom the heroine plays amanuensis in *A Counsel of Perfection* (1888), clerical men rarely escape criticism in Malet's stories. Nevertheless, despite the clear parody of Christian socialism at play in *Mrs. Lorimer*, it is through acts of charity and socialist endeavour that the titular heroine asserts control over her own destiny, and while this results in her death the reader is left in no doubt as to the emancipatory tenor of such acts. Similarly, it is via charitable socialism that the disabled protagonist in *Calmady* is reconciled with his own body and through which the sexual and social tensions at play in Malet's most infamous novel are ultimately resolved.

Imperial Politics

Like her complicated position—within the Kingsley dynasty yet largely opposed to the ideals embodied by her father—Malet's associations with empire were equally fraught. She travelled in India and had a dwindling interest in an Australian property left to herself and Rose after the death of their brother Grenville. Grenville's attempts to build a life for himself at the edge of the empire were unsuccessful, and the property became a financial burden on his sisters in later life (Lundberg 2003, 310). At Mary Henrietta Kingsley's request, Malet read the manuscript for her cousin's ethnographic study *Travels in West Africa* (1897), remembered today for its relatively sympathetic portrayal of African native customs. Malet, we are told by Kingsley's biographer, bestowed a "generally favourable opinion" (Frank 2005, 229) on the work, yet while Kingsley's critique of English colonial exploits survived to posterity, Malet's detailed novelistic accounts of imperialism have now largely disappeared from view. Malet fictionalised both the imperious Victorian father figure and the consequences of failing to flourish beyond the safety of British shores in *Damaris* (1916) and *Deadham Hard* (1919), both of which feature a father-daughter relationship that, at least in part, reconfigures that of the young Mary Kingsley with her own father.

Set in British India in 1864, *Damaris* explores several triangulations of illicit desire against the exotic backdrop of a restrictive yet only superficially conservative Anglo-Indian social sphere. The respected Commissioner of the Bhutpur Maidan and hero of the Indian mutiny, Charles Verity is a widowed father to five-year-old Damaris, whose mother, Agnes, he married in an act of misguided gallantry, despite his passion for the then-married Henrietta Pereira. When Henrietta—now on her second marriage to the dissolute Johnny Pereira—visits Bhutpur, she and the widowed Verity reminisce over the missed opportunities for their union as they contemplate an extramarital affair. Meanwhile, Damaris falls in love with the beautiful but cold-hearted Henrietta, an infatuation that will see her languish and her father renounce women for good. In a text rich with allusion to the workings of empire and Victorian patriarchy, Malet, as Lundberg has argued, bemoans the shallow hypocrisy of Anglo-Indian society and mercilessly lampoons its exponents (2003, 361). Nevertheless, *Damaris* depicts its colonial patriarch figure in highly romanticised, even nostalgic, terms, complicating a straightforward reading of the novel as a critique of imperialism.

Verity is "a man of heroic build, clear-sighted, unsparing of himself, tireless in action and in achievement as some paladin of old" (173), and his ruthless approach to colonial rule is imagined as far less problematic than one might expect in a text that elsewhere condemns the narrow mindedness of British colonialism. Verity explains,

> I was sent here to rule. I do rule. What's more, I civilize. I make a very fair measure of justice and decency prevail. When I came, four

> years ago, law and order were practically a dead letter. To day life and prosperity are—broadly speaking—as safe in Bhutpur district as in one of the English home counties. For the first time, probably, in history the peasants plough their fields and gather in their harvest in peace.
>
> (77)

While Verity admits, "I had to do a little hanging to begin with" (77) his activities are portrayed as necessary and correspond to the aptitude for leadership suggested by his physical, intellectual, and psychological vigour. He laments, rather than boasts, that "to sterilize efforts of revolt, he must adopt somewhat merciless methods" (291), and his absolute power goes unquestioned by his staff, his neighbours, and his daughter. Even when Verity violently manhandles Henrietta in a disturbingly aggressive amatory scene, his actions are excused as a form of virile masculine desirability that leaves Henrietta "without wish or will of her own" (180). What, then, must we make of Malet's fictional Charles: the oppressive, powerful patriarch who wields absolute power; the *de facto* hero of the novel; and the last bastion of a dying breed? If her feelings for her father were characterised by a shifting desire to diverge from his maxims and pay tribute to his canonical status, then her fictional exploration of the moral vagaries of the British imperial project in India works in much the same way. Malet both derides and romanticises Charles Verity; as a stand-in for her own father he constitutes a highly nostalgic rendering of a relationship that by all accounts was neither as distant or as difficult as that which Malet shared with Verity's real-life namesake.

Malet adopted an equivocal position on imperialist politics; she idealised the exploits of pioneers like General Gordon—a prototype for Charles Verity—whom she described, flatteringly, as "a fanatic, a fatalist and an ascetic" (1885, 396) but objected to the economic impetus for imperialism, a fact verified by Malet's friend, the historian Julia Cartwright Ady. According to Ady, Malet viewed the First Boer War as "a war of *Capitalists*" (Emanuel 1899, 245). Despite her reservations about the motive for the war in South Africa, Malet remained a committed patriot and supporter of British imperialism in a broader sense. After the First World War, she exhibited unwavering pride in the English nation, explaining in a 1920 *The Daily Telegraph* article that

> in as far as our own country and Empire is concerned … against the monstrous background of war, one fact stands out in clear and very beautiful relief—the fact the English race is neither degenerate nor effete, that its spirit is unbroken, its conscience sensitive, actively ready to affront momentous decisions and accept incalculable risks.
>
> (1920, 9)

While it seems that Malet, echoing nineteenth-century socialist understandings of imperialism, objected to England's pecuniary greed, she found very little else about colonisation particularly wrong. Malet continued to view the English 'race' as a sanitising force for moral authority in world affairs well into the twentieth century.

Dissident Pilgrim

In the early 1890s Malet separated from Harrison—a move she explained as a series of therapeutic visits to the Continent. Surviving family have suggested that Harrison struggled to come to terms with the increasingly subversive nature of Malet's writing, and letters from the late 1880s reveal that her residence with Harrison at their isolated Clovelly home took a heavy toll on her mental health (Lundberg 2003, 116–7). Harrison died in 1898.

In or around 1902 Malet converted to Catholicism, an audacious act which has been read both as a rebellion against the anti-Romanism and tenets of Christian manliness espoused by Kingsley and paradoxically a retreat into religious orthodoxy. Patricia Srebrnik, for instance, characterises Malet's conversion as both an anti-Oedipal impulse and a way to "achieve consolation … for the injuries of gender." But Srebrnik also argues that Malet's Catholicism ultimately "compelled [her…] to reassert many of her father's assumptions concerning appropriate gender roles …" (Srebrnik 1994, 206). This is perhaps too tidy an account of Malet's complex gender politics, which present a conservative edge long before her conversion, but Srebrnik's comments do tell us something of the ambivalence that constitutes Malet's *weltanschauung* or vision of life—a sense of dividedness the title of this volume strives to encapsulate.

In *The Far Horizon* (1906), Malet's circumspect hero, Dominic Iglesias, longs for the Catholicism of his parents' respective homelands as he confronts the meaninglessness of bourgeois values and the exacting physical and spiritual price demanded by the "monstrous mother" of London (1906, 32). He is devastated first by his mother's death, and then by his unexpected early retirement. Fastidious, celibate, and ascetic, he has devoted much of his adult life to the beautiful, ailing Mrs Iglesias and to the exploitative capitalist machine synecdochised in the bank from which he is unceremoniously discharged. Described through the alluring prism of Roman Catholic mysticism, Mrs Iglesias, we are told,

> … was ill, how deeply and in what manner [Dominic] could not tell. He shrank, indeed, from all clear thought, let alone speech, on the subject, as from something indelicate, in a way irreverent. Her beauty remained to her, notwithstanding a gradual wasting as of fever. A peculiar, very individual grace of dress and of bearing

> remained to her likewise. But she was uncertain in mood, the victim of strange fancies, a being almost alarmingly removed from the interests of ordinary life ... His mother had always been sacred. She remained so, even when her sympathies had become imperfect, and she moved in regions which his sane young imagination failed to penetrate.
>
> (1906, 10–2)

Dominic's mother, who dies following a long period of "madness," is a "dear saint and martyr" (55), revered as "that which was holy" (55). She both stands in for and complicates the Holy Virgin within the schema of Malet's vision of Catholic conversion. Mrs Iglesias's tireless support of her husband's dangerous revolutionary activities constitutes a perfect sacrificial gesture, her production of lacework the epitome of dedicated feminine industry. Such acts reflect her dual function: she embodies a distinctly Marian and highly aestheticised bodily appeal on the one hand and practices the ministries of her perfect faith through the tireless production of commodities on the other. Fetishised by her devoted son she is at once the Madonna, a saintly maternal presence, and a magnetic force that stifles Dominic's opportunities and consumes the best years of his life. In this way the extended metaphor of London in all her monstrous maternity stands in for the major relationship of the hero's life, and Mrs Iglesias comes to function as a potent Catholic symbol and a source of sexual, reproductive, and social anxiety.

In *The Far Horizon*, Malet was reluctant to venerate the self-sacrificing mother as an example of uncomplicated maternal perfection. Despite this, her clear disdain for the sorts of self-serving femininity embodied by women within her diegetic panorama—Charlotte Perry (*The Carissima*), Helen de Vallorbes (*Calmady*), Henrietta Pereira (*Damaris/ Deadham Hard*), and Mary-Louise Syme (*The Dogs of Want*)—is difficult to misinterpret. While her stance on women's primary duties as wives and mothers was surprisingly traditional, her exploration of Catholic practice, including the worship of the Holy Virgin, made some of her later work as thematically unorthodox as it was formally experimental.

Sapphic Modernism

In 1906, Malet adopted her nineteen-year-old second cousin, Gabrielle Vallings, and the two lived together until Malet's death in 1931. Vallings would go on to be an opera singer, socialist, and writer, completing and publishing Malet's own unfinished novel *The Private Life of Mr Justice Syme* in 1932. It appears likely their relationship was romantic in nature, but this has never been verified—a circumstance not helped by the fact that Vallings (at Malet's request) burned most of their personal letters after her death. As Patricia Lorimer Lundberg points out, it seems that Malet understood her sexuality and gender identity at least in part through the prism of contemporary sexological ideas surrounding 'sexual inversion.' During her interview with Mary Angela Dickens, in what is not only an allusion to her own 'masculine' characteristics but possibly a reference to Henry Kingsley's purported homosexuality, Rose Kingsley's accomplishments in shooting and riding, and Mary Henrietta Kingsley's African fieldwork, Malet reveals that she

> has one grave and fundamental quarrel with Fate. It turned her out a woman and not a man! She herself is of opinion that Nature jumbled things up altogether in the construction of her whole family and distributed male and female characteristics at random!
>
> (Dickens 1899, 522)

Malet expresses a similar sentiment in her 1905 essay "The Threatened Re-Subjection of Woman." Following a contentious prediction that it is only working-class women and "women of genius" that will capitalise on the freedoms made available by the women's movement, Malet argues that the latter (of which she certainly regards herself a specimen) should not entirely be envied since

> to possess the dual nature—a man's brain and ambitions, and a woman's capacity of loving and suffering along with that most intricate and capricious piece of mechanism, a woman's body—is, indeed, to dwell in a city divided against itself.
>
> (1905, 818)

Though "cruelly over-endowed" such hybrid beings do, according to Malet, possess an advantage in the field of fiction, an attitude mirrored by *The Survivors*' Lydia Alywin (818). In an oft-cited passage Lydia, a fledgling writer, reflects on the biform nature of her own creative mind: "the teller of tales and maker of stories is bisexual, hermaphrodite—he who begets, she who conceives, complete in one" (1923, 277). It is of note that Radclyffe Hall, author of the most famous literary treatment of 'sexual inversion,' *The Well of Loneliness* (1928), was an admirer of Malet's fiction. In a 1927 lecture delivered at Sion College, Hall praised Malet for the unshrinking realism of *The History of Sir Richard Calmady* (Lundberg 2003, 427). Later, in a 1942 letter—a response to a postcard sent by Evguenia Souline from Bramshill House, Hampshire—Hall writes, "I forget the Peerage to which the estate belongs but do you know that Bramshill was the house chosen by Lucas Malet for the setting of her really great book 'The History of Sir Richard Calmady'? Well it was" (Glasgow 1997, 255). In this novel, Richard Calmady's eventual wife, Honoria St. Quentin, is a mannish New Woman with a strong romantic attachment to Richard's mother, Katherine. Although Honoria's lesbian desire is ultimately contained within a heterosexual plot, Hall must have been drawn to the novel's candid moments of sapphic expression:

> "... has it never occurred to you, that I may be just every bit as greedy of your companionship as you of mine—more so, I fancy, because—because—"
>
> Honoria bowed her head and kissed the hand she held, once again.
>
> "You see—I know it sounds as if I was rather a beast—perhaps I am—but I never cared for anyone—really to care, I mean—till I cared for you."
>
> "My dear!"—Katherine said again, wondering, shrinking somewhat, at once touched and almost repulsed. The younger woman's attitude was so far removed from her own experience.
>
> "Does it displease you? Does it seem to you unnatural?" Honoria asked quickly.
>
> "A little," Lady Calmady answered, smiling, yet very tenderly.
>
> (2003, 281)

Honoria's speech is halting, euphemistic—the hanging conjunction, "because," giving way to a silence indicative of "unspeakable" homosexual desire. But for all its awkwardness, Honoria's is a daring revelation and one that produces real ambivalence within her auditor; Katherine was both "touched" and "repulsed," and shortly after, when Honoria "[i]mpulsively ... put her hands on Lady Calmady's hips [and] laid her head in her lap," Katherine "could not rouse herself to any immediate response" (282, 283). What is most striking about this exchange is not Honoria's romantic declaration but the fact that it is "so far removed" from Katherine's frame of sexual reference that she can no more reciprocate Honoria's affections, than understand them (281).

In a similar scene from *The Survivors,* the widow Amanda Levipolous lies in bed, while Lydia Alywin sits beside her in a saffron silk dressing gown—a gift from Amanda. The interaction becomes increasingly intimate, falling just short of erotic consummation. Lydia regales Amanda with some shockingly 'modern' views on their social set, and Amanda muses:

> How disconcertingly direct is your modern maiden! If the Victorians erred on the side of pruderies and hypocrises—as they did—hadn't Amanda herself bitterly suffered therefrom!—these neo-Georgians rushed to the opposite extreme, making you blush for them, or rather for your pre-Georgian remnant of outraged modesty...
>
> (1923, 240)

Though there is a temptation to read these intergenerational pairings as an expression of the Malet-Vallings relationship, there is a real sense in which they speak of Malet's conflicted sense of herself as a writer straddling Victorianism and modernism. At the margins of the spoken, sapphic experience becomes the site at which the modernity of the text is contested—it is a privileged space in which Malet's Victorian and contemporary selves enter into dialogue, with all the textual/sexual ambivalence that entails.

Curiously, Malet's twentieth-century critics not only overlooked the sapphic current of her writing but seriously misunderstood her relationship to her modernist contemporaries. In a review of *Deadham Hard*, *The Bystander* magazine, though praising "the author's great skill," laments that the novel "is not a tale of this new world which, we are told, is now in the process of becoming. It belongs very definitely to a past which, for all its stiff ways, many of us will regret" (Straus 1919, 873). The novel's nineteenth-century historical setting is a red herring since the book itself is a psychoanalytically conceived narrative of sexual becoming in which the heroine, Damaris Verity, discovers that Henrietta, the locus of her erotic energies, is a shallow ("frothy") specimen of womanhood. This epiphany is managed through the trope of digital penetration. At first, in defiance of a creeping awareness of Henrietta's triviality, Damaris "pushed one hand into that lady's muff and coaxed the slender pointed-fingers hiding in the comfortable pussy-warmth within" (1919, 211). Then later, when she pushes their confidence too far, Henrietta becomes aware that "in the pussy-warmth within her muff … Damaris's hand grew unresponsive, at once curiously stiff and curiously limp" (212). Giving the lie to the *Bystander* review, the sexual connotations are glaringly clear. Not only does Malet draw on well-established sexual slang, but Freud's 1905 exposition of fetishism had recently posited fur, of which the muff is composed, as a proxy for the hair-covered "*mons veneris*" (Freud 2001, 155). Damaris's sexual desire for Henrietta, like her father's, is predicated on a carefully crafted blindness to this woman's 'lighter' side. The realisation, when it comes, is tantamount to erectile dysfunction.

In many ways, Malet's handling of lesbian desire places her in league with modernist writers such as Katherine Mansfield, Virginia Woolf, and Elizabeth Bowen. Petra Rau points out that in the novels of the 1920s, sapphism became "a signifier of modernity" (Rau 2006, 217). Reframing the Victorian period's sublimated "non-realist forms of [sapphic] representation" around a "modernist esthetic" (Woolf's orgasmic "match burning in a crocus" is a trope *par excellence*), such writing "undermines the conventional heterosexual teleology of the realist novel" (217). But according to Rau, while sapphic experience "functions repeatedly as a nostalgic disruption of straight romance … it also ensures that this desire is temporary and that it does not prevent heterosexual teleologies, but merely makes them look desperate, bland, or implausible" (Rau 2006, 217–8). In Malet's writing lesbian desire is frequently (though not always) communicated through aestheticised, nonrealist figures. The infant Damaris's realisation of an erotic desire for Henrietta is schematised as a baby-soul "breaking free of the chrysalid stage" (1916, 3), and the trope of water, which, as Joseph Allen Boone points out, "figure[s] prominently in the symbolic geographies" of Chopin, Lawrence, and Freud, is one means through which Damaris achieves libidinal expression (Boone 1998, 64). Indeed, in a scene of erotic release, at the moment Damaris gives voice to her desire for Henrietta, "the monsoon broke ... already the smell and taste of wet, sweeping in between the slats of the bolted shutters, began to penetrate the air, bringing foretaste of alleviation and relief" (313). Despite these stunning moments of sapphic pleasure, romantic union between women is fleeting—subordinated to the claims of heterosexual romance or spinsterhood. Though such narrative teleologies certainly reveal, in Rau's words, "considerable ambivalence about the rules of engagement with sapphism," this is not to say that Malet's dénouements support a heterosexual agenda (217).

In *Deadham Hard*, Damaris makes up her mind to marry Carteret, her late father's second-in-command, because she determines to face up to the "distasteful" "question of [heterosexual] sex," a move she conceptualises as graduating in "the school of reality" (1919, 415). Turning her back on nascent literary aspirations, Damaris, unable to imagine a life outside the conventional marriage plot, asks herself, "what other possible school is it worthwhile to graduate?" (1919, 415). With such questionable motives, Damaris's marriage does not serve a heterosexualising function but is framed as a critique of Victorian social mores.

Stylistic and Formal Experiments

In Malet's last published novel, *The Dogs of Want* (1924), the protagonist, Barbara Heritage, is (both in name and nature) a symbol of Malet's Victorianism. A young, hard-up widow forced out of employment by returning troops, Barbara takes on the role of chaperone to Marie-Louise Syme, an unflattering specimen of 1920s femininity. One of a number of old-young female pairings—including Katherine Calmady-Honoria St. Quentin (*Calmady*), Henrietta Pereira-Damaris Verity (*Damaris/Deadham Hard*), and Amanda Levipoulos-Lydia Aylwin (*The Survivors*)—Barbara and Marie-Louise embody their respective cultural moments. After a fraught encounter in which Marie-Louise chillingly reveals somewhat her Machiavellian social tactics, Barbara watches her retreating figure:

> ... the young lady drifted away ... long-backed, hipless, bosomless, her straight white frock, without folds as, apparently, without seams, plastered around the loins with wide black silk sash, knotted at the

> side—The incarnation of an up-to-date fashion-plate possessed of strong opinions, purposes—
>
> II
>
> And a heart?
>
> (Malet 1924, 63)

Voguishly slim, Marie-Louise is an exemplar of those "modern canons of taste" which the novel more or less derides (65). She has the *sangfroid* of Lawrence's Gudrun Brangwen; ruthless ambition; and a sharp, ironical tongue. Her beauty is of the avant-garde sort, "more precious because recondite, appealing to the initiated rather than the vulgar" (65). At the mention of Marie-Louise's "strong opinions," Malet leaves the reader suspended as if pausing in contemplation of this curious development in female character, the claims of sentiment hesitantly—ashamedly?—surfacing after the chapter break. In contrast to Marie-Louise, Barbara's shapely outline is reminiscent of an earlier, Victorian moment. Looking in a full-length mirror:

> Barbara gave a half turn and fell into observing her figure in profile. Seen thus it represented undeniable contours, a swell of the bosom and a fall in the back condemned by the canons of modern fashion, though not as she comfortably reminded herself, by those of classic art. It could not be acclaimed modishly one-dimensional but neither could the most carping critics call her fat. The lines were long and suave and the contours, however much their existence might offend, were still absolutely in their right place.
>
> (228)

With an increasingly stylised, metonymic treatment of Barbara's body and its grammatical move from object to subject, the physical gives way to the textual. That is to say, Barbara's body becomes the pre*text* on which Malet inveighs against the "carping critics" who dismiss her as a practitioner of the Victorian grand manner. If we were in doubt as to her intention, a strange visual effect—light, shining through a window blind—transforms Barbara's hotel room into "a blank white page ruled with broad black lines" (231). Reviewers were evidently conscious of the inference. In a November 1924 edition of the *Times Literary Supplement* Orlo Williams remarks of the novel that "[t]here is a certain dignified amplitude in the method of narration which is deliberately, but quite successfully, adopted. Lucas Malet makes no bones about her dislike for certain modernities, whether of art, conversation, or contour." For Williams, Malet's style "has the undeniable contours of an older school" (Williams 1924, 705). While Denison Fisher, Barbara's secret lover, "is a little over rotund for a modern day," Marie-Louise, emissary of the new, has a pleasing "economy of line" (705). Similarly, in a review titled simply "Victorianism" the *Manchester Guardian* notes the "struggle between two periods," which manifests around Marie-Louise's "undulating line of body" (B.A.S. 1924, 7). Thus, for Malet and her critics, while the rarefied body of Marie-Louise stands in for high literary modernism, her unfashionable counterparts have the fleshlier aspect of Victorian prose. In noting its conflictedness, the *Manchester Guardian* dismisses the novel as "an old fashioned book thinly varnished with modernity," a view we should treat with extreme caution (B.A.S. 1924, 7).

The Dogs of Want registers an anxiety about its own modernity that renders it more, not less, worthy of attention. There is a fascinating unconscious irony in that at the very moment Malet seeks to defend old-fashioned narrative amplitude, her prose itself becomes "recondite," meta-critical, conspicuously *modern*. In fact, this whole episode of extended looking serves to communicate the ranging impressions of Barbara's "rudderless mind," from the psychological dislocation of her self-image to something like metaphysical crisis: "she realised the extraordinary apartness of each human life"; she was a "solitary spot of consciousness in the heart of universal vacancy" (230).

Such corporal rhetoric inevitably obtrudes itself into critical discussions about Malet's short stories, which were characterised, on the one hand, as turgid experiments in the short form and, on the other, as lamentably abbreviated specimens of the novel. An expression of her problematic positioning within a literary marketplace which increasingly privileged the short story in its magazine format is the 1909 publication of *The Score* (1909), a volume which contains the two apparently unrelated novella-length stories "Miserere Nobis" and "The Courage of Her Convictions." Critics did not quite know what to make of the volume, not least because the publisher, John Murray, failed to advertise it as a collection of stories. Writing in *The New Age* under the name Jacob Tonson, Arnold Bennett complains:

> I have noticed over and over again that the chief aim of a publisher, when he publishes a book of stories seems to be to conceal the horrid fact that that he has published a book of stories ... just recently Mr. John Murray has had the honour of publishing two volumes of stories by Mr. Eden Phillpotts and Lucas Malet... Mr Murray advertised the books as "works of fiction." Not a word to state that ... Lucas Malet's [contained] two separate stories!
>
> (Tonson 1909, 287)

Likewise, a review in *Vogue* objects that "[u]pon some principle of inclusion unrevealed to at least one reader, Mrs Harrison makes the title above given cover the two novelettes bound together in the volume thus named" ("What They Read" 1909, 474). Pitching her experiment in the short form as a halfway house between the novel and the short story, *The Score* led critics to the view that Malet was not suited to the demands of this increasingly popular format. *The Athenaeum* reported that "the short story does not give quite sufficient scope to this author's remarkable gifts," and similarly, *The Dublin Review* explains that the author's "literary habits are those of the realistic artist, who usually works in the form of the long novel"; regretfully "Lucas Malet is hampered by the narrow limits she has chosen" (S 1909, 429; "Short Stories" 1909, 206; S 1909, 429). By 1912 Malet had arrived at a similar conclusion. In a letter lamenting her comparative lack of success with American audiences, she admits, "I don't serialize well. I can't write short stories [… The Americans] think me old fashioned" (qtd. In Lundberg 2003, 347). Nonetheless in 1922 she published *Da Silva's Widow and Other Stories*. The collection received a more enthusiastic response, particularly from the *New York Times*, which praised the stories for their "sophistication" and "finesse" (Maunsell Field 1922, 51). Combined with the fact that John Cournos selected two of Malet's tales for his "best short stories of 1922–23," the collection's moderately warm reception led Lundberg to claim that "[n]ecessity has made of Malet a good short story writer" (Lundberg 2003, 398). The stories in *Da Silva's Widow* are, in fact, rather uneven.

Critical Fortunes

After the First World War, Malet's critical and commercial fortunes took a turn for the worse. A toxic combination of depression and poor physical health meant that she struggled to write. Financial difficulty also weighed heavy on her mind, and she began to cash in advances on as yet unwritten material. It is difficult precisely to say why an author who turned dining tables into battlefields at the turn of the century failed to realise decent returns on her twentieth-century writing. In *The Forgotten Female Aesthetes*, Talia Schaffer articulates the problem of Malet's critical neglect in the following terms:

> We know that some New Woman writers were neglected because their politics were too overt and their style was too journalistic. But this does not apply to Malet, whose politics were unobtrusive, whose style was consciously literary, and whose contemporaries admired her. To read Lucas Malet today is to participate in a history that demands a different explanation: a woman writer whose canonical imprimatur was later, apparently, revoked.
>
> (Schaffer 2000, 199)

Various possible explanations have been offered for Malet's eclipse: that there was a pervasive (but altogether erroneous) feeling that her novels became less incendiary following her conversion to Catholicism (Lundberg 2003, 6); that Malet's agent, A.P. Watt, failed to market her fiction to an appropriate audience (Gillies 2007, 80); that her "evolving modernist style met with sloppy reviews that endeavoured to push her back into Victorianism" (Lundberg 2003, 6); and finally that her equivocal position in relation to the women's movement made her an unattractive subject for recovery.

There exists much in Malet's fiction that overlaps with the work of the so-called New Woman writers of the *fin de siècle.* Her preoccupation with female, sometimes homosexual, desire; her dramatisation of unconventional relationships; and her contempt for sexual double standards connects her work to some of the biggest New Woman names of her day. In an 1888 letter to famous American socialite and bibliophile Isabella Stewart Gardner, Bernard Berenson, the art connoisseur, described Malet's *Mrs. Lorimer* as "the best English novel I have read" since "a remarkably intelligent woman attempts to really tell me what women of the average kind think and feel." He describes the work of the poets Michael Field as "exquisite" yet "very crude" and Elizabeth Barrett-Browning's writings as "uninteresting, half-masculine, half-hysterical aspirations" (1888, 16). However, he compares *Mrs. Lorimer* to his own semi-autobiographical short story "The Third Category" (1887), the tale of an epicurean and acolyte of Walter Pater, whose appreciation of beauty is uninhibited by moral scruples. Clearly, Malet was fully aligned with neither the experimental strain in *fin-de-siècle* poetry by women nor the hysterical femininity of the mid-Victorian novelistic tradition but with a third category that walked the line between the two.

In a 1921 review of her work the French critic Abel Chevalley praised Malet for having "devoted the better part of her talent to women's emancipation and marital problems," which, he adds, she had done "in the spirit of feminism" (qtd. in Lundberg 2003, 386). Regardless of what her readers may have thought, Malet certainly did not see herself as part of any feminist tradition since by her own admission she favoured works by so-called anti-feminists. In "The Progress of Woman: In Literature" (1888) she writes of Ouida—famous for her derisive reply to Sarah Grand's announcement of the arrival of the New Woman in 1894—that she is "endowed with splendid gifts, cruelly injured, alas!" since she is an author "with whom it is not the fashion to reckon as seriously as she deserves" (299). Along with anti-suffrage campaigner Eliza Lynn Linton, Malet singles out only Mary Elizabeth Braddon and Anne Isabella Thackeray as contemporary female authors worthy of praise. In 1888, the year Grand's explosive first novel, *Ideala*, was published; the year Amy Levy's *Reuben Sachs* and *The Romance of a Shop* appeared; the year Mona Caird's article "Marriage" caused a sensation in the *Westminster Review*; and five years after Olive Schreiner's *The Story of an African Farm* set the tone for a new breed of proto-feminist fiction, Malet fails to mention New Woman writers in her assessment of modern literary women.

Indeed, 'modern' women are largely unfavourably represented in Malet's oeuvre—Charlotte Perry in *The Carissima* (1896), Virginia Rivers in *The Gateless Barrier* (1900), Henrietta Pereira in *Damaris*, and Marie-Louise Syme in *The Dogs of Want* (1924) are all rendered unflatteringly in contrast to womanly—or 'Victorian'—women. In "The Threatened Re-Subjection of Woman" Malet labelled the New Woman "sexless, homeless, unmaternal" (1905, 816) and lamented the state of the English middle classes, whose women she indicted for prioritising their independence and valuing work over motherhood. An earlier version of the essay published in *The Daily Telegraph* in December 1904 entitled "The Wife and the Home" had cavilled at women in far less inflammatory terms. The article received so little attention that the later version—which accused middle-class women of "moral and physical indifference somewhat distressingly animal" and of being "infected by a greed of notoriety" (808–9)—may well have been calculated to provoke ire among the "*féministes*" from whom Malet carefully set herself apart. If Malet's aim in redrafting the essay was publicity, it certainly worked. In response to "The Threatened Re-Subjection of Woman" Mona Caird upbraided Malet, in an article entitled "The Duel of the Sexes" (1905), for ingratitude and pessimism—for undermining the progress made by her long-suffering female literary forebears.

In many ways, Malet's defence of domesticity and motherhood, and her horror at women's increasing desire for the sorts of hard work that made marriage, and thus ease and comfort, unlikely, seems disappointingly essentialist and at odds with the radical explorations of female agency in her fictional works. However, for this typology of the New Woman there was indeed precedent in the form of George Egerton (Mary Chavelita Dunne Bright), who held similar views on maternity and who was also equivocal about women's suffrage. Egerton's collections of short stories, entitled *Keynotes* (1893) and *Discords* (1894), caused a literary stir and moral panic ultimately leading to the demise of her short publishing career after the trial and conviction for gross indecency of Oscar Wilde in 1895. Like Egerton, Malet frankly depicted the seedier aspects of Victorian life and lambasted the sexual hypocrisy that made victims of both sexes. However, her career survived the moral censure of the late 1890s that stifled the creativity of controversial writers like Egerton, and she went on to publish a more sexually subversive offering in *Calmady* than either *Keynotes* or *Discords* had ever been.

Why then was Malet's work—ostensibly better able to weather the storm of outrage that surrounded allegedly 'decadent' women writers of the late 1890s—lost to contemporary scholars, while Egerton's has enjoyed such a resurgence of interest over the past two decades? If these female authors held similar views on the Woman Question, and published similarly seditious works, why did Malet enjoy the success in her own lifetime that eluded Egerton and others like her yet fail to surface as a natural candidate for feminist recovery in twentieth- or twenty-first-century scholarship? The answer is fourfold. Malet was a Kingsley, a representative of a much-loved dynasty with the connections and acumen to survive. She had gained enough literary prestige by 1901 that much of her controversial content went unnoticed by reviewers, who avoided the sorts of criticism that made other authors unreadable after 1895. Her texts were marketed very differently from Egerton's, whose provocative cover-illustrations and depictions of Beardsleyesque women immediately aligned her with controversial *Yellow Book* contributors like Wilde. Malet wrote mostly in the novel form, and her efforts at short story writing, the modus operandi of the New Woman literary movement, were frequently rejected by publishers and often attracted negative reviews. Since much of the research on women writers of the late nineteenth and early twentieth centuries has focused on the transition from the realist novel to shorter, experimental forms, Malet's extensive range of proto-modernist offerings seem to have escaped the attention afforded to authors like Grand, Caird, Egerton, Levy, Schreiner, Victoria Cross, and Vernon Lee. Like the influence of Agnes Rivers, the ghost with whom the married protagonist falls in love in *The Gateless Barrier*, the morality of Malet's ascetic hero in *The Far Horizon* provides cover for the questionable sexual conduct of her actress heroine. Conversely, controversial works by other late nineteenth-century woman writers were publicly denounced for the sort of anti-religious rhetoric that Malet's novels, even when concerned with purportedly 'deviant' forms of Christianity like Catholicism, were not. Seemingly, what shielded Malet's novels from censure and safeguarded her literary success in her own time—the traditionalism of the novel form and her reverence for the spiritual and the religious—may in part have contributed to her lack of appeal amongst contemporary students and scholars, who have better connected with the formal and thematic radicalism of some of her competitors.

§

This introduction endeavours to paint a portrait of a writer who occupied a central position in late nineteenth- and early twentieth-century literary networks; a writer who, in a career spanning fifty years, did not merely absorb changing literary trends but helped drive developments in style and actively flouted convention. As we point out, this is particularly true of her gender politics, which were subversive enough to attract censure from social conservatives and conservative enough to inflame social progressives—including 'feminists' like Mona Caird. Malet's preoccupation with the human body and, in particular, aberrant or pathological physical states, opened a gateway for her unflinching spiritual, moral, and psychological enquiry. She was also, latterly, a writer who wore her Catholicism on her sleeve and, contrary to popular opinion, continued to explore incendiary subjects within the framework of her religious fiction. To this end we have organised the collection into four sections, which articulate what we consider to be the principal pathways to an understanding of her oeuvre: "Maletian Bodies," "Dissident Women," "Malet and her Contemporaries," and "Catholic (Proto-)Modernism." Of course, there are aspects of Malet's work which fall outside the remit of this collection and stories, too, that we have not been in a position to explore, but it is our hope that this volume will build on the early critical interventions of Patricia Lorimer Lundberg, Talia Schaffer, Catherine Delyfer, and others to mark a clear turning point in the critical fortunes of Lucas Malet.

Part 1: Maletian Bodies

In a 1926 edition of *The Irish Journal of Medical Science,* an editorial piece on medicine in literature complains of the Victorians' "pathological proprieties" ("Editorial" 1926, 57). Drawing on the amusing (but not entirely accurate) adage that "nobody in a Victorian novel ever died of anything below the diaphragm," the editor laments that even a writer so "iconoclastic" as Sarah Grand forbears from using the word "syphilis" in *The Heavenly Twins* (1893), a novel which offers an otherwise radical exploration of the social and physical effects of the disease. By contrast, Lucas Malet's *The History of Sir Richard Calmady* is praised as an "astonishing" story which uses candid portrayals of "physical deformity to account for the progressive moral deterioration of a subject" (57). The editorial evidently carries the taint of twentieth-century repudiations of Victorian "modesty," but nonetheless the editor (who, like Malet, regards physician and novelist as kindred occupations) draws attention to what it is that sets Malet apart from her contemporaries: her trenchant exploration of human pathology. Nonnormative bodies and bodily experience are a privileged theme in her oeuvre and extend far beyond depictions of disability in her most prominent novel. The three chapters in this section explore Malet's abiding preoccupation with the human body and consider how ideas of disability, disease, and decay shape her narrative practice and sense of herself as a woman writer bridging realism, the gothic, and naturalism.

In Chapter 1 Louise Benson James positions Malet's writing between the realist (specifically Eliotean) tradition of scientific enquiry and a gothic aesthetic which schematises human bodies as "disordered," "perverse," or "marginal" (33). With reference to *The Wages of Sin* (1891) and *The Survivors* (1923), novels which practically bookend Malet's career, Benson James reveals Malet's long-standing commitment to "materialise medical fears about bodily rupture, impairment and disfigurement" (34). As Benson James points out, Malet frequently focuses on *male* pathology and psychological disorder, a strategy which serves to upend gendered ideas about sick, unruly, and hysterical female bodies, and disrupt Cartesian understandings of the human form as the empty husk within which the soul resided. Indeed, as Benson James shows, Malet's remarkable attention to synergies of bodily and mental pathology in her medical gothic texts is both imaginative and stylistic, the space of the operating room or the symptoms of nervous disorder standing in for Malet's views on the act of authorship itself.

Framed as an inherited curse, Sir Richard Calmady's disability is often read as a rejection of Charles Kingsley's valorisation of a physically robust, heterosexual masculinity. In Chapter 2, Clare Walker Gore posits a more dialogic relationship with Malet's "paternal inheritance" (52) and considers how Kingsley's legacy is managed through equestrian motifs. Indeed, Richard struggles with his late father's injunction that he learn to "ride straight," (52), a term which conveniently carries associations with heterosexuality and direct, unmediated inheritance. Focusing on the trope of "adaptation" established in Sir Richard's bespoke riding saddle, Walker Gore argues that his disabled body expresses not a rejection but a rerouting of "inherited traditions" (53).

Bodily alterity and fragility are also a central concern of Alani Hicks-Bartlett's essay on *The Far Horizon*, a novel which traces the movements of Dominic Iglesias, a retired bank clerk with Irish and Spanish heritage. In her chapter, Hicks-Bartlett considers how the novel offers a "strategic recodification of the bildungsroman" (83) genre in the wake of Malet's conversion to Catholicism. In contrast to traditional novels of development, which tend to follow a youthful protagonist's journey from social margins to the social core, *The Far Horizon* depicts Iglesias's "vertiginous back-and-forth" between an "oneiric, illusive past" and "an otherworldly, divine future" (73). Hicks-Bartlett demonstrates that in restructuring the bildungsroman around a character "whose liminality, corporeal fragility and ... old age" would traditionally have excluded him from the role of protagonist, Malet launches a critique of the "exclusionary" tactics of English Protestant society.

Part 2: Dissident Women

Writing in 1909, Edith Searle Grossman describes, in a *Westminster Review* article entitled "The New Sex Psychology," the shift from a Victorian "ascetic presentment of moral problems" to a modernist "questioning of the old basis of morality" (Grossman 1909, 508) at the end of the nineteenth century. Identifying Malet as an author across whose works such a shift can be traced, Grossman cites the "distant prospect of new foundations" for the relationship between the sexes that Malet's works were negotiating as early as 1896 in *The Carissima*. One of a handful of popular authors whose opus captures the uneasy transition between distinctive philosophies of "Woman," Malet, according to Grossman, was a writer who imagined a range of possibilities for women who dared to want more. The essays in this section discuss female characters who attempt to 'have it all': wealth as well as independence, freedom from control as well as a happy marriage, and a professional life as well as romantic love. From a range of narrative, generic, national, and historical perspectives these dissident female figures personify nineteenth-century concerns about women's bodies and desires, and their changing place in the social and political order. For Malet, however, these concerns were both multifarious and inextricable. The inscrutability of her shifting views is exemplified by the development of what might easily be read as both proto-feminist *and* anti-feminist rhetoric in the three novels examined, respectively, by Alexandra Gray, Catherine Delyfer, and Crescent Rainwater.

In Chapter 4 Gray disentangles Malet's alleged 'feminism' from the New Woman politics of her day. Focusing on *The Carissima*, an 1896 gothic tale about a hallucinatory demon dog, Gray argues that the grotesque (in particular, animalistic images of feminised men and lurid images of sexual women) is deployed by Malet to destabilise polarised thinking about gender—thinking which actually emerges in essentialist New Woman critiques of the sexual double standard. Importantly, this essay uncovers striking similarities between *The Carissima* and Arthur Conan Doyle's own demon-dog mystery *The Hound of the Baskervilles* (1902). As Gray points out, while Doyle's hound was "applauded ... as a narrative device," Malet's own canine offering was perceived to be derivative (except, tellingly, by a reviewer who believed Malet to be male (91)). Gray therefore not only reassesses Malet's place in the canon of nineteenth-century 'feminist' authors but also considers how her gender may have coloured the critical reception of this novel.

In Chapter 5 Delyfer explores the fate of two women who yearn for more, one English, one French, whose efforts at navigating nineteenth-century social and cultural norms are read through the prism of national, political, and religious differences. Delyfer's essay seeks to question the notion of a happy ending in Malet's works and posits *Adrian Savage* as an example of the author's subversion of the formal and thematic conventions of both romance and realism. Tracing a range of early twentieth-century feminist crosscurrents, Delyfer considers the exploits of the novel's heroines as a caution against the dangers of underestimating women's desires. Similarly, in Chapter 6 Rainwater investigates Malet's dramatic reworking of the bildungsroman to challenge literary traditions placing masculine adventure and self-discovery at the heart of the Victorian novel. Making "striking claims about women's independence ... that emerge largely through the narrative structure rather than overt polemic" (129) Rainwater investigates the unstable equilibrium of the heroine's burgeoning sexuality against her desire to succeed as an author.

The essay traces the tensions between femininity and cultural production in a text featuring a fictional reworking of Malet's own emergence from the shadow of her famous father's literary legacy.

Part 3: Malet and Her Contemporaries

Malet's engagement in the gender debates of the late nineteenth and early twentieth centuries, evidenced in essays by Gray, Delyfer, and Rainwater, constitutes an important piece of the puzzle of her relation to her literary contemporaries. Malet came under fire from her peers for subversive portrayals of transgressive women as well as for her seemingly anti-suffrage politics. She was also, at times, accused by reviewers of plagiarising the work of her male rivals. Critics were far less attuned to the various ways in which Malet's own efforts were appropriated by male authors, a disappointing fissure in critical assessments of her that chapters by Jill Ehnenn and Talia Schaffer set out to address. In Chapter 7 Ehnenn observes that both Lucas Malet and Thomas Hardy deploy the bildungsroman to cleverly reorient their characters towards nontraditional identities. In doing so, Ehnenn situates *Calmady* as part of a tradition of *fin-de-siècle* authorship responsible for undermining Victorian ideals of normalcy. Malet's 1901 novel is thus imagined not as a response to, or appropriation of, *Jude the Obscure* but as part of a discursive continuum of candid explorations of alterity that cleared the way for future literary portrayals of disability and homosexuality.

In Chapter 8 Schaffer points out the multidirectional quality of Malet's influence on, and by, Henry James. Although direct influence is impossible to prove, in reading James's unpublished ghost story *The Sense of the Past* alongside Malet's *The Gateless Barrier*, Schaffer argues, the relative positions of a male and female author can be traced in their treatment of the same themes and plot. What Schaffer is careful to point out is that, far from pilfering material from James, Malet's work likely inspired him at a time when he was particularly concerned with the influence of both his reading habits and his creative legacy on his continuing contributions to cultural history. Performing more than just a comparison of male versus female vantage points, Schaffer's essay considers the extent to which both texts' metaphors of imprisonment, haunting, and female creative agency represent the concerns of two authors at different stages in their respective careers and, in Malet's case, prophesise the fate of the neglected female author during the hundred years that followed.

Part 4: Catholic (Proto-)Modernism

In an oft-cited passage from his *Oxford Introduction to Modern Verse*, W.B. Yeats humorously declared that after 1900, "everybody got down off his stilts; henceforth nobody drank absinthe with his black coffee;

nobody went mad, nobody committed suicide; nobody joined the Catholic Church; or if they did I have forgotten" (Yeats 1936, xi). Of course, there were several modernist Catholic converts, including, notably, Ford Madox Ford and Evelyn Waugh. However, as Timothy J. Sutton persuasively demonstrates, Catholic modernists frequently had less to do with aesthetic and Newmanite forms of Victorian Catholicism than a recusant Catholic tradition which emphasised discreet devotional practices and English nationalism (2010, 13–31). Malet's Catholic sensibility contributed to the modernist development of her prose, but the overt ideology of her faith and its explicitly anti-English character align her more closely with figures like Hilaire Belloc and G.K. Chesterton (an admirer of her work) than with prominent Catholic modernists. In fact, Malet was a close personal friend of Belloc's sister, the writer Marie Belloc Lowndes, and like Belloc Malet believed that the Reformation and imposition of national barriers between Christian adherents, ushered in a great number of social and economic ills. The two chapters in this section, then, explore the stylistic development of Malet's fiction in the twentieth century, looking particularly at how her Catholicism informed her negotiations with an emerging modernist aesthetic.

In Chapter 9, Holly Laird argues that *The Far Horizon* registers the generic and stylistic "cross currents of the early twentieth century," merging "turn-of the-century realism and satire with modernist anti-conventialism" (185). As Laird demonstrates, the novel's "proto-modernism" is informed by a religious ideology which, in yearning for a "pre-modern past," censures the narrowly nationalistic spirit of English Protestantism (187). But Laird is careful to point out that the "*The Far Horizon* does not represent Malet's most radical vision of human possibility," reproducing, as it does, English assumptions about class, race, and decorum. In her chapter on *The Survivors*, Jane Ford similarly points out that the modernist development of Malet's style, far from representing a kind of modish opportunism, is rooted in theological ideas which loom large in her earlier, conversion-period work. Ford argues that the novel's representations of telepathy—a literary trope which, because of its unstable psychic qualities, has frequently been aligned with modernist experiments in style and narrative—is positioned as an analogue of divine revelation. Ford suggests that the First World War and the opportunities for "spiritual performance and charlatanism" (218) it created presents a useful backdrop for Malet, who persistently seeks to juxtapose corrupted forms of terrestrial communication with the edifying (but still epistemologically challenged) possibilities of the Word.

Appendix

In the final section of this volume we include the transcript of "In Memoriam, Ernest D. Chesterfield," a previously unpublished short story now housed in the L. Tom Perry Special Collections at Brigham Young University. The story is written in the form of a eulogy for the narrator's mentor: a Wildean aesthete, who exerted a "singular influence" over his younger Cambridge peers. The manuscript is undated, but it bears a striking resemblance to Malet's 1922 short story "The Birth of a Masterpiece," which similarly explores themes of aesthetic discipleship and egoism. It may be that "Ernest D" predates the 1922 story, the latter expanding and reworking ideas initially explored in this manuscript.

"Ernest D" certainly showcases Malet's quirky sense of humour (the few fragments relating to Ernest's infancy are the lines "it is very red. It cries a great deal. I hope to goodness poor Charlotte is not going to have a large family"), but more importantly it reveals a deeply ambivalent attitude towards aestheticism or, at least, the movement's most prominent, male practitioners (221). This is important, particularly given that existing critical efforts to recover Malet rely heavily on Talia Schaffer's reading of her as a "forgotten female aesthete" (Schaffer 2000). Indeed, as Ruth Robbins argues in her accompanying essay "Retelling the Untold Stories: Lucas Malet's Critique of an Aesthetic Trope," Malet not only applied the techniques and "borrowed the plumes" of aestheticism but satirised the "useless lives of egocentric men," their "false idols and foolish disciples," and their "unconsummated artistic endeavour" (232).

Robbins questions, through a reading of the two stories, whether Lucas Malet can be called an aesthete at all. Like Schaffer and Ehnenn, whose own contributions to this collection examine Malet's connection to her male contemporaries, and Gray and Ford, whose respective essays also note the networks of literary influence at the centre of which Malet often found herself, Robbins highlights the Wildean, Paterian pastiche central to "In Ernest D," one that would seem to anticipate and, arguably, exceed Malet's scathing indictment of male aesthetes in "The Birth of a Masterpiece" yet never found its way into the hands of the public.

Works Cited

Alden, William L. 1901. "London Letter." *New York Times*, 28 September, 9.

Barry, William. 1901. "Lucas Malet's Challenge." *The Bookman* 21(121): 20–21.

Berenson, Bernard. 1987. "Letter to Mrs Gardener, Feb 25th 1888." In *The Letters of Bernard Berenson and Isabella Stewart Gardner, 1887–1924, with Correspondence by Mary Berenson*, edited by R. Van N. Hadley. Lebanon: Northeastern University Press.

Boone, Joseph Allen. 1998. *Libidinal Currents: Sexuality and the Shaping of Modernism*. Chicago, IL: Chicago University Press.

Caird, Mona. 1905. "The Duel of the Sexes: A Comment." *The Fortnightly Review*, 78: 109–22.

Delyfer, Catherine. 2010. "Lucas Malet's Subversive Late-Gothic: Humanizing the Monster in *The History of Sir Richard Calmady*." In *Demons of the Body and Mind: Essays on Disability in Gothic Literature*, edited by Ruth Bienstock Anolik, 80–96. Jefferson: McFarland.

———. 2011. *Art and Womanhood in Fin-de-Siècle Writing: The Fiction of Lucas Malet: 1880–1931*. London: Pickering & Chatto.

Dickens, Mary Angela. 1899. "A Talk with Lucas Malet." *The Windsor Magazine* 10: 522–4.

Dolman, Frederick. 1896. "'Lucas Malet' at Home: A Chat with the Daughter of Charles Kingsley." *The Young Woman: A Monthly Journal and Review* 4: 145–9.

"Editorial." 1926. *Irish Journal of Medical Science* 1(2): 57–60.

Ellis, Havelock. 1932. "A Note on Paul Bourget." In *Views and Reviews: A Selection of Uncollected Articles 1884–1932*, 48–60. London: Desmond Harmsworth.

Emanuel, Angela. 1989. "Introduction." In *A Bright Remembrance: The Diaries of Julia Cartwright 1851–1924*, edited by Angela Emanuel. London: Wiedenfeld & Nicholson.

Frank, Katherine. 2005. *A Voyager Out: The Life of Mary Kingsley*. New York: Tauris.

Freud, Sigmund. 2001. "Three Essays on the Theory of Sexuality (1905), I, The Sexual Aberrations." In *The Standard Edition of the Complete Psychological Works of Sigmund Freud, Vol. VII (1901–1905)*, translated by James Strachey, 135–72. London: Vintage.

Gillies, Mary Ann. 2007. *The Professional Literary Agent in Britain 1880–1920*. Toronto, ON: University of Toronto Press.

Glasgow, Joanne (ed.). 1997. *Your John: The Love Letters of Radclyffe Hall*. New York: New York University Press.

Grossman, Edith Searle. 1909. "The New Sex Psychology." *Westminster Review* 172(5): 497–510.

Hogarth, Janet F. 1902. "Lucas Malet's Novels." *The Fortnightly Review* 71(423): 532–40.

Lorimer Lundberg, Patricia. 2003. *An Inward Necessity: The Writer's Life of Lucas Malet*. New York: Peter Lang.

Malet, Lucas. 1883. *Mrs. Lorimer: A Sketch in Black and White* (2nd ed.). London: Macmillan and Co.

———. 1888a. "The Progress of Woman: In Literature." *The Universal Review* 2(7): 295–301.

———. 1888b. *A Counsel of Perfection*. London: Kegan Paul, Trench & Co.

———. 1904. "The Wife and the Home." *The Daily Telegraph*, 20 December, 9.

———. 1905. "The Threatened Re-Subjection of Woman." *The Fortnightly Review* 77: 806–19.

———. 1906. *The Far Horizon*. London: Hutchinson.

———. 1910. *The Wreck of the Golden Galleon*. London: Hodder and Stoughton.

———. 1916. *Damaris*. London: Hutchinson.

———. 1919. *Deadham Hard: A Romance*. London: Methuen.

———. 1920. "Is it a New World? The Ancient Wisdom." *The Daily Telegraph*. 26 August, 9.

———. 1923. *The Survivors: A Novel*. London: Cassell and Company.

———. 1924. *The Dogs of Want: A Modern Comedy of Errors*. London: Hutchinson.

———. 2003. *The History of Sir Richard Calmady*, edited by Talia Schaffer. Birmingham: Birmingham University Press.

Maunsell Field, Louise. 1922. "Latest Works of Fiction." *New York Times*, 9 July, 51.

Miller, Kathleen A. 2012. "'Your Loving Is Unlike Any Other': Romance and the Disabled Body in the Gothic Fiction of Edith Nesbit and Lucas Malet." In *Writing Women of the Fin de Siècle: Authors of Change*, edited by Adrienne E. Gavin and Carolyn de la Oulton, 193–203. New York: Palgrave Macmillan.

O'Connell, Rachel. 2012. "'That Cruel Spectacle': The Extraordinary Body Eroticized in Lucas Malet's *The History of Sir Richard Calmady*." In *Sex and Disability*, edited by Robert McRuer and Anna Mollow, 108–22. Durham, NC: Duke University Press.

Paul, Herbert. 1902. "Art and Eccentricity." *The Nineteenth Century: A Monthly Review* 51: 252–62.

Rau, Petra. 2006. "Telling It Straight: The Rhetorics of Conversion in Elizabeth Bowen's *The Hotel* and Freud's *Psychogenesis*." In *Sapphic Modernities: Sexuality, Women and National Culture*, edited by Laura Doan and Jane Garrity, 217–31. New York: Palgrave Macmillan.

"Review of New Books." 1896. *Morning Oregonian*, 29 November, 19.

Ruskin, John. 1853. *The Stones of Venice, vol. 3: The Fall*. London: Smith, Elder & Co.

S. 1909. "The Score." *The Dublin Review* 145(290): 429–30.

Schaffer, Talia. 1996. "Some Chapter of Some Other Story: Henry James, Lucas Malet, and the Real Past of the Sense of the Past." *The Henry James Review* 17(2): 109–28.

———. 2000. *The Forgotten Female Aesthetes: Literary Culture in Late Victorian England*. Charlottesville: University Press of Virginia.

Sherwood, Mary Elizabeth Wilson 1901. "Mrs Sherwood." *New York Times*, 23 November, 854.

"Short Stories." 1909. *The Athenaeum* 4269: 206.

Srebrnik, Patricia. 1994. "The Threatened Re-Subjection of 'Lucas Malet': Charles Kingsley's Daughter and the Response to Muscular Christianity." In *Muscular Christianity: Embodying the Victorian Age*, edited by Donald E. Hall, 194–214. Cambridge: Cambridge University Press.

Straus, Ralph. 1919. "A New Literary 'Log.'" 24 September, 873.

Sutton, Timothy J. 2010. *Catholic Modernists, English Nationalists*. Newark, NJ: University of Delaware Press.

Thorp, Margaret, F. 1975. *Charles Kingsley*. London: Constable.

Tonson, Jacob [Arnold Bennett]. 1909. "Books and Persons (An Occasional Causerie)." *The New Age*, 5 August, 286–7.

Walker Gore, Clare. 2014. "Noble Lives: Writing Disability and Masculinity in the Late Nineteenth-Century." *Nineteenth-Century Contexts* 36(4): 363–75.

"Well-Known Women." 1899. *The London Journal* 32: 578.

"What they Read." 1909. *Vogue*, 25 September, 474.

Whitelock, William Wallace. 1901. "A Visit to the Home of Charles Kingsley's Daughter and a Talk with Her." *New York Times Saturday Review*, 26 October, 784.

Willcocks, M. P. 1916. "The Flaw in the Idol." *The Bookman* 51(303): 97–98.

Williams, Orlo. 1924. "New Novels: The Dogs of Want." *The Times Literary Supplement* 6 November.

Yeats, William Butler. 1936. *The Oxford Book of Modern Verse, 1892–1935*. New York: Oxford University Press.

Part 1

Maletian Bodies

1 Hysterical Bodies and Gothic Spaces

Lucas Malet's "moral dissecting-room"

Louise Benson James

The narrator of Lucas Malet's second novel, *Colonel Enderby's Wife* (1885), invokes a metaphorical "moral dissecting-room," with "all its ugly sights, all its humiliating revelations of the weakness, disease, and incompleteness of fallen humanity" (Malet 1908, 176). In this room, those "who are cursed with a necessity to look below the surface, and haunted with an insatiable desire to see things as they really are," apply their scalpel to "moral and mental obliquity" (176–7). This is a statement of Malet's authorial vision: the novel is the "moral dissecting-room," the novelist a purveyor of truth, dismantling the "human obliquity" of the subject and society (176). Patricia Lorimer Lundberg points to this metaphor as signalling Malet's engagement with the realist project: literature that performs a scientific study of human motives (Lundberg 2003, 100). Lundberg highlights Malet's admiration for George Eliot, whom she praised as a novelist "scientific to the core" (Malet 1888, 298). Indeed, we can see echoes of the microscope of *Middlemarch* (1871) in the moral dissecting-room. Yet Malet's surgical scalpel differs from Eliot's variable microscopic lens; it is penetrative, invasive, and corporeal. Dissection, surgical or anatomical, implies the presence of a body or a corpse. Yet Malet obscures this association by designating "obliquity" as the subject under the knife, engaging in evasion and contradiction while promising revelation or insight. This encapsulates a marked feature of Malet's writing: troubling objective 'truth' and established binaries. The repeated use of the word "obliquity" emphasises Malet's fascination with the perverse, strange, and marginal, and her contention that the nature of humanity is essentially deviant.

The moral dissecting-room signposts the significance of the medical and the gothic to Malet's writing. The objective nature of medical practice and the Hippocratic oath are rendered suspect if the drive to dissect is a gothic haunting or curse, an "insatiable" compulsion, the purpose to extract revelations rather than to heal. This chapter will demonstrate how fears about medicine, surgery, dissection, and the vulnerability of the pathologised body manifest throughout Malet's oeuvre, not just as a metaphor for the process of writing, but in objects, events, and characters. It looks at two themes which demonstrate the frequent union of the gothic and medical in Malet's fiction: unruly hysterical bodies, and spaces of illness, surgery, and death. Malet's characters exhibit symptoms, behaviours, and maladies which draw on contemporary medical understandings of hysteria: psychological angst translated into involuntary physical symptoms. Her writing is preoccupied with how the subject is represented by the body, and the body as out of control, even betraying the self, during episodes of disorder. When the body's stability breaks down, the afflicted individual is often confined to a room. Rooms of illness, surgery, and death are the extreme realisation of Malet's impulse to materialise medical fears about bodily rupture, impairment, and disfigurement. The metaphorical moral dissecting-room is invoked in spaces ostensibly for healing, but which reveal themselves to be spaces of pathology, destruction, and death.

The conflation of the gothic and medical is also employed stylistically. Malet indulges in excessive, iterative, histrionic language, tempered by a controlled, scientific, observant narrative voice. This experimental duality reflects Malet's conception and presentation of herself as a writer. The scientific is central not just to Malet's fiction but to her methodology, her determination to write, as she insisted to Janet Hogarth in 1902, "like the man of science, register[ing] the results of my observation and experience" (J. Courtney 1932, 238).[1] In "The Progress of Woman: In Literature" Malet praised science and democracy in literature above all and insisted that women must write "under these two banners" (Malet 1888, 298). In an 1899 interview, discussing believability of character, Malet said, "I suppose it comes of a scientific reasoning faculty—one argues things out with a deadly precision. Given certain premises, certain results are inevitable" (Dickens 1899, 524). This reinforces the image of Malet as a writer analogous to a scientist or surgeon, extracting a logical truth; at least, this was what she presented in public interviews and essays. In a private letter to her brother-in-law Clifford Harrison in 1884, while writing *Colonel Enderby's Wife*, Malet disclosed, "I have been a little troubled lest my own book should become a trifle hysterical, lest we should sit shrieking at agony point" (qtd. in Lundberg 2003, 97). Malet may be referring to her own lifelong struggle with shattered nerves. Yet the move from "my" to "we" in this sentence suggests transmission from the individual to the collective, a sense of oneness with, or influence upon, her readership. It implies danger of contagion via the novel, much as Max Nordau would admonish "degenerate" fiction eight years later. The dichotomy of writing as the "man of science" and writing hysterically is channelled into Malet's fiction, narrativised as a formal and thematic device.

My analysis centres on two novels, produced in different historical moments with distinctive cultural anxieties, but which illustrate Malet's recurring interest in hysterical bodies, physical impairment, and human obliquity. The first is *The Wages of Sin* (1891), a *fin-de-siècle* text that incorporates hysteria as localised physical symptoms; convulsions, mydriasis, and stammering. The novel's protagonist James Colthurst is a struggling young artist, encumbered with a debilitating stammer. While visiting Devon he begins an affair with local girl, Jenny Parris. Meanwhile the twelve-year-old child, Mary Crookenden, is traumatised by the shooting of a rabbit. The narrative moves forward in time by six years, and Colthurst is a successful and celebrated artist with a painting hanging in the Royal Academy. He has been supporting Jenny and their child but refuses to marry her. During a less auspicious time, when they were close to starving in Paris, Jenny turned to prostitution in order to feed them. Colthurst cannot forgive her for this and regards her with disgust and contempt. He falls in love with Mary Crookenden, now a charming young socialite, who attends the art school where he teaches. Their brief idyll is disrupted by the revelation of the existence of his mistress and child. Yet Jenny has consumption, and returns to Devon, where Mary and Colthurst attend her deathbed and witness her final breath. Colthurst then falls, or is pushed, to his death from the cliffs, and Mary is left to wander the world aimlessly.

The second novel I will examine in detail is *The Survivors* (1923), set in an atmosphere of post-war cultural malaise, in which the fragility and flaws of humanity are somatised in a wounded soldier and vampiric hospital matron. *The Survivors* is a gothic story about the pathologising effect of war on the home front. The North Downs village of Maidsworthy and its inhabitants are affected by the "roll of ghostly drums" (Malet 1923, 29); these sounds of war from across the Channel disturb their nerves and behaviour: "it seems to drive you out of yourself and make you want to do any sort of mad thing to give you something else to think about" (86). Meanwhile, Lady Sybella Aylwin runs a hospital for convalescing wounded soldiers on Hampstead Heath. She has become infatuated with war-ravaged soldier Braybrooke and subjects him to the unnecessary amputation of a leg. Fifteen years her junior, Braybrooke will be reliant on Sybella forever and will be prevented from "running away" (216). "Moral dissection" is subverted and materialised in this act of surgical maiming, and Malet's use of the gothic transforms the supernatural or metaphorical into sadistic body horror.

Helen King comments of medical hysteria that throughout history "the message remains the same: women are sick, and men write their bodies" (King 1993, 64). As a woman author writing about 'sick,' unstable, or damaged male bodies, Malet enacts an inversion of this pattern. The *Survivors* hospital surgeon McNaughten states, "when you box up sick men and well women together in a circumscribed area" it creates "a hotbed of unwholesome emotions" (Malet 1923, 215). This encapsulates the transgressive interactions that occur within circumscribed spaces, where bodies and binaries are destabilised. Malet's artistic depictions of disordered bodies explore tensions between uncomfortable dualities, challenge received ideas about bodily integrity signifying morality, and trouble binary stereotypes of men as strong and controlled, and women as sick and unstable. Her frequent uniting of medical and gothic discourse is accompanied by increasing materialism, suggesting a fascination with the corporeal that transcends the metaphor of the moral dissecting-room and forms a distinctly Maletian medical gothic.

"broken human crockery": Bodies in Malet's Fiction

William Courtney and Janet Hogarth both followed Malet's career, and both objected to Malet's "marked tendency to dwell on physical peculiarities" (Hogarth 1902, 537). They list repetitive mannerisms that her characters display across several novels: sticking out the underlip, protruding the jaw, stammering, running into people, puckering lips, and grunting, in other words, tics, spasms, and compulsive repetitive actions. For Hogarth, this tendency in Malet's work documents "a natural history of the birth and growth of a taste for the abnormal" (Hogarth 1902, 532). She objects to Malet's "insistent dwelling upon physical pain" (536), commenting, "one cannot acquit Lucas Malet of a certain predilection for ugliness. All these little personal peculiarities are just the awkward, unsightly tricks which have an unhealthy fascination for us when our nerves are out of order" (537–8). While explaining the addictive quality of Malet's writing—the draw of the macabre and morbid as vicariously satisfying for the reader—Hogarth also implies that Malet's fiction is responsible for exacerbating nervous disorder.[2]

William Courtney discerns "physical peculiarities" to be part of Malet's "artistic study of life," evidence of "certain tendencies in the direction of the corporeal, the physical, the material" (W. Courtney 1904, 94). For Courtney, this is essential to Malet's development as a writer. His account of her oeuvre perceives that her

> careful and conscientious study of the spiritual, the unseen world … tends more and more to materialism—an imaginative handling, not of the abstract and imperceptible, but of the things which can only be its outward husk, crust, and emblematic figure.
>
> (W. Courtney 1904)

Courtney's observation of Malet's increasing materialism rings true; Malet's depiction of physical peculiarities suggests a medical interest in bodies, a scientific observation of physical symptoms and behaviours. However, his construction of materialism accords with Cartesian models of embodiment that see the body as a vehicle, vessel, or "husk," to the spiritual self. In contrast, Malet's novels signify the centrality of bodily experiences, the body as a complex system in which the mind is involved. Colthurst's stammer is an involuntary and compulsive hysterical symptom which defines his character and acts as a key plot device. Indeed, problems of utterance pervade the novel: muteness, inarticulate sounds, garbled expression. Often these struggles to articulate are resolved by communicating through alternative forms of body language, which Freud later defined as the function of hysteria. In later novels, characters are increasingly subjected to escalating bodily impairment, fleshly damage, and destruction. In *The Survivors*, Braybrooke's war-mutilated body is further disassembled by the combined forces of his lover's sadism and modern surgery. In Malet's novels the body is an unstable site in which crises are manifested; self and subjectivity are called into question by the presence of uncontrollable symptoms or physical rupture.

The second chapter of *Wages* opens with the protagonist Mary Crookenden, at this point twelve years old, "lying face downwards in the short crisp heath, while her poor, gaudily-clad, little shoulders quivered convulsively" (Malet 1895, 19). She has witnessed the shooting of a rabbit by her cousin Lancelot. Recounting the story to her Uncle Kent, Mary processes her emotions: "I cried because of the rabbit Lance shot. It squeaked, and that made me feel badly, and I was ever so angry" (28). The narrator tells us that "Unfortunately, however, Mary's imagination was powerful. The remembrance of the rabbit's death shriek, of the scattered tufts of soft grey fur, of the shuddering blood-stained little body, was too much for her" (29). That Mary's reaction is to some extent a performance is suggested by her gaudy outfit, her anger at Lance, and her statement of resolve: "I shall cry just all I want" (19). Yet her physical weeping and convulsion are also uncontrollable physical responses to what she has witnessed. The rabbit's shuddering little body is mirrored in Mary's little shoulders quivering convulsively. She mimics its death with her body, recalling the way in which Jean-Martin Charcot's hysterics mimicked epileptic seizures, forming the distinctive full-body fits of *grande hysterie* which became the definitive hysterical symptom within the walls of the Salpêtrière during the 1880s. These hysterics famously performed for audiences, publicly staging their symptoms. Mary's shuddering adolescent body reveals to Lance "the mystery, the glory, the cruel riddle and tragedy of sex" (22), at once an emergence from childhood, and anticipation of the sexualised hysterical body.

The traumatic impact of the rabbit's death-shriek resonates through Mary's life; she is overwhelmed by pathos whenever she witnesses physical pain in animals and humans alike. She is described as "wilfully blind" to inward mental suffering, while "physical suffering … affected her very differently" (248). Mary, like Malet, is more concerned with the external body than the "abstract and imperceptible" self. The dénouement to the formative episode of the rabbit's death sees Mary, tearstained on the hillside, encounter James Colthurst for the first time. When they meet again, like the rabbit's shriek, Colthurst's own tortured utterance, his pronounced stammer, produces an involuntary bodily response in Mary. When he tells her that he loves her, she "put one hand over her eyes with a sort of shuddering sigh" (255). As she hears him begin to stammer at a party, she "drew up her hands with a quick shuddering motion, covered her eyes with her fan" (348). The repeated "shudder" indicates a return to the scene of her childhood trauma, awakening of sexual awareness, and the onset of her instinctive mimetic response to physical suffering.

Catherine Delyfer notes that Mary "develops a peculiar eye condition: a form of mydriasis which becomes especially acute whenever Colthurst is in her vicinity" (Delyfer 2011, 68). Delyfer sees this dilation of the pupils as a metaphor for the expansion of Mary's aesthetic awareness due to her artistic relationship with Colthurst. Yet Mary's mydriasis can also be read as an involuntary hysterical symptom, the overturning of her emotional blindness: "Miss Crookenden was attentive. Her eyes were growing responsive, dilating, deepening in colour" (Malet 1895, 148). Seeing Colthurst from across the room at a party, "as she gazed her expression softened, her eyes dilated, kindled" (347). The combination of desire and repulsion that she feels for Colthurst is embodied in this simultaneous dilation and shuddering. Mary attempts to hide the part of her body that betrays her emotions, covering her eyes in a repetition of positioning herself "face downwards" as a child (Malet 1895, 19). In adulthood, Mary's sympathy for physical suffering finds a subject in Colthurst's physical and audible affliction. Colthurst's stammer is therefore integral to his potential future happiness and to the resolution of the romantic plot, which itself stops, starts, is interrupted, and falters several times, like his stammered speech.

Stammering is an involuntary bodily symptom with no obvious physiological cause. Late nineteenth-century doctors were somewhat baffled by it; while perceived as a muscular dysfunction that the muscles could be trained to overcome, stammering was also considered to be rooted in lifestyle and bad habits. The ambiguity about the physiological, psychological, or moral causes of this disorder aligns it with hysteria. In his studies of male hysterics, Charcot "often isolated language disorders in these cases, such as slurring of speech, stuttering, aphonia, and mutism, all of a hysterical nature" (Micale 2008, 159). Stammering was a symptom which frustrated the gender stereotypes of hysteria. Doctors could not avoid the fact—still true today—that stammering affects many more men than women, despite women's perceived proclivity towards nervousness and emotional and physical volatility. This involuntary, spasmodic affliction, reluctantly diagnosed as a hysterical symptom, challenged the gender assumptions about inherently unstable bodies.

Colthurst's stammer is described as a conflict between the physical and the unseen, the body and the mind. He attempts to jump to his death from a window, but the dramatic tension is subverted into bathos as he falls backwards into the room instead of forwards. Encountering Mary, his body continues to rebel:

> Colthurst tried to answer that nothing had happened, nothing was the matter, but his stammer got altogether the better of him. At no time was it a noisy stammer; it was not noisy now, but it was persistent, absolute. Fight against it as he might, wrench at his shirt collar, put forth all the energy left in him to overcome it, he could not articulate an intelligible word ... this revolt on the part of his body, this refusal of obedience, this breaking of the natural connection between the material and mental parts of himself in his present overwrought, highly nervous condition, was frightful. The city was divided against itself; his foes, in the most literal and practical sense of the phrase, were of his own household.
>
> (Malet 1895, 248)

This passage depicts the components of the self as a separate yet collaborative mind and body, a relationship which for Colthurst has become frighteningly inharmonious. His stammer is the body not simply out of control but overpowering. This negates the idea of body as a mere vessel, placing it at the centre of experiential subjectivity. The uncontrollable nature of the stammer and emphasis on nervousness reflect late nineteenth-century medical perspectives on hysteria, a disorder which encapsulates the volatile nature of the body like no other. Science and medicine increasingly framed the body as a conduit for hereditary disorders which may emerge at any moment: foes within one's own household. Malet's own heredity influenced her depiction of Colthurst; her father Charles Kingsley is one of history's famous stammerers. Both Kingsley and Colthurst describe their disorder as "a thorn in the flesh" (Kingsley qtd. in Lee 2008, 6; Malet 1895, 32), an apt biblical reference. The ambiguity about how literally the thorn should be understood reflects the uncertainty about the physiological causes of stammering. Malet attributed her "scientific reasoning faculty" to her father's training, yet also fictionalised his hysterical symptom in her male protagonist. In Malet's novel, Kinglsey, as both authority on science and experiential sufferer, is fictionalised as both the man of science and the hysterical masculine body.

Malet emphasises how the body is marked by social customs as well as medical discourses. Colthurst's wrenching of his shirt collar is a repeated compulsive action throughout the novel. While it simulates his struggle to manipulate the muscles of his throat, as though trying to speak or fighting for breath, it also reflects his self-imposed conformity to a rigid dress code, symbolising the performance of class, and the social conventions which oppress him. As Mary clasps Colthurst's hand, an act which transgresses convention, the "rage of living, stilled for the time being in Colthurst, began to stir in Mary Crookenden; - passed into her, perhaps (my sense of probability is not greatly staggered by the supposition), through the steady clasp of his hand" (250). Talia Schaffer notes of this passage that "he feels increasingly purified by her touch, but she feels increasingly aroused by his" (Schaffer 2000, 229). Yet it also indicates the double-edged nature of physical contact, which can affect healing, but also contagion. The narrator's parenthetical comment is scientific and sceptical, restoring a voice of narrative control. This contrast to the out-of-control bodies of the characters discourages a romanticised misreading of the situation. Colthurst regains his voice through Mary's healing touch: "he spoke low, in rapidly uttered sentences, hesitating distressingly at first, almost giving way again, yet he spoke" (252). His muteness transfers to Mary, who is silent for several pages, "her faculties paralysed by the strangeness of the position" (256). This epidermal experience affects both bodies, transferring not just "rage of living," or arousal, but also the power of speech. The sole witnesses to this scene between Mary and Colthurst are "an anatomical figure exalted on its pedestal, [and] a skeleton hanging meekly hideous from its little wooden gallows," defined as "not being companions of the talkative sort" (249). These figures parody the muteness of Mary and Colthurst. They are ungendered representations of the internal body, underlining the significance of the medical to the contested question of what constitutes the self in this scene. Rather than ascribing to or directly challenging hysterical gender stereotypes, Malet medicalises hysteria as an array of classifiable symptoms. She implies that all bodies are unstable and afflicted; whether male or female, all bodies are essentially anatomy when language is taken away.

Post-war, the mind-body relationship was redefined as soldiers returned from the front, often wounded physically, but also by the invisible wounds of trauma. Anxieties about the self were crystallised through increasingly frequent encounters with damaged bodies and traumatised minds, the undeniable evidence that the body's experiences in war could provoke devastating and disturbing transformations. War-damaged bodies challenged Lombrosian assertions that the body's physical stigmata were external signs of interior immorality and degeneracy; that, as Lennard J. Davis states in *The Body and Physical Difference* (1997), "the unwhole body is the unholy body" (Davis 1997, 57). *The Survivors* is a fictional depiction of this cultural shift. Braybrooke's maimed body, missing a foot and two fingers, is demarcated as a site of trauma; it evokes a range of emotions. Rupert Secker feels an instinctive horror of the damaged body: "to Rupert Secker, fastidious, idealist, devout adherent of beauty, physical disfigurement was indescribably distressing and repellent. His face blanched" (227). Secker's old-fashioned romanticism is disrupted by the war-ravaged body to the extent that he cannot find the language to process or articulate his response; his own body reacts by involuntarily turning white. For Francis Secker, Rupert's nephew, Braybrooke's body provokes guilt about his own wholeness; he

> would have been only too thankful to fall on his knees before this maimed, tormented former schoolfellow and implore pardon for his own immunity from the foul ravage of war ... disgraceful, yes, scandalous in presence of this infinitely piteous human wreck.
>
> (145)

These different narrative perspectives dramatise how one person, body, or self is constituted by numerous competing perspectives. Braybrooke's body acts as a cipher for Rupert's fears, Francis's guilt, and Lady Sybella Aylwin's erotic passion. In contrast to his male peers, she remains undisturbed by his injuries. Braybrooke

> drew away the poor, maimed hand and, opening his eyes wide, watched in his turn, half appealing, half curiously, while he placed it over her hand, clasping it, clawlike. Sybella did not wince as his fingers contracted, three dry hot bars as of metal closing on her soft flesh. The ghost of a smile crossed Braybrooke's face.
>
> (166)

Mirroring the clasping of hands in *Wages*, this physical contact transgresses social boundaries: medical professional and patient, older woman and younger man, whole body and damaged body. The male character in this later novel has suffered a more material loss, of thumb and finger rather than voice. Braybrooke observes his own action from a detached narrative perspective that reflects the detachment of his body, into parts which are here rendered clawlike and metallic, animal, and inorganic. They contrast Lady Aylwin's "soft flesh," reinforcing the less-than-human nature of his diminished form. He is further fragmented into wide eyes, a face, and a smile that is itself insubstantial and inhuman. The fragmentation of Braybrooke does not end when he returns from war but is extended by the allegedly healing practices of medicine and surgery. The hospital surgeon, McNaughten, states, "I've set my professional affections on that leg. Rammed every ounce of science I possess into the saving of it" (133). Braybrooke's leg, isolated and amputated in dialogue before it is physically detached, becomes an object commodity over which McNaughten and Lady Aylwin wrangle for ownership. The leg comes to signify the surgeon's reputation, and the matron's aim for "possession, namely, of a certain human life, of a certain human body (all which remained of it or soon would remain) in perpetuity" (134). His lack of wholeness and symbolic castration render Braybrooke a fearful symbol of men's vulnerability, and an object to possess.

Sybella Aylwin is an indifferent mother to her daughter Lydia, but to the wounded soldiers she is the Holy Mother, "Dear Lady of Good Counsel" as Braybrooke nicknames her (67). She is better at performing a symbolic maternal role, playing on images of religious idolatry, a performance which becomes increasingly grotesque as her sadism is made apparent, largely through her daughter's testimony. Sybella envisions herself as a "brimming vase of selfless devotion" (172). Yet Lydia provides an alternate reading: "my mother appears, to the uninitiated, to overflow. She never really overflows. Every drop is measured. She's economical" (236). The Virgin Mother, ideal model of femininity, mildness, and overflowing goodness, is supplanted by a more cynical image of economics and calculation. Lydia's view is substantiated by the interaction between Sybella and McNaughten as they dispute the amputation. McNaughten repeatedly denotes Sybella as hysterical: he was "touched by her words and the graceful spectacle of her very genuine distress, a little alarmed, too, by that hysterical threatening" (137). Sybella's argument escalates "to a cry, verging on hysterical" (136), she "sigh[s], an hysteric catch in her breath" (141), then faints. This appears to indicate a return to old-fashioned conceptions of the hysterical female body. However, the word hysteria is only applied directly to female characters through McNaughten's perspective. When the indirect discourse switches to Sybella, her interior monologue reveals that "she controlled every nerve, every sense, to the suppression of all outward signs of emotion and excitement" (133). She performs and exploits stereotypes of the female body as virginal, maternal, overflowing, and hysterical, in order to manipulate the surgeon and achieve her goal.

Sybella's self-characterisation as a vase recalls Malet's 1901 novel *The History of Sir Richard Calmady,* whose Doctor Knott has a "greed of riveting broken human crockery" (Malet 2003, 404). The medical drive to heal and fix, the Hippocratic oath, is inverted in Sybella, whose "greed" is for pain, suffering, and further dismantling rather than "riveting" broken bodies. Lydia states that while the wounded soldiers are

> bolstered up by drugs to ensure those pangs—and sometimes they can't endure, simply crumple up and die of them—my wonderful mother grows sleek on pangs, blooms upon maimings and lengthy, painful reconstructions. She is so well, looks so young and so bewitchingly pretty.
>
> (Malet 1923, 35)

Sybella is physically affected by her encounters with damaged bodies; her body thrives on their deterioration. This is a form of epidermal exchange which evokes the vampire rather than the vase. Sybella's vampiric nature is reiterated by the text; as she watches Braybrooke in pain, "the muscles of his handsome throat contract in a sudden spasm now and again. It fascinated her so that she watched for it with her teeth set, her nostrils dilated" (171). The figure of the vampire disrupts boundaries of subjectivity through its penetration of other bodies, and its transformation of those bodies into creatures which perpetuate its own appetites, desires, and needs. The vampire is a perversion of the mother figure in that it is also a progenitor but through acts of consumption and infection. In *The Survivors,* such gothic anxieties are linked to medical ones; fear of penetration is displaced onto the figure of the surgeon, another invader of the body, as Braybrooke voices his hatred of "that old butcher McNaughten and his knife" (173). Lydia's flippant description of her mother feeding on the soldiers' pain may be unscientific, yet this gothic image takes on a medical reality through Sybella's use of modern surgery to transform the body she intends to possess.

"stained with living scarlet": Malet's Red Rooms

Spaces of illness and death—sickrooms, deathbeds, operating theatres—appear often in Malet's fiction. They are medical sites, but also gothic spaces, containing the "horror of blood," graphic death, or macabre disfigurement (Malet 1895, 433). *Wages of Sin* describes the final, fatal utterances of a blood-soaked consumptive from her deathbed, and *The History of Sir Richard Calmady* details a preanaesthetic surgical amputation in the drawing room of a stately home. These rooms are characterised by their red or blood-soaked furnishings, "red rooms" which invoke and transcend *Jane Eyre*'s symbolic site of hysteria. Brontë's red room is an archetypal trope of the female gothic, a space of childhood punishment haunted by the patriarchal figure of Jane's uncle, or, following Gilbert and Gubar, the site of an adolescent hysterical fit brought on by the shock of menarche. In "The Progress of Woman: In Literature," Malet criticised Brontë for believing "in the divine right of man, with the whole force of her hot, stormy heart" (Malet 1888, 297). Malet sabotages and subverts the patriarchal spatiality of the red room, into a space where male bodies are subjected to fear, pain, and irreversible damage. In *The Survivors*, Victorian sickrooms are replaced by the modern operating theatre. Traditional gender dynamics are reversed—both that of the medical authority/patient and that of the gothic patriarch/female victim—with male patients at the mercy of the tyrannical hospital matron. The metaphorical moral dissecting-room is incarnated in real operating theatres, contested spaces of healing or destruction. Spatially locating these sites of physical trauma seems an attempt to confine sickness, mutilation, and death, compartmentalising and sterilising the horrors of medical deconstruction and bodily damage. Yet the narrative undermines this, suggesting the futility of attempting to contain either conceptual or physical disintegration.

Jenny Parris is Colthurst's model, "the face that had made his fortune. The face he had painted in his now famous 'Road to Ruin'" (Malet 1895, 238). Elisabeth Bronfen asserts that when the female body is sublimated into art, the model/muse is "killed," by her transformation into "a perfect, inanimate image, a dead 'figure'" (Bronfen 1992, 64). Jenny's reduction to a dead figure is reflected by Colthurst's repeated verbal reduction of her to a face or form, and her status as mistress and prostitute renders her "the skeleton of a dead love and a living sin" (173). Jenny arrives at Colthurst's art school, unbeknownst to him, to model for his students in the "red-walled theatre" (214). Colthurst finds himself surrounded by images of Jenny, in an episode reminiscent of Christina Rossetti's 1856 poem "In an Artist's Studio": "one face looks out from all his canvases" (Rossetti 2001).[3] His students' easels dissect and multiply parts of Jenny's body; her brow, her cheek, her chin, the nape of her neck and shoulder, her profile, the front of her face, her eyes, raised arm and drooping hand: "everywhere, wherever he looked, Jenny, Jenny, Jenny. A world of Jennies ... And in the midst of them, uplifted, enthroned, silent, motionless, sphinx-like, Jenny herself, the living, breathing woman" (232). Jenny's concurrent dissection and multiplication creates a nightmarish vision for Colthurst, "one of those terrible, ever-changing, yet ever stable forms and faces seen in delirium" (231). Still but breathing, dead but living, she embodies the male fear of the mutable, unreadable, and disorderly female body, which—as in hysteria—refuses to stay within its bounds, contagious and proliferating, resisting the imposition of artistic death.

As Jenny lies dying of consumption at the end of the novel, she again resists sublimation into a picturesque death. The ever-scientific narrator informs us, "respiration is hardly comfortable work when you have to spit up the larger half of one lung and the vessels of the other are clogged by matter and blood" (403). When Colthurst arrives, Jenny emits a hysterical laugh, which "sent the blood welling up from her lacerated lungs, flowing down from her poor laughing mouth over the bosom of her nightgown onto the sheet" (433). This deathbed laugher has fatal medical consequences. It colours the scene with blood, associating Jenny's small room with the red-walled space of the model's platform in the art school. Mary "bent over Jenny trying to sop it up with the towel and hide this horror of blood" (433). When Colthurst takes her place, Mary finds it "almost intolerable" to watch his hands "busied in repulsive, menial, sick-room offices, holding a little cracked pudding basin, wringing out a bloody sponge" (434). A gothic "horror of blood" converges with tedious medical processes in this space of dying and death, encapsulating Malet's almost compulsive drive to literalise gothic metaphors. This visceral encounter with a consumptive death, replete with aural and visual gruesomeness, disallows romantic perceptions of the illness; Malet forces us to see the ubiquitous blood and Jenny's eyes "staring half open as at some sight of unearthly terror," and hear "a rattling now and again in her throat, too, between the panting, choking breaths" (435). This intensely medical scene challenges artistic and religious ideals of the female body, of dying, and of death. Medical language pervades the narrative and the characters' interior monologues, as if they are pervious to the atmosphere in the room. The sound of Colthurst arriving is "cruel to Mary Crookenden as the first incision of the surgeon's knife cutting down into the quivering, shrinking flesh" (430–1). As he approaches Jenny's deathbed, Colthurst's "senses were preternaturally acute; were flayed, so to speak, offering a surface all quick to the lightest touch" (426). Within this room, senses become comparable to the splitting of flesh and the violent stripping of skin. This defleshing is a visual deconstruction of the characters; they become once more the anatomical figure and the skeleton, stripped of their artistic ideals by the spectacle of Jenny's dying.

I will briefly mention *The History of Sir Richard Calmady* to demonstrate the continuum of the red room as a Maletian construct. As Clare Walker Gore explains in her contribution to this collection, the foundational episode of Book I sees the protagonist's father, the elder Richard Calmady, trampled by a horse. Doctor Knott determines that "amputation of the right leg was imperative ... they must operate, he said, and operate immediately" (Malet 2003, 28). Malet temporally locates the reader by referring to medical advances: "it must be remembered that in 1842 anaesthetics had not robbed the operating room of half its horrors. The victim went to execution wide-awake, with no mercy of deadened senses and dulled brain" (28). Historical surgery is presented as traumatic and horrific rather than a necessarily healing process, to which "victims" rather than "patients" are subjected. The operation is spatially located in "the red drawing room on the ground floor" (26). Calmady's wife Katherine paces outside, "hearing at intervals, through the closed doors, the short peremptory tones of the surgeons, fearing she heard more and worse sounds than those. They were hurting him, sorely, sorely, dismembering and disfiguring the dear, living body which she loved" (28). In contrast to the bloody detail in *Wages*, neither Katherine nor the reader witness the amputation. We are left to imagine the blood, as Katherine does; upon entering the room, her imagination perceives the redness of furniture and fire contaminating the entirety, "splashed, and stained with living scarlet," a "universal redness" (29). A biological agency is attributed to the spreading stain, and Katherine's imagination of the operation has a biological effect; the child in her womb is subject to "spontaneous amputation" (42). The site of trauma remanifests in the womb—the archetypal red room—and in the body of the younger Sir Richard. The theory of maternal impressions is at once medical and gothic, scientific and supernatural. The female imagination is as dangerous as the surgeon's knife, powerful enough to enact physical maiming.

This attempt to compartmentalise body horror is ineffectual; like the spreading stain it spills out of the bodies and rooms to contaminate other bodies and spaces.

In *The Survivors*, Lady Aylwin's private war hospital is a space which is described variously as gothic, medical, and pathological. Lady Aylwin imagines it "peopled with phantoms" (Malet 1923, 162). Lydia describes it as outwardly "a model ... It's perfect; fairyland, with the last word of modern sanitation and applied surgical science thrown in" (33). Her choice of words parallels the scientific with nonrealist language, invention, and fantasy. Lydia has escaped the atmosphere there which she describes as "over-blown" and "over-charged" with "the smirched business of sex" (28). McNaughten reiterates that beneath the surface, war hospitals are "forcing houses for sexual neurosis" (217). This circumscribed area, supposedly a space of healing, is inhabited by the "phantoms of war scenes", the peacocking of war heroics, and women who become obsessed with the image of themselves as saviour: an ideal environment for the propagation of pathology (162).

The operating room in the hospital is intrinsic to the plot, yet the reader is not party to what occurs there. Delyfer points out the narrative's careful avoidance of direct description of Braybrooke's surgery. She observes that the three times the surgical procedure is mentioned, "these descriptions are always suspended and incomplete, the characters being unwilling, or unable, fully to put into words what will/has happen[ed]" (Delyfer 2011, 135). We are readmitted to the narrative directly following the operation:

> The assistant surgeons had made their bow and, after a little professional gossip, departed. Stripped of his soiled white-linen overalls and other ritual accessories, McNaughten passed, in an atmosphere redolent of iodoform and ether, from an inner sanctuary, whence came a continuous sound of running water, into the vestibule—polished, pale-green painted walls, polished grey, black, and drab tessellated pavement, somewhat drearily lighted from above through bottle-glass roofing—which adjoined the operating theatre.
>
> (210)

The peripheral space of the vestibule is described in detail as the narrative hovers on the threshold of the operating theatre. The sanitised smells of antiseptic and anaesthetic are emphasised. McNaughten is divested of any sign of the operation, and immediately dries his hands, and begins "carefully paring and scraping his finger nails" (212). Meanwhile, from beyond the closed door, we hear not the sounds of surgery and pain, but sounds of cleaning: "the continuous tinkle of running water from the inner sanctuary, along with confused sounds—swish of a mop, ring of a pail, scrape of moved furniture" (214). McNaughten reflects on the operation: "never could he remember to have operated with finer address, with greater dispatch or greater coolness. He felt an artist's pride in his own triumphant skill" (210). Braybrooke's anaesthetised body is a canvas on which the doctor executes his skill; the patient rather than the model is dehumanised into art. The operating theatre is described as an inner sanctuary twice; along with McNaughten's ritualised accessories, this demarcates it as an abstract, even religious space, creating a sense of mysticism which masks the reality of the event. We are told "Captain Braybrooke is coming out of the anaesthetic beautifully" and that "the loss of blood was negligible" (211). Blood is mentioned only once, in order to stress its insignificance. In this peripheral area, McNaughten acknowledges Sybella's reason for demanding the surgery, so that Braybrooke will not "run after strange flesh—younger, fresher flesh" (216). The mention of flesh in this surgical space, especially fresh flesh, is a grotesque echo, a Freudian slip, of the unseen piece of young Braybrooke's flesh, freshly severed, surgically estranged from his body.

Operations are sanitised in this modern medical space. The anaesthetising of the patient means that the experience is no longer defined by the colour red; they never see the blood. The reader is also anaesthetised by the narrative's suppression of this significant event in the plot. The last we hear of Braybrooke before this involves him taking a sleeping draught and requesting that no one talk to him about the operation, and the reader joins him in his selective oblivion, sleep, and anaesthetisation. The two chapters that follow are an interlude in the "humbler, less volcanic pastures" (182) of Maidsworthy, and we rejoin the hospital narrative in this post-surgery moment with the unsettling feeling that part of the story is missing. Likewise, the sanitisation itself becomes fearful, a cover-up. Braybrooke comments, "I own to being rather fed up with white, always white, just at present. It seems to carry superfluous reminders of the operating theatre" (174). Like McNaughten's "soiled white-linen overalls" (216), and the sanitised hospital as "smirched" (28) with the sexuality of war heroics, traditional associations of white with purity and innocence are sullied. The repeated emphasis on sterilisation reveals the whitewashing of darker impulses, which McNaughten refers to as "intimate feminine defilements," and a "degraded predilection for carrion" (216–7), contrasting the cleanliness of the surgical space with the perceived uncleanliness of interior femininity and appetites.

The surgical and narrative fragmentation of the human subject in the operating theatre is informed by Malet's careful engagement with contemporary medicine. The apparent trajectory of intensifying physical horror in the novels is countered by increasingly distancing the reader from the spaces in which the bodily damage occurs; from being inside the room, to beyond the door, to a space devoid of pain and blood. The plot of *The Survivors* performs a narrative whitewashing by avoiding describing the operation. Yet as Delyfer comments, this has the adverse effect of making the event more tangible. She notes, "paradoxically, Malet's use of aposiopesis, which by-passes verbalisation, is highly effective in making the senseless butchery bewilderingly visible, forcing the reader to rely on her imagination or mental gaze" (Delyfer 2011, 135). As in the metaphor of the moral dissecting-room, the body is strikingly absent from the scene. The lack of description is a departure from the shock tactic of evoking revulsion, as in gothic horror, to a more nuanced gothic terror, engendering apprehension and dread. The reader's heightened awareness mirrors the state Rupert Secker diagnoses in himself early in the novel, an "abnormally perceptive condition" (8) which leads to a "morbidly active imagination" (16), an "accursed super-perceptive, super-sensitive condition" (28). Malet is encouraging the reader to be likewise super-attuned, or, borrowing the language of hysteria, hyperaesthetic—"excessively or morbidly sensitive" (*OED*). The man of science and the hysteric converge in this practice of observation and awareness that Malet encourages in her reader.

In Malet's fiction, both rooms and bodies are unstable sites, susceptible to permeation, leakage, or overflowing. The breakdown of the body as container is a recurring theme: involuntary hysterical symptoms, flowing blood, missing limbs, amputations, contagion, epidermal exchanges, maternal impressions, imagery of flaying and defleshing, the internal made external. Bodily vulnerability finds its most extreme expression in rooms and spaces where the body is dismantled. Yet these rooms also fail to contain, compartmentalise, or sanitise medical fears, infection, or death. Malet structures in binaries and plays around inversions; scientific and hysterical, male and female, mind and body, objective and subjective, stability and breakdown, literal and metaphorical. This dualistic thinking is marked and self-conscious; these binaries are simultaneously reiterated and disturbed as they converge in unruly or damaged bodies and gothic medical spaces. The narratives echo this, locked into binary constructs and anaphoric structures even as these are troubled, as if trapped into a pattern of repetition compulsion.

Malet's characters project their bodily symptoms, disabilities, and neuroses onto the body politic. Colthurst envisages wider society as afflicted with speech disorders, perceiving mass muteness, collective convulsions, and problems with articulation affecting the "hideous jostling crowd of things struggling to be born; struggling to make themselves heard and felt; struggling to push something else aside so as to make their word, their want, their meaning known" (Malet 1895, 240). The repetition of the word struggle implies an inability to break from a lexicon of desperate toil and reflects the iterative nature of the stammer. Yet this frustrated narrative style is not confined to Colthurst or to *Wages*; triplets, escalation, and repetition proliferate in Malet's writing. Richard Calmady also projects his disability onto the masses, using similar narrative formation: "that hideous apprehension of universal mutilation, of maimed purposes, maimed happenings, of a world peopled by beings maimed as he was himself" (Malet 2003, 310). If these projections are attempts to heal the self, they are ineffectual, instead transmitting individual maladies, conceiving a damaged homogenous social body.

However, an alternative reading is that the characters are able to perceive societal disorders through the sympathy and understanding engendered by their bodily experience. Colthurst acknowledges the silencing of the masses because he understands what it is like to be gagged by his misbehaving body. Calmady perceives social inequality and the plight of the lower classes because of his lived experience of disability. As such, they become diagnosticians and thus channel Malet's authorial vision. Malet's moral dissection of the body politic can be read as an act of simultaneous vivisection and healing, seeking to both dissect and restore. Like Colthurst, Malet wants to capture and elevate baseness and depravity as artistic subjects: "I want to show that, if intelligently looked at, poverty, disease, sorrow, decay, death, sin—yes I am not much afraid of the word—are ideally beautiful too, paintable too, intrinsically and enduringly poetic" (Malet 1895, 134). Implicit in Malet's penetrating analysis of human obliquity is the awareness that while the surgical knife can be used to dissect and deconstruct, it can also be used as a tool of healing. Just as moral doctrine acts to both disassemble and recuperate the self, the forces of science, medicine, psychological analysis, and fiction act to fragment and dislocate, and can either pathologise or heal the human subject.

In "The Threatened Re-Subjection of Woman," Malet discusses "the woman of genius," whom she purports to neither pity nor envy:

> to possess the dual nature—a man's brain and ambitions, and woman's capacity of loving and suffering along with that most intricate and capricious piece of mechanism, a woman's body—is, indeed, to dwell in a city divided against itself.
>
> (Malet 1905, 818)

Malet distances herself from the woman of genius, yet an intimate understanding of the feeling of being divided and dually gendered is implicit; she uses the same metaphor as Colthurst of the self as a divided city. This passage reflects the psychic battle of Malet's identity and her feelings about gender, crystallised in her literary persona, and her complex relationship with and depiction of masculinity. For Malet, possessing the capacities of the man of science alongside a "capricious" female body creates a dual nature, that of both "broken human" and purveyor of truth. Occupying the position of both hysterical patient and scientific observer lends Malet the quality of hyperacuity, both haunted and undisturbed by the drive "to look beneath the surface" and "to see things as they really are" (Malet 1908, 177).

Notes

1 Janet Hogarth married William Leonard Courtney in 1911, becoming Janet Courtney.

2 Reviewers noted that the description of artist James Colthurst's naturalist aesthetic in *The Wages of Sin* seemed to describe Malet's own style: "Colthurst revelled in incongruities. There was unquestionably a sinister vein in him, a rather morbid enjoyment of all that is strange, jarring, unexpected, abnormal. Some persons, indeed, have gone so far as to accuse him of a love of actual physical deformity and a relish of horror for mere horror's sake" (Malet 1895, 33).

3 Christina Rossetti wrote "In An Artist's Studio" about her brother Dante Gabriel Rossetti's paintings. We might also consider links to his poem 'Jenny,' which describes a sleeping prostitute; surely it is no coincidence that Malet's character shares this name.

Works Cited

Bronfen, Elisabeth. 1992. *Over Her Dead Body: Death, Femininity and the Aesthetic*. Manchester: Manchester University Press.

Brontë, Charlotte. 1996. *Jane Eyre, Case Studies in Contemporary Criticism*, edited by Beth Newman. Boston, MA: Bedford Books.

Courtney, Janet E. (née Hogarth). 1932. "A Novelist of the 'Nineties." *Fortnightly Review* 131: 230–41.

Courtney, William Leonard. 1904. *The Feminine Note in Fiction*. London: Chapman & Hall.

Davis, Lennard J. 1997. "Nude Venuses, Medusa's Body, and Phantom Limbs: Disability and Visuality." In *Body and Physical Difference: Discourses of Disability in the Humanities*, edited by David T. Mitchell and Sharon L. Snyder, 51–70. Michigan: University of Michigan Press.

Delyfer, Catherine. 2011. *Art and Womanhood in Fin-de-Siècle Writing: The Fiction of Lucas Malet, 1880–1931*. London: Pickering & Chatto.

Dickens, Mary Angela. 1899. "A Talk with Lucas Malet." *The Windsor Magazine* 10: 522–4.

Hogarth, Janet. 1895. "Literary Degenerates." *Fortnightly Review* 57: 586–92.

———. 1902. "Lucas Malet's Novels." *Fortnightly Review* 71: 532–40.

King, Helen. 1993. "Once upon a Text: Hysteria from Hippocrates." In *Hysteria Beyond Freud*, edited by Sander L. Gilman, Helen King, Roy Porter, G.S. Rousseau, Elaine Showalter. 1–90. Oxford: University of California Press.

Lee, Louise. 2008. "Voicing, De-voicing and Self-Silencing: Charles Kingsley's Stuttering Christian Manliness." *Journal of Victorian Culture* 13(1): 1–17.

Lundberg, Patricia Lorimer. 2003. *"An Inward Necessity": The Writer's Life of Lucas Malet*. New York: Peter Lang.

Malet, Lucas. 1888. "The Progress of Woman: In Literature." *The Universal Review* 2(7): 295–301.

———. 1895. *The Wages of Sin*. London: Swan Sonnenschein & Co.

———. 1905. "The Threatened Re-Subjection of Woman." *Fortnightly Review* 77: 806–19.

———. 1908. *Colonel Enderby's Wife*, Newnes Illustrated Edition. London: George Newnes.

———. 1923. *The Survivors*. London: Cassell and Company.

———. 2003. *The History of Sir Richard Calmady*, edited by Talia Schaffer. Birmingham: Birmingham University Press.

Micale, Mark. 2008. *Hysterical Men: The Hidden History of Male Nervous Illness*. London: Harvard University Press.

Rossetti, Christina. 2001. "In An Artist's Studio." In *Christina Rossetti: The Complete Poems*, edited by R. W. Crump; notes and introduction by Betty S. Flowers. London: Penguin.

Schaffer, Talia. 2000. *The Forgotten Female Aesthetes: Literary Culture in Late-Victorian England*. Charlottesville: University Press of Virginia.

2 "[T]hat very ugly saddle"

Disability, Adaptation, and Paternal Inheritance in *The History of Sir Richard Calmady*

Clare Walker Gore

> "Look here, darling," he said, "you'll let the stables go on just as usual ... I should like to know nothing was changed at the stables. They've been a great hobby of mine, and if—if the baby is a boy, he may take after me and care for them. Make him ride straight, Roger. And teach him to love sport for its own sake, dear old man, as a gentleman should ... You'll call the boy after me, Kitty, won't you? I want there to be another Richard Calmady."
>
> (Malet 2003, 33)

Like so many heroes of bildungsromane before him, the eponymous protagonist of Lucas Malet's *The History of Sir Richard Calmady* (1901) is fatherless. Yet there can be few novelistic heroes whose relationship with an absent father is more highly vexed, for the first Sir Richard's dying wishes turn out to be cruelly contradictory. It is precisely because he takes after his father that the second Sir Richard is born with his feet growing directly out of his knees, his drastically foreshortened lower legs mirroring the fatal injuries and surgical amputation his father suffered after falling from his horse. This disability does not prevent the second Richard from riding, but it makes it impossible for him to "ride straight." This is something his uncle Roger—the man tasked with teaching him to "ride straight"—underlines for the reader when he learns of his nephew's disability and reflects bitterly, "And this was the boy whom they had so longed for ... the boy who should ... ride straight ...!" (43). By a grimly ironic twist, the disability that prevents Richard from embodying the "straight" masculine ideals his father espoused is also his patrimony, an inheritance from his father.

Unlike Richard and his family, the reader is also aware at this point that Richard's disability represents his paternal inheritance in a second sense. We know that his body is marked not only by his father's riding but also by his ancestor Sir Denzil's: it is because Sir Denzil carelessly rode his horses over the legs of his illegitimate infant son that his legitimate male heirs were cursed to die young and violently. The curse will be lifted, we are told, only when "a fatherless babe to the birth shall have come," with "a foot that shall never know stocking or shoe. / If he opens his purse to the lamenter's cry, / Then the woe shall lift and be laid for aye" (19). Knowing this, the reader is aware from the beginning that Richard's disability is charged with redemptive possibility, not simply a curse for his paternal ancestor's crimes but a potential cure. For Richard, however, it is for most of the novel the unbearable mark of his inadequacy, the difference which makes it impossible for him to "keep straight" (203).

Repeatedly used to stand for everything that the disabled, feminised Richard cannot be, the word "straight" gains ever more traction as the narrative progresses, and comes to seem ever more restrictive, as Malet works to alienate us from the stiflingly narrow conception of masculinity which it evokes. Ultimately, it is only by giving up the desire to "ride straight" that Richard can learn to be happy riding in his adapted saddle, a way of riding which Malet encourages us to see as more truly satisfying. At the novel's romantic climax, Richard's cousin Honoria declares her love by "put[ting] her hand on the peak of that very ugly saddle" (414), a gesture of acceptance which marks the culmination of the novel's long drawn out struggle to come to terms with disability, capturing Honoria and Richard's newfound tolerance and tenderness for that which diverges from the "straight" ideal. The male-identified Honoria has previously described herself as "not what you call a marrying man" (277) and has stood out—even amongst Richard's intolerant friends and relatives—for the strength of her aversion to Richard's disability. Her gesture in touching his adapted saddle is therefore charged with significance, making a fitting climax to a love scene which is unconventional in more ways than one: in a departure from the strictly gendered script of both nineteenth-century and modern marriage plot novels, she proposes to him. In a conclusion that is both radical and romantic, Richard and Honoria are shown to find not only a new way to be married, but new ways to be men and women, to be Christians, and to be aristocrats. This new settlement, like Richard's saddle, is shaped around disability. It represents not a rejection but an adaptation of inherited traditions, allowing Richard to be not "another Richard Calmady" but an *other* Richard Calmady.

Given her father's fame, and the prevailing tendency of contemporary critics to read her work in the light of his, it is hardly surprising that Malet should have been preoccupied with paternal inheritance. But whereas contemporary critics tended to see this novel as a straight repudiation of her father's ideas, I want to argue that Malet's engagement with her paternal inheritance is better understood through the prism of adaptation, a motif which she develops through the images of horse riding which run through the novel.[1] If we follow this narrative thread, it becomes clear that through depicting the second Richard's struggle to live with disability, Malet stages a complex struggle between the ideals of the father and the experience of the son—not a straight repudiation, but an involved, fraught, and ultimately creative relationship. Although the second Richard's predicament is clearly analogous to that of the woman writer struggling to be creative in a patriarchal literary culture and bearing the burden of internalised misogyny—as Patricia Lorimer Lundberg (2003, 1), Catherine Delyfer (2010, 89), and Patricia Srebnik (1994, 200) have pointed out—I will try to resist the straight translation of disability *into* gender, in order to explore what I see as the complex connections between the two. Similarly, while my reading highlights the gender trouble introduced into the novel by Richard's disability, and sees the novel's romantic conclusion as queering "straight" romantic norms, I will not be reading disability as a metaphor for same-sex desire. Instead, I will suggest that Malet uses disability to expose the nexus of ideas which together make up the "straight" male ideal, embodied by the first Sir Richard.[2]

The Sins of the Fathers?

It might at first glance seem perverse to think about *Calmady* as a novel primarily about paternal inheritance, when the first Sir Richard dies so near the beginning, and the novel's major characters, apart from the protagonist himself, are female. Most existing studies of the novel stress Richard's relationship with a triumvirate of powerful women: his noble mother Katherine, his wicked cousin Helen, and his androgynous, politically radical cousin Honoria, who stand in complex and interesting relation to one another (Delyfer 2011, 81; O'Connell 2012, 108–9). However, I would argue that Richard's relationship to these women is shaped by his relationship with his absent father, who embodies the ideals against which Richard judges himself and is judged by others, and exerts a powerful influence on the novel's plot from beyond the grave.

Malet greatly strengthens our sense of this influence through tightly coordinating the imagery that surrounds the first Sir Richard. He is so insistently associated with horse riding that although his appearance in the novel is brief, any future mention of horses or of horse riding conjures up his ghost. The first thing we learn about him is that he is a famous rider (7), and it seems cruelly fitting that, characterised as he is entirely through his relationship with horses, he receives the injury that proves fatal to him in a riding accident. Even as he lies dying, in his own mind he is "riding, riding, whole and vigorous ... towards a great light on the far horizon, which streamed forth, as he knew, from the throne of Almighty God" (33). It is therefore no surprise that his deathbed wishes relate to horses, and that his hopes for his son revolve around riding.

Within the world of the novel, there is a direct connection between Richard's disability and his father's riding accident. It is assumed by all the family, and even by the doctor, that the unborn Richard has been literally shaped by his mother's trauma upon looking at his father's injured body: as Katherine puts it, "she was herself, in a sense, accountable ... the greatness of her love for the father had maimed the child" (50).[3] While the theory of maternal impressions—which held that anything which made a strong mental impression on an expectant mother could make a physical impression on her unborn child—was indeed widely held in the 1840s when this part of the novel is set (Stoddard Holmes 2004, 65), readers in 1901 might have been more sceptical.[4] Perhaps with this in mind, Malet stresses the poetic rather than the scientific truth of the situation by having the strictly rational Dr Knott explain the connection in emotional terms: "love," he says, "is an incalculably great, natural force ... In this case it has worked strangely against itself—at once for irreparable injury and for perfection" (43).

The idea that the strength of Katherine's love for the first Sir Richard is an injury to the second gains traction as the plot develops, and we see how greatly she values her son's likeness to his father, and how absolutely unwilling she is to accept his difference. Any deviation from the example set by the first Sir Richard is, in Katherine's eyes, regrettable; his way of riding is totemic for the way he lived, which is established not simply as desirable, but as ideal. The first Sir Richard has therefore doubly injured his son, not only by the catastrophic failure in riding that is the source of both their injuries, but by defining the ideal kind of riding in such a way that Richard's own riding can only be understood as inadequate.

The reader has already been primed, however, to see the first Sir Richard as himself a victim of his paternal inheritance. The narrator reveals in the very first chapter that the heirs of Brockhurst all suffer early and violent deaths (3), and in the third, we are allowed to read over the shoulder of the family priest Julius as he discovers a seventeenth-century chapbook which tells the terrible tale of Sir Denzil's wrongdoings. The short life expectancy that is part of the Calmady inheritance turns out to be due to the curse laid on Sir Denzil for his callous treatment of his forester's daughter, whom he seduced with false promises of marriage, and then of their illegitimate son, who died after being trampled by Sir Denzil's carriage horses. The fact that it was the boy's legs which were trampled, "almost sever[ed]... just above the knee" (19), makes the first Richard's accident, and the second Richard's disability, peculiarly redolent of their forefather's crime. More subtly, Sir Denzil's devil-may-care riding holds up a dark mirror to the first Richard's celebrated horsemanship, showing us the other side of aristocratic male power and privilege—not the attractive "vigour" of the debonair Sir Richard (18), but a selfish carelessness, a brutal disregard for the vulnerable and a willingness to trample the inconvenient.

Although there is never any suggestion that the first Sir Richard resembles Sir Denzil in his "perfidy and lust" (19), Malet makes it impossible for us fully to disentangle their legacies. We see the first Sir Richard not only as closely resembling Sir Denzil in his talents, and described in terms which strongly evoke those used of Sir Denzil (1, 7), but as enjoying possession of his estate on terms which do not seem to be so very different. Malet emphasises that there has been no break with the past at Brockhurst. She has the second Sir Richard sit as a magistrate on the local bench, ruling on the case of a young unmarried mother whose position strongly recalls the forester's daughter (126). The privileges enjoyed by those who benefit from a grossly unjust social and economic structure are never disentangled from their potential for abuse, and both are written onto the second Richard's body. In being both a physical copy of his father, heir to the Calmady estates, and of the "ideally beautiful" child who was maimed by Sir Denzil, Richard embodies both victim and perpetrator of injustice. Ultimately, it is this embodiment which enables Richard to reconcile his inherited position with his desire for social justice, but in order to reach this point, he has to recognise the problematic aspects of his inheritance, and to accept his difference from, as well as his likeness to, his idealised father.

The Struggle to "keep straight"

When the first Richard Calmady imagines a child who will "ride straight," there seems to be no doubt in his mind that this child will be male. The association between horse riding and masculinity is subtle but insistent; although we do see female characters on horseback, it is the male-identified characters who define themselves through their riding. Tellingly, Katherine Calmady reveals her pregnancy by telling her husband that she "'ought not to ride now—for a time'" (11), and this giving up of horse riding seems the final development in the feminising process that she has undergone through her relationship with Richard. Malet describes their relationship in extravagantly romantic and firmly, even brutally gendered terms, and it therefore seems natural that in marrying Richard, the great horse rider, Katherine herself should have to give up riding. The woman in the novel who is repeatedly associated with riding is the masculine Honoria: as she tells her unsuccessful suitor Ludovic, she "can meet men pretty well on their own ground" because she "can ride as straight as [they] can" (338). Not coincidentally, she also feels "instinctive repulsion" (120) when she first sees Richard riding in his adapted saddle, closely echoing the "repulsion" Roger Ormiston feels upon first learning of Richard's disability (43).

In fact, Roger's feelings for his brother-in-law and close friend, the first Richard, undergo serious modification after his injury. Malet dwells less upon his compassion for the dying man than upon his terror in the face of bodily injury and pain:

> It struck him as an intolerable humiliation and outrage that Richard Calmady, splendid fellow as he was, gifted, high-bred gentleman, should, of all men, come to this sorry pass! ... Would he, Roger Ormiston, one day, find himself thus weak and broken ... ? ... It knocked all the manhood out of him. But for very shame, before those two calm, devoted women, he would have broken down and wept.
>
> (30)

Just as his unwillingness to look upon his friend's broken body is rooted in fear of his own vulnerability, and this fearfulness is connected to his masculinity, so too his revulsion from the second Richard's disabled body is made continuous with his "straight" masculine identity, as the narrator explains: "Like all sound and healthy-minded men he had an inherent suspicion of the abnormal" (67). Although he is soon reassured that Richard's "nature was wholesome enough," it is surely not coincidental that Roger's entrance into Richard's life coincides with Richard's newfound sense of himself as inadequate. As a child, he does not see his difference as a mark of inferiority; it is not until he thinks of his father, and imagines his father's friend and acting substitute, Roger, watching him walk, that he feels "glad my father never saw me!" (67). Richard's growing desire to be a man like Roger is, of course, expressed as the desire to ride: as he tells his mother, "riding is just the one thing to—to make up—to make a man of me" (101).

Given her husband's gruesome end, Katherine is understandably reluctant to see her son in the saddle, and Richard's riding thus involves a separation of himself from his mother, the "first conflict" between them (101). Katherine's unwillingness to let Richard ride is significant on several levels; as well as being psychologically convincing, it strengthens the connection between riding and masculinity, enabling Malet to stress that his desire to ride is part of Richard's paternal inheritance, "the special heritage of English*men* of gentle blood" (101) [emphasis added]. It also relates to Katherine's unwillingness to accept Richard's difference from his father, since allowing Richard to ride means allowing him to ride in an adapted saddle, and this is an idea that Katherine initially finds unbearable. Several critics have commented on the incestuous note that Malet strikes in her depictions the passionate love between mother and son (Schaffer 2000, 206; Delyfer 2010, 81; O'Connell 2012, 109); for my purposes, what is interesting in these scenes is Katherine's desire to make Richard a substitute for his father, and therefore to avoid recognising his physical difference from the first Richard. She encourages him to keep his legs covered at all times when he is sitting or lying down, and never to be seen walking or standing, in what she considers "a practice of self-respecting concealment" (243). The idea of his riding strikes her most powerfully as a form of self-display:

> the vision of poor Richard—her darling, whom she had striven so jealously to shield ever since the day, over thirteen years ago, when undressing her baby she had first looked upon its malformed limbs—Richard riding forth for all the staring, mocking world to see, arose before her.
>
> (101)

The idea that Richard might make a spectacle of himself by riding is gruesomely underlined on his expedition to order his adapted saddle, when he rides past a travelling fair and sees a picture on a signboard which shocks him so deeply that he never names what he has seen. Malet chooses not to do so either, allowing the image to remain for the reader—as it is for Richard—an unspeakable trauma, but it is clear from the context that it is an advertisement for a freak show. After seeing this advertisement, Richard seeks reassurance from his mother that his position is unassailable, explaining that he has seen "things" which "made [him] understand that it is safer for anyone—well, anyone like—me—don't you know, to be rich" (109). Choking with indirections, euphemisms, and ellipses, this speech is typical of Richard's exchanges with his mother about his disability. Just as naming the freak show would somehow summon its presence and allow it to intrude upon the sanctuary of Brockhurst, they both behave as if the only way of avoiding the humiliating public display of Richard's body as a curiosity is to avoid directly acknowledging its difference, even in private.[5]

The belief that concealment is the only alternative to dehumanising display informs Richard's attitude to riding even after he has persuaded his mother that he should learn. There is a grim irony in the description of his riding "fearlessly" and with "audacity" (111), given that he fears his riding being seen by others so much that he lacks the audacity to venture outside his private estate on horseback (115). Despite being a capable, even brilliant rider, his riding continues to be a source of shame and anxiety. These contradictions are captured by his adapted saddle, which brings "happiness and health to the owner of it," but is simultaneously described as "singularly ugly." Its "complicated system of straps and buckles," the "contrivances" which serve "in place of stirrups," are treated not as practical adaptations to be welcomed, but as deviations from the norm which imbue the saddle with tremendous emotional power (111). The mere sight of it causes Mary Cathcart to weep, Roger Ormiston to exclaim, and Honoria to recoil, "as in approach to fear" (120). As these reactions suggest, the saddle serves as a synecdoche for

Richard's inability to embody normative masculinity, and characters respond accordingly. Fascinatingly, Richard seems to be angered by Honoria's response primarily because it disrupts the hierarchical relationship which he believes their relative genders should naturally create between them: he is humiliated by Honoria's revulsion because "after all, he was a man, and his critic merely a woman" (120). At this point in the novel, Richard fundamentally shares Honoria's attitude to his disability, he just regards her expression of it as an abrogation of a masculine position which is rightfully his.

Upholding his father's values means that Richard is forced both to despise and to deny his own embodiment, trapping him in a shameful stalemate of unspeakable self-hatred. As he tells his mother, "it's almost impossible always to carry something about with you which—which you hate, and not let it infect your attitude of mind and, in a degree, your speech" (126). Richard seeks to break out of this position through marriage—not, as we might expect, because he seeks acceptance and recognition in a love relationship, but as a way of transcending what he sees as the imperfection of his body through reproduction. Although his choice of his best friend's sister, Constance, perfectly accords with the conventions of the Victorian marriage plot—and in her passivity, beauty, and childishness she fulfils many of the criteria for the heroine of such a plot—Richard never claims to have fallen in love with Constance. Instead, as he explicitly explains to his mother, he wants to marry because he "want[s] a son" (202).

Although Richard's sexuality is a vexed subject—and one that we shall return to presently—it is important to note here that it is not the case that Richard has no experience of heterosexual desire at this point in the novel. In fact, he has already fallen wildly in love with his married cousin, the wicked temptress Helen de Vallorbes, and has enjoyed with her a series of decadently sensual scenes. Richard is not innocent of heterosexual desire, but rather imagines marriage as entirely separate from it. His desire is not for Constance, in her difference from himself, but for a son who will be a perfected copy of himself—which is to say, a copy of his father. In explaining this desire to his mother, he repeatedly characterises it as a desire to "keep straight" before turning, once again, to the image of riding:

> to be good I want a wife, that I may have my boy. I could keep straight for him, mother, though I'm afraid I can't keep straight for myself, and simply because it's right, much longer. I want him to have just all that I am denied. I want him to restore the balance, both for you and for me… He shall run, and he shall swim, and he shall fence, and he shall row,' he said. 'He shall learn all the gallant sports, as becomes an English gentleman. And he shall ride,—not as I ride, God forbid! like a monkey strapped on a dog at a fair, but as

> a centaur, as a young demi-god. We will set him, stark naked, on a bare-backed horse, and see that he's clean-limbed, perfect, without spot or blemish, from head to foot.
>
> (203–4)

Richard's pleasure in imagining an ideally handsome young man "stark naked, on a bare-backed horse" is likely to strike a modern reader as a very queer kind of straightening-out, but it does, in a sense, represent the acme of straight, patriarchal desire, sidelining women and overlooking pleasure in anything but the continuity of the male line. Constance herself is nowhere in this fantasy: Richard's putative bride is merely a vessel for the reproduction of perfect masculinity, the means of begetting "another Richard Calmady," as his father put it. Whereas the first Richard's desire for a son was mixed with desire for his wife, the second Richard seems to imagine a pure—by which I mean purely masculine—form of reproduction, entirely untouched by femininity, safe from imperfection and uninvolved with human frailty. The son he imagines is a perfected version of his father, like him in everything but his vulnerability to injury, symbolically riding, not even in a normal saddle, but "bare-backed." Tellingly, he pictures this son as "an entirely sound and healthy human *animal*... a centaur, a young demi-god" (203) [emphasis added], terms which force us to imagine this perfect son as something both more and less than fully human. It is not, I would suggest, the first or the second Richard who is monstrous, but this fantastical offspring, "clean-limbed" and inhuman. When Malet thwarts this marriage plot, then, I do not think she is pandering to eugenic anxieties about disabled people's reproductive capacity. Instead, she is wrenching the plot of patriarchal reproduction off course, saving Richard from his own desires in order to redirect them in a more ultimately satisfying direction. Although Honoria's intervention to prevent the marriage is surely influenced by her "instinctive repulsion" for Richard (225), the novel's plotting casts her not in the role of avenging angel of eugenics, interposing her fiery sword between the disabled Richard and his matrimonial desires, but as the defender of romantic love. Ensuring that Richard's desire for a perfected copy of his father is thwarted, she preserves his potential to desire something different, and keeps open the space in his life which she will eventually fill.

The Joys of "queer unsteadiness"

Humiliated by Constance's appeal that he break their engagement, Richard decisively abandons his doomed attempt to "keep straight," embracing instead an outright rebellion against the law of God the Father. Richard declares his intention to "break what men hold to be His laws, wherever and whenever I can... make hay of His so-called natural and moral order, just as often as I get the chance... curse, and again curse, back" (250) and embarks on a career of dissipation around Europe. This culminates in a night of passion with his wicked cousin which forces him to recognise her vicious character (about which he has hitherto deluded himself) and how far he has sunk in his own estimation.

Wallowing in "dishonour and desolation" (317), he reaches the nadir of his career when he attends the opera in Naples that night and has a vision, not only of Helen's soul—a "black... reeking... lascivious" thing (325)—but of his own relation to the working-class spectators he looks down on in the stalls. In an extraordinary, hallucinogenic scene, he sees himself as the representative of a parasitical class, and the workers as his "preordained executioners" (323). Although the near-fatal beating he then suffers is actually at the hands of Helen's jealous lover, Destournelles—and is the result of his rejection of Helen, not his identity as an aristocrat—Malet structures the scene so that it seems equally the result of Richard's own conception of himself as a pointless relic of past social forms who deserves to be swept away by the coming tide of revolution.[6] It is, in a sense, Richard's final and most drastic moment of alienation from the values of his father: not only has he abandoned the code of personal honour by which Richard Calmady defined himself, but he now rejects the idea that an aristocrat, a Richard Calmady, *can* be anything other than a social menace and an undesirable throwback. In willing his own destruction, he seeks definitively to end the chain of patriarchal reproduction, the continuity of the Calmady line.

The revolution Richard envisages, however, is not the one Malet's plot provides. Far from being the sign of an unreformable system, Richard becomes the agent of reform, uniquely fitted by his embodiment to adapt aristocratic power and privilege so that they become bearable for himself, and useful to others. While there seemed to be no hope for Richard in the purely secular social revolution he foresaw at the opera, Malet offers him a new way of understanding himself by reintroducing the Christianity he temporarily abandoned during his rebellion. First, Richard's reconciliation with his estranged mother is figured as a *pietà*, in which Katherine cradles Richard's broken body as the Madonna cradles the crucified Christ (346). Then, as Katherine nurses him back to health, Richard casts himself, not as Christ, but as the Prodigal Son—as he claims, in an almost exact quotation from Luke 15:18–19, "I have sinned against heaven and before thee, and am no more worthy to be called thy son" (350)—allowing Katherine, in her turn, to play the role of Christ, freely offering him the grace of forgiveness. The Christian imagery used in these passages suggests that Richard's suffering, even to the point of complete breakdown, has been a necessary condition for his growth, and thus prepares us to reencounter the chapbook legend. This time, we read it alongside Richard himself, and it is interpreted typologically.

The curse laid on the Calmadys by Sir Denzil's victim becomes, in this reading, analogous to the curse of original sin, and Richard's disability, his cross and remedy in one.[7] Recognising that "sorrow, pain and death ... are, after all, the fashioners and teachers of humanity," and "only the Man of Sorrows can truly be the Son of God," Richard is suddenly able to see his physical impairments as valuable—useful, even, since he immediately sees these theological ideas as socially significant (370). Rather than denying his experience of marginalisation, stigma, and suffering as incompatible with the aristocratic masculinity he has longed to embody, Richard sees that this very incompatibility is what makes his disability valuable: "By the fact of his deformity he was emancipated from the delusions of his class" (371). This new understanding enables Richard to approach both his own body and his social role differently. He ceases to hide his legs and takes to moving around the house on crutches and riding where he can be seen by others. He also starts to manage his estate for the benefit of his tenants and sets up a home for injured and disabled workmen, which, as he explains to Honoria, will be run "not on the lines of a charitable institution, which must inevitably be a rather mechanical, step-mother kind of arrangement at best, but on the lines of family affection, of personal friendship" (389). Honoria is so moved by this idea, which she tearfully describes as going "back to the Gospels," that she is filled with the desire to remain at Brockhurst, where she is temporarily staying, and "assist in these experiments made in the name of holy charity" (406). Within a few chapters, she has communicated this desire to Richard, and the pair embark on a career of philanthropy together.

If this was all there was to the final part of the novel, we might say that Malet was offering a pretty straightforward endorsement of Christian socialism—was returning, in fact, to the values of her own father. Work as the cure for spiritual malaise, "personal friendship" as the answer to class conflict, radical idealism redirected towards the gradual reform of society rather than towards revolution—all this sounds strongly Kingsleyan. But this is only half the story Malet tells. Although many of her critics felt that she *should* have left Richard single (Barry 1901, 21; "The History of Sir Richard Calmady: A Romance." 1901, 339), she chose not to do so. Richard and Honoria become not just collaborators, but lovers.

Their relationship has been read as sexless by most contemporary critics (Miller 2012, 102–3; O'Connell 2012, 109), but I think this is a mistake. What Honoria says about wanting to stay at Brockhurst to work with Richard might sound platonic until we take into account the rest of this passage:

> She longed inexpressibly to remain here, to assist in these experiments made in the name of holy charity. She longed inexpressibly

> to—And there Honoria paused, even in thought. Yet she glanced at the young man riding beside her—at the handsome profile, still and set in outline, the suggestion, it was no more, of a scar running downward across the left cheek; at the well-made, upright, broad-shouldered figure, and then at the saddle, peaked, back and front, with oddly-shaped appendages to it resembling old-fashioned holsters. And, as yesterday on the bridge, the ache of a pain at once sweet and terrible laid hold of her, making her feel queerly faint.
>
> (406)

Honoria's contemplation of Richard's body is here unmistakably charged with erotic feeling. She does not overlook his disability in this passage; in fact, in a return to and revision of her first encounter with the adult Richard, she actively looks at his adapted saddle, but whereas the first time, she "recoiled" (120), her sensations now are "sweet and terrible" (406). We have already been offered an erotic view of Richard's body, of course, by Helen de Vallorbes, but whereas she fetishised his physical difference—accepting the idea that his body was degraded by deformity and finding erotic excitement in that degradation—Honoria sees Richard whole, and loves all of what she sees.

One of the reasons critics have perhaps resisted recognising the erotic charge between Honoria and Richard is that it could be seen as a straightening-out of two queer characters. Honoria has consistently identified herself as a man trapped in a woman's body, and has expressed romantic attachments only to women, most powerfully of all to Richard's mother, Katherine. As she explained to Dr Knott, when he suggested that she might be the one woman suited to marry Richard, she is "not what you call a marrying man" (277). Given Malet's own remarks about her sense of herself as male, it is of course tempting to read Honoria as an avatar for Malet herself in this regard, and we might well feel disappointed that Malet's fantasy for this New Woman involves at least a partial reconciliation with "straight" gender identity. Honoria gradually abandons the radical feminism she espouses towards the beginning of the novel, telling her would-be suitor Ludovic Quayle that she has been forced to "give up the fiction of [woman's] superiority, and admit that woman already has her political, domestic, and social deserts" (338).[8] As she explains, this has tempered what used to be the "anti-matrimonial tendency" (225) of her ideas, leading her to aspire to a marriage like the one Katherine enjoyed with the first Richard Calmady. Indeed, loving Katherine proves a preparation for loving Richard, as she is drawn towards Katherine's essentialist ideas about romance, marriage, and gender; once Katherine has "let in the light" by opening Honoria's heart to love, she is ready for what Katherine calls "the other half" of the lesson, the "doxology which … neither I, nor any other woman, can teach you" (282). As these exchanges show, Malet is by no means condemnatory about Honoria's lesbian attachment to Katherine—and in addition to its tolerant treatment of same-sex desire, the text also contains a sympathetic portrayal of celibacy, embraced by the family chaplain Julius—but conjugal love is given a special status as uniquely satisfying, and uniquely sacred. It is also emphatically heterosexual: integral to Honoria's discovery of a "grand passion" (399) with Richard is her acceptance of what she calls "the woman in her," whom she has hitherto "condemned to solitary confinement in the back attic" of her psyche (382).

Yet if Honoria's reorientation towards Richard involves a liberation of her repressed femininity, it also involves his acceptance of what is masculine in her. Throughout the novel, Richard has treated not only himself, but Honoria too, as an ugly freak; now that he can accept his own divergence from normative, masculine embodiment, he finds himself able to see Honoria, too, as beautiful in her uniqueness. Malet explicitly draws a parallel between her acceptance of his disability and his acceptance of her androgyny, having Richard turn to look at Honoria after she has put her hand on his crutch, because "[g]enerosity should be met by generosity," and seeing as if for the first time "[h]er transparent sincerity, her superb chastity … of manner and movement, even of outline—the slight angularity of strong muscle as opposed to soft roundness of flesh—these arrested and impressed him" (382). Later, as she contemplates his body with love, he looks back at her and recognises that while she is still the "nymph whom he had first known, who had baffled and crossed him … a woman was here too, of finest fibre" (408). Although Richard's feelings for Honoria are at this point cast as the "desires of the natural man" (408), they are not, as these descriptions demonstrate, based on her adherence to feminine norms, nor on her embodiment of a type of ideal woman. Instead, they involve a recognition and celebration of particularity, of difference.

Such feelings cannot, therefore, be seamlessly fitted into a "straight" narrative, even though they are leading the couple towards marriage. When Honoria speaks with "queer unsteadiness," and feels "queerly faint" (382, 406), Malet may not necessarily have intended the adjective to carry connotations of same-sex desire (a usage only just emerging during the period of the novel's composition), but it would certainly have invoked that which was not "straight": the odd, the unusual, the nonnormative. Fittingly, Honoria inverts the conventional script of the marriage plot novel's proposal scene and proposes to Richard, declaring her own masculinity as she does so:

> "Richard," she cried fiercely, "if you don't care for me, if you don't want me, be honourable, tell me so straight out and let us have done with it! I am strong enough, I am man enough for that. For Heaven's

> sake don't take me out of pity. I would never forgive you. There's a good deal of both of us, one way and another, and we should give each other a hell of a time if I was in love and you were not. But" — she put her hand on the peak of that very ugly saddle again— "but, if you do care, here I am. I have never failed anyone yet. I will never fail you. I am yours body and soul. Marry me," she said.
>
> (414)

Reading this scene, it becomes clear that the critical consensus around the lack of eroticism in Richard and Honoria's relationship exists not *because* Malet is reticent in depicting passion between the pair, but *in spite of* repeated and vehement declarations of love. One possible explanation is that the dominant narratives in our own culture around romance are still so strongly hierarchical and rigidly gendered, so firmly based on an active man and a passive woman, that this meeting of equals, with its shifting gender roles, has not registered as romantic. In fact, I would suggest that it is a genuinely radical depiction of a relationship based on tenderness and respect, acknowledging likeness—"There's a good deal of both of us"—as well as difference. By laying her hand on Richard's adapted saddle, Honoria declares her desire for that which she once found despicable; it is a gesture which takes us back to the first scene between Richard and Honoria, only to mark how far both have travelled since then.

It is a fitting gesture to initiate a relationship which, although radical, is rooted in old forms, and involves no clean break with the past. Honoria and Richard's adapted marriage plot is one in which shared work is as vital as shared attraction, and in which masculine and feminine traits are shared out between husband and wife. In the next and final chapter, we see Honoria and Richard living together at Brockhurst, with a third Richard—their nephew, Roger Ormiston's son—alongside them. We might be tempted to read the fact that this third Richard is not a Calmady as representing the ultimate break in the chain of paternal inheritance, but in fact, Malet leaves open the possibility that Richard might yet have a biological heir. In their nephew's (seemingly uncharacteristic) anxiety about Honoria's delicacy (416), and in Katherine Calmady's recollections of how exactly this evening resembles the one on which she told her husband of her pregnancy (417), I think we can read at least the suggestion that Honoria is pregnant, and conclude that this final scene takes us back to the novel's opening, and marks another turning in the cycle of the history of Richard Calmadys.

It is, however, a return with a difference. The family the second Richard has made seems more flexibly constructed than that of the first. Since the curse on the Calmady heirs has been lifted, it no longer seems critical whether Richard's heir will be his son by choice or by blood. Retaining his title and his possession of the family estates, but committing his life to fighting poverty and acknowledging fellowship with his tenants; remaining a Christian, but reshaping his faith around disability; becoming a married man, but marrying a woman whose masculinity is a part of her charm for him—*The History of Richard Calmady* turns out to be the history of one man's transformation of a burdensome inheritance into the materials from which a life worth living can be made. I would argue that it is also a triumphant reworking of Malet's own literary, political, and social inheritance, a novel in which deviance becomes difference, and an adapted saddle the symbol of a better way forward.

Notes

1 For a sample of contemporary reviewers' reactions, see Lundberg 2003, 238–41.
2 Robert McRuer has argued that the dis/ability system, which stigmatises those whose bodies are deemed abnormal and insists on the superiority of the 'able' body, is analogous to the system of compulsory heterosexuality, suggesting that "the system of compulsory able-bodiedness, which in a sense produces disability, is thoroughly interwoven with the system of compulsory heterosexuality that produces queerness: that, in fact, compulsory heterosexuality is contingent on compulsory able-bodiedness, and vice versa" (McRuer 2006, 2). The way Malet imbricates "straight" masculinity, able-bodiedness, and heterosexuality suggests that she, too, perceived these ideals as mutually dependent, and I would argue that her conclusion queers the marriage plot as thoroughly as it crips aristocratic masculinity.
3 Reading this in the twenty-first century, the overtones of the Freudian family romance are unmissable, and this impression is only strengthened by Malet's subsequent depiction of Richard's quasi-erotic feelings for his mother as he grows up. Since Freud's theories about the Oedipus complex had not been published in 1901 (Blass and Simon 1991), it seems unlikely that Malet could have been influenced by Freud, but their shared experience of the nineteenth-century patriarchal bourgeois family seems to have led them to some similar conclusions about the male psyche.
4 Karen Bourrier suggests that the attempt to treat Richard's orthopaedic disability through mechanical means, rather than surgery, is "purposefully and accurately anachronistic" (2014, 11), reflecting the medical science of the 1840s rather than the 1900s. The same explanation could be offered for Malet's inclusion of this mid-Victorian theory of the circumstantial causes of disability, although, as I hope to demonstrate, it is also vital to the novel's plotting.
5 In a compelling reading which stresses the voyeuristic elements of the text, Rachel O'Connor argues that the novel "thematizes and draws on the conventions of the freak show, describing Richard's body in visual terms and posing him in tableaux dripping with emotional significance, so that the novel as a whole becomes a kind of textual stage upon which Richard is displayed as a freak" (O'Connell 2012, 109). O'Connor underestimates the extent to which the reader is encouraged to share Richard's perspective, to look not just at him but *with* him. In making us share both Richard's terror of exposure and his experience of self-concealment, I would argue that the novel attempts to offer an alternative and superior way of understanding the

body, ultimately leading us away from both horror and titillation, towards a religious viewpoint which sees Richard's body in a typological light.

6 For an extended discussion of Malet's treatment of revolutionary socialism, see Ford (2015).

7 For further discussion of this passage, see Delyfer (2011, 93).

8 Malet was similarly equivocal about the feminist movement in her non-fictional writing. In her 1905 essay, "The Threatened Re-Subjection of Woman," she argued that the movement had "run its course" and while many of its gains were to be celebrated, it was natural that most women would want to devote their lives to the care of husbands and children (Malet 1905, 817–19). Edward Carpenter—socialist, pacifist, feminist and all-round radical proponent of the joys of same-sex love—expressed very similar ideas about the New Woman in *Love's Coming-of-Age* (1896), lamenting her "deficiency in maternal instinct" (Carpenter 2010, 57), even while he celebrated the crumbling of the worn-out edifices of marriage and the binary division of gender.

Works Cited

Barry, William. 1901. "Lucas Malet's Challenge." *The Bookman* 21(121): 20–21.

Blass, Rachel B., and Bennett Simon. 1991. "The Development and Vicissitudes of Freud's Ideas on the Oedipus Complex." In *Cambridge Companion to Freud*, edited by Jerome Neu, 161–74. Cambridge: Cambridge University Press.

Bourrier, Karen. 2014. "Orthopaedic Disability and the Nineteenth-Century Novel." *Nineteenth-Century Contexts* 36(1): 1–17.

Carpenter, Edward. 2010. *Love's Coming-of-Age: A Series of Papers on the Relations of the Sexes by Edward Carpenter.* Facsimile of 1912 ed. Montana: Kessinger Books.

Delyfer, Catherine. 2010. "Lucas Malet's Subversive Late-Gothic: Humanizing the Monster in The History of Sir Richard Calmady." In *Demons of the Body and Mind: Essays on Disability in Gothic Literature*, edited by Ruth Bienstock Anolik, 80–96. Jefferson: McFarland.

———. 2011. *Art and Womanhood in Fin-de-Siècle Writing: The Fiction of Lucas Malet, 1880–1931.* London: Pickering & Chatto.

Ford, Jane. 2015. "Socialism, Capitalism and the Fiction of Lucas Malet: 'The Spirit of the Hive.'" *English Literature in Transition, 1880–1920* 58(4): 551–71.

Lundberg, Patricia Lorimer. 2003. *'An Inward Necessity': The Writer's Life of Lucas Malet.* New York: Peter Lang.

Malet, Lucas. 1905. "The Threatened Re-Subjection of Woman." *Fortnightly Review* 77(461): 806–19.

———. 2003. *The History of Sir Richard Calmady*, edited by Talia Schaffer. Birmingham: University of Birmingham Press.

McRuer, Robert. 2006. *Crip Theory: Cultural Signs of Queerness and Disability.* Cultural Front. New York: New York University Press.

Miller, Kathleen A. 2012. "'Your Loving Is Unlike Any Other:' Romance and the Disabled Body in the Gothic Fiction of Edith Nesbit and Lucas Malet." In *Writing Women of the Fin de Siècle: Authors of Change*, edited by Carolyn Oulton and Adrienne E. Gavin, 193–203. Basingstoke: Palgrave Macmillan.

O'Connell, Rachel. 2012. "'That Cruel Spectacle': The Extraordinary Body Eroticized in Lucas Malet's *The History of Sir Richard Calmady*." In *Sex and Disability*, edited by Robert McRuer and Anna Mollow, 108–22. Durham: Duke University Press.

Schaffer, Talia. 2000. *The Forgotten Female Aesthetes: Literary Culture in Late-Victorian England*. Charlottesville: University Press of Virginia.

Srebrnik, Patricia. 1994. "The Re-Subjection of 'Lucas Malet': Charles Kingsley's Daughter and the Response to Muscular Christianity." In *Muscular Christianity: Embodying the Victorian Age*, edited by Donald E. Hall, 194–214. Cambridge: Cambridge University Press.

Stoddard Holmes, Martha. 2004. *Fictions of Affliction: Physical Disability in Victorian Culture*. Ann Arbor: University of Michigan Press.

3 “Vanity of vanities”

The Bildungsroman, Corporeal Fragility, and the Aesthetic Ideal in *The Far Horizon*

Alani Hicks-Bartlett

The desire for an ‘educational’ process that leads to personal, spiritual, and artistic development is one of the obsessive concerns of Lucas Malet’s *The Far Horizon*. Published in 1906, less than five years after Malet is understood to have converted to Catholicism, the novel recounts the forced retirement of the bank clerk, Dominic Iglesias; his discomfort with his newfound leisure; and the religious awakening that ultimately leads him to (re-)embrace Catholicism.[1] However, Dominic’s tardy yet profound ideological transformation contrasts the insufficient social education he has received. Having been raised in a climate that has forced him to trade his healthy, active nature for a restricted, private world of “acquiescent sickness,” “intangible sadness”, and “haunting melancholy” (Malet 1906, 11), Dominic is left ill-equipped to weather the prejudices and limitations of English Protestant society.

Even after Dominic learns more about his origins and “touch[es] the key to the riddle” (8) that shrouds his past and youth in mystery, rather than being able to rejoin the society he feels has abandoned him, Dominic finds that even more distance separates him from it. *The Far Horizon*’s dénouement, which traces Dominic’s mounting sense of melancholy and his concern that he has little to show for his many years of life, emphasises this cleavage and disorientation. The novel details how the guidance that Dominic has received from those in his immediate family, as well as those in his professional and social milieux, has been wholly insufficient. Since Dominic has always shunned the attention of others while drifting through his “laborious, monotonous, and … very virtuous life” (5), he has never benefited from constructive guidance, nor has he received an appropriate model from his elders. Subsequently, his isolation and difficulty finding a favourable direction prevent him from obtaining the tranquillity, peace, and advancement he desires. Both literally and metaphorically, Dominic’s loss of bearings forces him down a stilted path that confounds the edifying trajectory he hoped to take, miring him in ideological, artistic, and amorous conflicts. It is not until he is set on the proper path by the actress Poppy St. John (who serves as his platonic ideal and sparks his delight in aesthetic pleasures), and by the Catholic Church, (which provides spiritual inspiration and redirects his attentions from his fragile body to his eternal soul) that he is able to achieve his personal, religious, and aesthetic objectives.

Despite *The Far Horizon*'s engagement of popular literary trends fundamental to the development of the novel and reprisal of themes explored in Malet's more favoured works, it has been largely understudied.[2] The reasons behind the novel's inconsistent reception are numerous yet primarily correspond to a fundamental evolution in Malet's ideological and generic objectives, seen in her seamless transition from a Victorian modality to a modernist one, from her "lush late-Victorian style to the spare yet psychologically intense and subjective Modern style" (Lundberg 2003, 332). Yet "as Modernism began to assert the need to break with a Victorian past now coded as genteel and stifling, Malet fell on the wrong side of that divide" (Schaffer 2001), contributing to the perception that she was far more Victorian than modern.[3]

Probing the temporal gulf separating Malet's work from modern authors, Patricia Srebrnik, Mary Anne Gillies, Talia Schaffer, and Catherine Delyfer examine the correlation between Malet's declining popularity and esteem, and her rather controversial religious conversion. Malet's earlier novels granted her an innovative space for authorial self-fashioning (Demoor 2004, 7, 14), allowing her to meticulously investigate liminal and nonnormative subjectivities. However, her 1902 conversion marked a vital turn in terms of the content, tone, and reception of her work. Delyfer helpfully traces the decline in Malet's readership post-conversion, shedding light on the "especially suspicious" stance of readers towards *The Far Horizon*'s "explicit Catholic theme" (Delyfer 2011, 114). As such, while Malet's conversion marked an increased interest in exploring more fundamentally religious arguments, it also triggered a renegotiation of her authorial agency, as her faith granted her a new independence that resonated on religious, literary, and familial levels. As it establishes distance between herself and the staunchly Protestant doctrine of her father, Malet's conversion can be understood as "a highly controversial choice coming from the daughter of the most virulent Victorian opponent of Catholicism" (Delyfer 2011, 114).[4]

Malet's ideological, spiritual, and physical distance from paternal authoritarian models freed her to explore a new religious telos—or, per Ford, a "spiritual or evolutionary *telos*" (Ford 2015, 565). Despite this freedom, Malet's reorientation led her, at least superficially, to choose less disarming subject matters since she wanted to be in greater alignment with the dogmata of the Catholic Church. Given Protestantism's stronghold in early twentieth-century England, and a pervasive hostility towards Catholicism, it is no wonder that critical and popular assessments of Malet's works also became less auspicious, leading to the "deterioration" of her "reputation and readership ... in the 1910s and 1920s" (Delyfer 2011, 114).

When combined with the rigidity that thrusts Dominic into an anachronistic relationship with his contemporaries (making him seem as if he were "left behind" and "born five or six centuries out of [his] time" (279), the novel's "heavy handedness" ("Glimpses of New Books" 1907, 47–48) can be read as a symptom of the inimical societal mores and resulting sense of alienation and disconcertment that plagues its protagonist. Certainly, by following a narrative arc that showcases professional and social shortcomings along with frustrated attempts at integration and positive development, Malet offers a perspicacious yet acerbic critique of society's hostility and the empirical and didactic failures that Dominic consequently experiences.

The more Dominic learns about the inner workings of a cold, capitalist, and calculating society in which he discovers he is but a mere cog, the more isolated and disoriented he feels. Though he continues to search for purpose, direction, and seeks reorientation, he ultimately withdraws, having learned only that his rigidity makes him ill-suited for the contemporary world that has oppressed and failed him: "'The routine has gone on too long,' … 'I have lost my pliability, lost my humanity. I am a machine not a man'" (28). Rather than the social integration usually sought by the protagonists of bildungsromane Dominic prefers isolation, renunciation, and retreat. Even his late-won spiritual development directs him away from earthly life, producing a trajectory that contravenes the typical orientation of bildungsromane and other novels of development.

Describing himself alternately as a boat that is stranded or adrift, with neither a clear orientation nor a well-defined "shore" in sight, Dominic is trapped between competing extremes prior to his spiritual awakening. He is encumbered by: the contradiction between financial liberty and professional and moral obligation; an artistic and sentimental asceticism and newly sparked amorous possibilities; a nostalgic desire for a remote past and a spiritual penchant for a more promising future. Yet, it is not until readers examine the protagonist's difficult development, and study how these vacillations contribute to the epistemological stagnation that leaves Dominic feeling distanced from the world around him, that a new approach to *The Far Horizon* can be charted. In this context, the novel can be understood as an innovative novel of formation that critiques the exclusionary, disinterested Protestant society that causes the protagonist's failure, and recodifies the bildungsroman genre itself.

Bildungsromane commonly take the protagonist's metaphorical exile or loss of familiar bearings as their point of departure. However, for the unsettled and grave protagonist of *The Far Horizon*, the losses that he has suffered are even more monumental than spatial disorientation or expulsion. After a jarring and "hurried exodus" (6) from Spain that he can barely recall, Dominic loses both of his parents under unusually painful circumstances. His secretive and distant social anarchist father, who "was deeply involved in revolutionary intrigue" (8) disappears under mysterious conditions during Dominic's youth. Decades later, Dominic loses his pious and sickly mother, who has suffered throughout her life from obscure mental and physical ailments that he prefers not to voice. The death of the tormented woman, whom Dominic regards as "wholly exquisite" (7), and "sacred" (11), and around whose presence he has always oriented himself, leaves Dominic with no family of his own, compounding the pervasive loneliness he has long experienced.

Opening *in medias res* to underscore the confusing disorientation that Dominic is made to endure, the novel's first scenes describe how he has been forced from his only permanent job. The sudden liberty that is rather shamefully forced upon him leaves him confused and reeling. He is

> still very sore, the heat of anger past, but the smart of it remaining ... And not only that after-smart, but a perplexity held him. For two strange faces had looked into his during the last few hours—those of Loneliness and Freedom.
>
> (21)

Once Dominic finally accepts an unanticipated freedom from his profession, he swiftly loses it again; subsequently, he loses his only friends and the genial rapport he has with other residents of his boarding house. He finds himself profoundly alone, regretting that his only companions are "Old Age," "Loneliness," and "Death," and becomes increasingly aware of the painful distance that separates him from his past, his acquaintances, and even from a country he believed he could call his own.

The unique combination of disorientation and loss that Dominic experiences from childhood—"that a sense of mystery, of large issues, of things at once strong and hidden, impenetrable to his understanding and concerning which no questions might be asked ... " (7)—reveals that the profundity of his past losses has only set him up for future damages and contraventions. This, we are told, "resulted in an atmosphere of seriousness and responsibility which inevitably reacted on the boy, making him sober beyond his years, tempering his natural vivacity with watchfulness, and pitching even his laughter in a minor key" (7–8). Rather than being oriented towards future development, the "minor key" that has affected Dominic's entire life, "the public danger, the private strain and stress which had surrounded his childhood and early youth" (8), along with his self-abnegation, morbid thoughts, disorientation, and his profound nostalgia cause him to be firmly oriented towards the past.

Susan Fraiman's analysis of female bildungsromane in *Unbecoming Women: British Women Writers and the Novel of Development* (1993) can be applied to Dominic's epistemologically and physically frustrated situation, particularly given his rather ascetic and asexual characterisation. Fraiman identifies the circularity that characterises nostalgic turns to the past as evidence of "obstructed ... development" symptomising the "logic of impediment" and the nightmarish "holding patterns" in which female protagonists find themselves when situations, memories, and other manifestations of stunted growth force their orientation towards the past (34–40). While Fraiman's work is helpful in understanding both the comfort Dominic finds in nostalgic remembrances and the impediments that repeatedly stunt him, *The Far Horizon* is unique in that it is not the contemporary world that attracts Dominic, nor is it where he will achieve social progression. Instead of a cycle, Dominic can be understood as being caught in a vertiginous back-and-forth. He distances himself from the contemporary world, looking only towards the comforts of an oneiric, illusive past, or to the excitement of an otherworldly, divine future.

As certain critics have identified a certain fractious quality to *The Far Horizon*, reading the novel in light of the bildungsroman genre helps elucidate the changes that Dominic undergoes in regard to his unexpected maturation—specifically, his spiritual, romantic, and personal development. Given the dramatic social context of *fin-de-siècle* literature, the genre of the bildungsroman offered a framework to many authors for the exploration of social commentary and analyses of self-determination. However, by replicating many of the signposts of the bildungsroman only to take noteworthy departures from it, Malet's modifications reveal both a new preoccupation with the subjectivity of her protagonist and a critique of her society's patriarchal modes of identity, literary, and ideological representation.

In her contribution to this volume, Jill Ehnenn persuasively demonstrates how Malet's acceptance of notions of difference and nonnormativity offers unique renegotiations of a genre that traditionally works for the erasure of difference and strangeness by resisting the impulse to "enforce normalcy."[5] Although Dominic's corporeal alterity is presented in a subtler manner in *The Far Horizon* than in the novels Ehnenn discusses, both his nonnormative body and ideals render his "foreign" nature metaphoric. Described numerous times as "unusual," "exotic," and "foreign," Dominic is "marked" differently than others, due to his "young figure, his thin shapely hands and feet, his blue-black Irish eyes and black hair, his energetic colourless face, his ready yet reticent speech" (13); twice he is referred to as "unusual and exotic" (13) and is described as having "something exotic, aloof, unusual about him" (199). Similarly, foreignness is a problem that creates discord and singularity. Dominic has a "foreign name" (13, 67), engages in "foreign ... practice" (217), and is a "foreign being" (243). In more oblique references to "unpleasant foreign bodies" (212), foreignness is continually disparaged in the novel. On the positive side, Dominic is "unusually considerate" (179), and Poppy St. John finds him appealing precisely because of "the exotic and foreign elements in him, which captivated her fancy, endowing him with an effect of mystery, making him seem to hail from some region of legend and high romance" (281).

Dominic feels that he is irrevocably marked by a shameful alterity: "Everything, he feared, was against him—his youth, his foreign name, his limited acquaintance, the impossibility of giving definite information regarding his father's past occupations or present whereabouts" (13). Though professions of faith do not correspond to a physical change, Dominic's alterity mounts when he definitively adopts Catholicism; once other members of his social milieu discover his change of religion, they use it as both symptom and reinforcement of his foreign background and fundamental difference. For instance, an acquaintance laments Dominic's conversion, taking it as proof of foreignness and of a callous disregard for British manners: "[o]f course, the change of religion is dreadful, particularly in one who should have known better, though a foreigner, having had the advantage of being brought up in England" (302). This incongruence between external appearance and internal reality critiques a bigoted Protestant society, allowing Malet to insist upon the greatness of the transformation that Catholicism effectuates.

Dominic's unique background, his corporeal singularity, and the ensuing friction defines his relationships with others, frustrating the 'educational' trajectory he undertakes. His progress neither foments advancement nor leads to an easily won societal integration, and it is only once Dominic moves past his desire to be integrated with his contemporaries and begins prioritising his spiritual development, that he is able to progress. Naturally, in addition to his "unusual and exotic" aspect, Dominic's difference is rendered all the more noteworthy as his physical maturity foregrounds his alterity even within the bildungsroman genre. His eventual illness and physical wasting notwithstanding, his age sets him down a path already distanced from the vim and excitement experienced by the immature youths of traditional novels of formation.

Malet's innovative use of the bildungsroman genre and the way in which she recodifies it such that it embraces characters whose liminality, corporal fragility, and even old age would traditionally have precluded them from being protagonists, underscores her valorisation of difference and the "revolutionary potential of the extraordinary body" as a "vehicle of the future" (Delyfer 2010, 92). That is, rather than insisting on the normalisation of her characters Malet proffers an original understanding of progress that largely depends upon the uniqueness and unpredictability of the human body and experience. Rather than adhering to the pattern of traditional novels of formation by highlighting assimilation and "normalcy," *The Far Horizon* interrogates questionable extant modes of representation. In this respect, her choice of protagonist is significant and evidences her commitment to investigating "corporeal otherness" (Delyfer 2010, 87), and valorising marginalised voices and overlooked perspectives. By taking these notions of alterity understood as problematic and upending them through the socially restorative heroism, moral development, and 'martyrdom' of the main character, Malet gives a new visibility to the capacity and strengths of marginalised bodies.

Dominic is indeed primarily regarded as an outsider with a suspect, transgressive, and ultimately unproductive body. The difficulties he encounters feeling at ease with others and even finding a job are attributed to his unique body and his "exotic" origins. Indeed, London treats Dominic "in a very cynical fashion," and his potential employers "distrus[t] the distinctness of his personality," "for the unusual and exotic the British employer of labour—of whatever sort—has, it must be conceded, but little use" (13). Notably, in terms of reproduction and marriage, Dominic is deemed odd or described as an "enemy" (337) for shunning marriage, yet also obliquely lauded on several occasions for not marrying, which is deemed a safer option. Rather than following the traditional bildungsroman trajectory that charts protagonists' overall adherence to the straightforward progression of more successful and common developmental processes, Malet relishes dramatising the moments of nonconformity of her characters' experience. Thus, the 'monstrosity' of style and genre that her work betrays underscores the hybrid terrain that readers should understand as her reprisal and rewriting of the bildungsroman, while her focus on generic diversity and modification shows an appreciation for the broader potential of the genre.

Furthermore, traditional bildungsromane often take an instance of loss, a pervasive sense of displacement, or a fundamental immaturity as the catalyst for physical and emotional development. Yet instead of commencing with the expulsion from one's home or familiar land that is necessary for a protagonist to gain entry into society and find his place in the world, *The Far Horizon* begins with Dominic's recognition of defeat and affective estrangement. Rather than portraying a young protagonist's development into a wiser adult or his increased ability to overcome the disorientation of inhospitable environments, the novel's reprioritised attentions recount the slow maturation and delayed 'education' of a man well past his prime and his frustrated efforts to recuperate the past. Given his obsessive, oneiric nostalgia for a past that haunts him with memories that "stick, stick like a leech" (324), Dominic's losses have indubitably stunted him. As Poppy observes tenderly, "You're the veriest infant. One has only to look into your face to see that … You belong to another order of doctrine and practice to that current in contemporary society" (105). In addition to a certain lack of maturity. Dominic lives chastely and tries to mollify his passions: "Temperate in all things, he was temperate in enjoyment" (313). Although he describes himself as "a perfectly normal piece of flesh and blood, with a man's normal passions, and his natural craving for wife, and child, home, family, and the like," he details how pressing preoccupations and responsibilities continually took precedence over any amorous awakening or self-preserving desires: "during my mother's lifetime I was bound to other service than that of marriage" (313, 320).[6]

Staging the extent to which Dominic is ill at ease with his world, the novel's opening scene details how the aging protagonist is lost and confused; in an attempt to regather his bearings, he decides to turn away from his usual companions, preferring his restless, anxious solitude to the banality of their company. Unsure of what has sparked his emotional *désarroi*, Dominic has difficulty seeing how he can advance or what his appropriate trajectory should be. He knows only that he has been suddenly and tardily set loose in the world, freed from the "monstrous mother" and "awful" "living creature" that London ("so long his task-mistress and gaoler") represents. Despite being "cast ... off," Dominic is left feeling "agitated and hurt," and no longer knows what to do "with that which remained to him of life" (15).

Dominic's disorientation and feelings of disconnection are compounded by his stilted 'educational' path and the withdrawal that accompanies a lifetime marked by sacrifice, distance, and isolation. And indeed, as for Dominic's point of departure, his phenomenological orientation and the first definitive action readers see him take is one of retreat rather than advancement. Malet's reversal of order, therefore, the attention she gives to withdrawal and retraction, the prioritisation of a character so resistant to development and progress that he refers to himself as a "nobody" and regards his circumstances as "incapable of alteration and development" (163), are innovative choices that purposefully trouble the usual starting point and course of novels of formation.

Likewise, while Dominic's uncertainty shares commonalities with the neophyte youths of standard bildungsromane, he is neither being introduced to a new environment nor does he have any direct assistance in navigating a challenging terrain. The initial nervousness typical of traditional iterations is usually a more felicitous anxiety paired with excitement for the future rather than trepidation. Though as a child Dominic feels "eagerly ambitious to make his way in the world" (6), this motivation is fleeting. His adulthood is marked by an anxiety so physically and mentally consuming it leads to lassitude, collapse, and death. Even sensorial difficulties accentuate the overwhelming epistemological and visual disequilibrium with which Dominic grapples. Highlighting his subjugation to a mutinous division between body and mind, Dominic is described as "tired in body," though his mind is "eminently, consciously awake, to the point of restlessness" (1), while his "thought" and sight are wild and uncontrollable, "refus[ing] ... limits, and rang[ing] outward" (1). Simultaneously, however, the pervasive sense of alienation and strangeness that distracts and reroutes his thoughts, further costs him perspective, agency, and clarity: "His own thoughts, his own life, filled his entire horizon, leaving no space for the thoughts or lives of others" (5). Dominic feels that his entire existence has been dramatically altered and that he has been abruptly thrust from his expected course. Consequently, as his familiar environment has become profoundly unfamiliar, the only path he feels comfortable taking is one that allows him to withdraw and direct himself towards a more familiar, though still murky, past.

Dominic's physical and social withdrawal is also represented atmospherically as he stands gazing over a gloomy Trimmer's Green at the nervous transition between of day and night. Not only do mentions of "twilight," and "night" conjure up classical literary references to sleep, decrepitude, and the corporeal fragility that leads to death, they draw attention to Dominic's advanced age and the feelings of lassitude that further orient him against the typical path of bildungsromane. Finally, appearing potentially merciful but threatening bellicosity, just as the "face of heaven" is ready to burst into an aggressive storm, Dominic wonders if the "strange appearance" altering his existence "was destined to prove that of a friend or of an enemy" (4). Recalling the traditional bildungsroman's neophytes who are too trusting to properly decipher the signs and codes of the vibrant new society into which they have been introduced, Dominic labours to understand a society with which he has long been familiar and struggles to determine whether the forces in vigour are friendly or inimical. The "darkening" light around Dominic therefore proffers another indication of the difficult negotiation of perspicacity and confusion, of perspectival amplitude and frustrated or restricted "vision" that will plague him throughout the novel as he struggles to grasp intangible matters situated on a distanced plane, on a far horizon.

Dominic's surroundings both on the Green and at Cedar Lodge, where he resides, appear "wholly pacific," connote "suburban security," and are auspiciously introduced as offering him the "maximum of comfort and advantage" (2). These depictions of domestic ease and societal comfort are offset by foreboding descriptions of his mounting discomfiture: "All day thunder had threatened but had not broken. And even yet the face of heaven seemed less peaceful than remonstrant, a sullenness holding it as of troops in retreat denied satisfaction of imminent battle" (1). Dominic experiences a certain emotional disquietude and perceives a latent threat in his tempestuous environment, one that prophetically gestures to the ominous social, amorous, and religious troubles that have long been storming within him.

To fully emphasise how great the risks of Dominic's disorientation are, and the passivity and uncertainty that deprive him of agency, Malet illustrates his "mental incoherence," his "bewildering activity of vision" (5), and the impending sense of menace that disorient him by combining visual vocabulary with nautical terminology. The rapidly changing terrain that catches Dominic unawares is not simply an unsettling experience, but one that precludes him from finding the bearings and advancement as he desires:

> More than once before in the course of his laborious, monotonous, and, as men go, very virtuous life had this same thing happened to him—the tides of the obvious and accustomed suddenly receding and leaving him stranded, as on some barren sand-bank, uncertain whether the ship of his individual fate would lie there wind-swept and sun-bleached till rusty rivets fell out and planks parted, disclosing the ribs of her unsightly nakedness, or whether the kindly tide, rising, would float her off into blue water and she would sail hopefully once again.
>
> (5)

Explicitly gesturing towards the notions of disorder and loss, that are frequent tropes in novels of formation, the "ship of [Dominic's] fate" is thrice described as "stranded" in the first chapter alone.

Throughout the rest of the novel, there are many mentions of sailing and ships that are adrift, stranded, lost at sea, or beset by tempests. In a revealing description of his stunted trajectory, for example, Dominic's lack of progress is a ship unable to set sail: "Thus did the ship of poor Dominic's fate appear to be stranded or ever it had fairly set sail at all" (13). Similarly, much later in the novel he is advised "not to go sail off on a wrong tack" (249) or be careless about his trajectory. When Dominic's devoutly Protestant friend George Lovegrove discovers that Dominic has embraced Catholicism, Lovegrove also recurs to nautical terminology. In this instance, however, Lovegrove uses allusions to nautical failure and the economic losses suggested therein (such as botched seizure, and unachieved mooring), to express his disappointment and surprise: "My mind refuses to grasp it. I would rather have lost five hundred pounds than have heard this. I declare I am fairly unmanned. I have never received a greater shock" (241). Lovegrove's physical and linguistic response to the news of Dominic's 'Romanism' feeds in to the idea of an improper (emotional/narrative) trajectory or alignment. The exchange is mediated through Lovegrove's attempts to reorient himself towards a more familiar path:

> 'I think if you will kindly excuse me, I will go no farther,' [Lovegrove] faltered. 'What you say may be true—I am sure I don't know. It is all beyond me ... Nothing does come between people like religion,' he added with unconscious irony. 'So I think, if you will kindly excuse me, I will just go away, Dominic.
>
> (242)

Lovegrove no longer wishes to walk with Dominic and his language becomes stunted, repetitive, and awkward as he makes his retreat from the friend he once held in such high regard. Lovegrove stumbles away "blindly," underscoring the myopia that causes him to no longer see "his beloved friend" as before (243). Dominic cannot be "the faithful comrade of more than half a lifetime," since he is now a "foreign being." Lovegrove, we are told, is "frightened," since his "everyday, comfortable, jog-trot, little odd and end of a local parochial suburban middle-class world was literally turned upside down and inside out" (242).

Particularly in light of the difficulty Dominic has finding the orientation he desires, and the relief, acceptance, and safety he experiences once he has found it, Malet's frequent use of nautical metaphors recall biblical references to ships and sailing, and the importance of both in the Christian church. In addition to the salvific function of the ark during the great flood (Genesis 5:32-10:1), or the plea in Psalm 69 to be saved from wreckage, ships and shipwrecks are explicitly connected to moments of religious doubt and (re)assertions of faith that speak to Dominic's return to the religion so prized by his mother. These connections to faith, direction, and succour make the ship an apt metaphor for the Church qua "ark of salvation" (Genesis 6:14–16), particularly given that imagery related to ships frequently represented the path towards salvation in interpretations of Christian life as a trajectory. Dominic's concern that he is "adrift" or that his "ship" is not headed towards the appropriate port is directly offset by the surety, safety, and proper orientation he feels once he has returned to the Church.

Reworking the bildungsroman's obsession with proper orientation as we have seen, Dominic's trajectory is imprecise, troubled, and largely uncharted. Even the tediousness of his career recalls the monotonous lapping of waves and ships adrift—imagery that is problematic for the implicit lack of agency and control that Dominic has over such an important element of his life and for the speed with which his menial labours consume him. When Dominic is forced to leave his job to avail space to "men younger and more in touch with modern methods" (19), he "drifts" even more and is "frightened by the greatness of the emptiness, within and about him" (28). Later, when he briefly returns to tender professional assistance to the same company that rejected him, his noble mien and generosity towards the company are described as "righting" and "saving a stranded ship" (278, 284). Yet once Dominic has resolved the company's financial difficulty and again takes up retirement, he lists, finding himself directionless and stranded once more.[7]

After losing his mother (who had provided him with a constant aesthetic, social, and spiritual orientation despite her ailing body and eternal martyrdom), and his career (which had granted him a certain professional direction, however problematic), the only two forces giving

Dominic guidance or propulsion are Poppy St. John and the Catholic church. Recasting Dominic's reliance upon his job to give meaning to his life in a more positive light, the text shows that once Dominic feels that he can trust Poppy, he depends upon her as one would a lodestar. When he feels that she has "given him his dismissal" (183)—much like Barking Brothers & Barking had done—Dominic regrets the loss of a safe harbourage and feels that a "foul miasma" is distorting his world and confounding his sight. Drawing attention to Dominic's phenomenological orientation around Poppy's presence, the void and obstructed vision that losing Poppy represents reveal how Dominic has situated her as the beacon he hopes to use for guidance and direction:

> ... it remained indisputable that the Lady of the Windswept Dust had given him his dismissal. Out of his daily life a joy had gone, a constant object of thought and interest. Out of his heart a living presence had gone, leaving a void more harsh than death. ... In short, Dominic Iglesias had lost sight of the far horizon which is touched by the glory of the Uncreated Light; and, so doing, dwelt in outer darkness once again, infinitely desolate.
>
> (183)

Of course, the darkness lifts, and when Dominic comes to understand that he is still in Poppy's good graces his eyes can perceive the horizon again. In addition to emphasising the salubrious and restorative effect Poppy has upon him—"I am rested. And more than that, I am alive and awake, strangely awake and full of vision—thanks to you" (318)—Dominic insists upon her importance to him: " ... save for my love for my mother—such as the throne is or ever has been—you reign alone" (321). By granting Poppy such supremacy, not only does Dominic align her with the "sacred" mother who represents "the one perfect relationship he had known" (88), the adored, elevated throne he grants to her is suggestive of religious contemplation, hyperdulia, and the Catholic church's veneration of the Virgin Mary.

This is the precise dynamic repeated in Malet's descriptions of Dominic's rapprochement to the Catholic church—though constant and supreme, the Church never fails him, nor does his faith, once regained, falter. Like the comfort he seeks in Poppy, what Dominic desires of the Church is simple and specific—the instruction, support, and guidance necessary for him to choose the right path:

> He merely desired, earnestly yet humbly, to be given grace to find the road—however archaic in the eyes of the modern world that road might be—which leads to the light on the far horizon and beyond to the presence of God.
>
> (227)

Indeed, Dominic's adoption of Catholicism is described in terms of trajectory and orientation: when he embraces Catholicism as an adult, "as one who comes by long-established right" (232), he feels rerouted and welcomed.

Not only does Dominic's conversion render him fundamentally different from the naïve, perplexed man readers first encountered, he finally feels comfortable, finding that the world has opened a "definite place" for him, bestowing upon him "the perfect freedom, namely, freedom of soul, freedom of heavenly citizenship" (293). Moreover, he is able to look forward to the future, rather than solely regarding it as indicative of a vast and dark "emptiness," as he previously believed: "For in the last nine months Dominic Iglesias' habits and outlook had changed notably. The values were altered" (273). It should be noted that these dramatic alterations are not only exterior; rather, they are specifically presented as fundamental interior changes as well. Certainly, as the alterations are situated within a period of nine months, they become suggestive of a gestational period that dramatises Dominic's rebirth in God, while also emphasising the matrix of women—both living and sacred, both intercessors and *genetrices*, so to speak—who have facilitated Dominic's new (Catholic) life.

Exploiting maritime tropes once again, the attribution of a new significance to Dominic's habitual gaze reveals the developmental changes that his maturation has generated. In other words, while his eyes continue to be drawn towards the far horizon, he no longer feels the bleak sense of menace and disorientation he once experienced. Rather, the horizon's scopic economies become almost aesthetic; they are grounding, orienting, and even exciting. As Dominic's path has been righted and granted a new purpose, no longer does he worry about the sense of loss and waywardness that once afflicted him so profoundly:

> Loneliness, the emptiness induced by absence of definite employment, no longer oppressed him. Holy Church had cured all that, giving him a definite place, and definite purpose, beautiful duties of prayer and worship, the restrained, yet continuous, excitement of the pushing forward of soul and spirit upon the fair, strange, daily, hourly journey towards the far horizon and the friendship of Almighty God.
>
> (273)

Having traded his fears of emptiness for a newly purposeful excitement about the future, Dominic is eager to embrace a new objective. Although the far horizon is increasingly synonymous with death as the novel draws to its conclusion, the direction and reinvigoration that Poppy and the Church provide make Dominic excited for his mortal end, rather than fearful.

Furthermore, Dominic's mounting corporal fragility, along with the emotional disorientation and sense of loss and misdirection that previously plagued him have entirely ceased to register as concerns. His mind is "at rest," and he is redirected and secure, focused solely "on matters of vital, because of eternal, importance": "The ship of his individual fate no longer drifted rudderless or risked danger of stranding, but steered steadily, fearlessly, towards the promise of a secure and lovely harbourage" (330). Dominic is able to use his new eternal orientation and spiritual objective as an epistemological telos to understand the overall trajectory his life has taken. The redirection and reorientation that Poppy and Catholicism have extended to him have also adjusted his vantage point, providing him with new, divinely oriented bearings.

As Dominic confesses to Poppy, reflecting on her ennobling, edifying love, and the impact that the Church has had upon him,

> The last few months have been the happiest I remember since my childhood. ... And for the rest, dearest friend, as one draws near to the edge of the great shadow, which we call death, one begins to trust more and fuss less; looking to the next step only ....
>
> (381–2)

No longer fearing the darkness around him, Dominic has full access to the orientation that guides him, with clarity, towards the only horizon that matters—eternal life.

Finally, the detail that it is a "secure and lovely harbourage" towards which Dominic sails again elucidates Malet's reworking of the traditional bildungsroman. It reaffirms the link between Dominic's conversion to Catholicism and the profoundly educational and transformative opportunity to redirect the remainder of his life. It allows him to embrace a vastly new identity as he casts off his anxiety-ridden status as a disoriented "*débutant*," who, despite the youth and the novitiate status implied therein, is physically mature and paradoxically feels that "[n]othing is left, ... nothing," perceiving his future to be "as blank as the present" (184). Nevertheless, while his newfound devotion and spiritual development do grant him a new and productive direction on a spiritual level, his late-learned sense of fulfilment, his late-blooming appreciation for beauty and other aesthetic pleasures (which he perceives as manifestations of the divine), his recognition of the vanity of earthly life, and his veneration of the far horizon and what death can bring all come too late to be useful to Dominic in the mortal world. Thus, they are yet another example of how Malet upends the traditional bildungsroman genre for the skills that Dominic acquires and the values that he comes to appreciate cannot even be fully applied during his life. Fragile and ephemeral, they emphasise how insignificant and vain mortal life is.

This reversal of direction and the ideological prioritisation of Catholicism is perhaps the most significant element of Malet's strategic recodification of the bildungsroman. Rather than structuring her novel such that it inaugurates her protagonist's entry into urban life or high society, Malet's adaptation of the genre illuminates Dominic's *failures* at entering into this world and the epistemological disorientation and distance from others that he experiences. By focusing on discomfiture and malaise and marking Dominic's early attempts to function well in modern life with failure, Malet is able to give greater attention to the vital impact that "the recognition not merely of religion, but of Christianity, as a supreme factor in earthly existence" has for Dominic (224).

Indeed, dramatising the sense of delay, confusion, and purposelessness that have always conditioned Dominic's life, it is well past both the midway point of the novel and the midway point of his life, when he identifies the spiritual despair that sparks his new religiosity as the transformative catalyst that gives purpose to what remains to him of life. "[N]o fugitive experience," it signals

> the starting-point of a journey the prosecution of which promised not only to be the main occupation of his remaining years here in time, but, the river of death once crossed, to stretch onward and onward through realms, at present inconceivable, of beauty, of knowledge, and of love.
>
> (224)

Drawing upon the language of development and orientation, Dominic declares "I fulfilled the main object I had in view" (164), acknowledging his vital though late-learned religiosity, his dedication to eternal life, and his subsequent felicitous withdrawal from the vanities of earthly life.

Notes

1 There is some contention about the date of Malet's conversion. Most situate it in 1902, but Lundberg traces it to a 1906 letter from the Jesuit Thomas Rigby to Malet's cousin, Lilian Mary Vallings, which suggests that "instruction" for the conversion process was still ongoing for both women (2003, 292).

2 For recent critical reassessments of this text see Delyfer (2016) and Ford (2015).

3 The waning appeal of Malet and her works was exacerbated further by the rather shocking inefficacy of her literary agent, A.P. Watt, who "simply failed to understand the kind of fiction that she was writing and the market for which it would be suitable" (Gillies 2007, 83). Despite her best efforts, therefore, and categorised as being much more aligned with a Victorian *weltanschauung* during a time in which modernism was increasingly gaining terrain, Malet started being associated, to her detriment, with a bygone period identified as "genteel and stifling," "unfashionably traditional" (Schaffer 2001), and "obsolete and outmoded" (Delyfer 2011, 114–15).

4 Srebrnik understands this as an act of rebellion against Muscular Christianity in particular since "her conversion came as no surprise to her friends, for 'Lucas' ... had long been a rebel against 'Muscular Christianity'" (1995b, 194).

5 Ehnenn borrows the term "enforcing normalcy" from Lennard Davis (1995) and draws from Sara Ahmed's helpful discussion of phenomenological orientation in her theoretical application of the term (2019, 150).

6 For more on Dominic's quasi-monastic discipline and asceticism, see Delyfer (2016). Regenia Gagnier's *The Insatiability of Human Wants* shows how extreme ascesis can develop from and alongside consumer culture; additionally, Gagnier's argument helps to understand Dominic's epicene nature and (un)productive body (2000, 90–114, 115–46).

7 In her short novel *The Wreck of The Golden Galleon* (1910), Malet also depends heavily on the trope of the ship, which directly recalls *The Far Horizon*'s recurrence to nautical imagery and language, and the alignment of the ship with the ebb and flow of Dominic's emotions. In *The Wreck of The Golden Galleon*, the ship is even more central, particularly in regards to the education in social and political hardship that the suffering protagonist receives. Rather than emphasising the charting of a trajectory, *The Golden Galleon*'s frequently personified ship is both fundamental to the plot as a tangible object—it is an "old-world toy" the main character adores—and an exteriorised reflection of the protagonist's emotions.

Works Cited

Ahmed, Sara. 2006. *Queer Phenomenology: Orientations, Objects, Others.* Durham: Duke University Press.

Davis, Lennard. 1995. *Enforcing Normalcy: Disability, Deafness and the Body.* New York: Verso.

Delyfer, Catherine. 2010. "Lucas Malet's Subversive Late-Gothic: Humanizing the Monster in The History of Sir Richard Calmady." In *Demons of the Body and Mind: Essays on Disability in Gothic Culture*, edited by Ruth Anolik, 80–96. Jefferson: McFarland.

———. 2011. *Art and Womanhood in Fin-de-Siècle Writing: The Fiction of Lucas Malet, 1880–1931.* London and New York. Routledge.

———. 2016. "The Aesthete, the Banker, and the Saint: Economies of Gift and Desire in Lucas Malet's *The Far Horizon* (1906)." In *Economies of Desire at the Fin-de-Siècle: Libidinal Lives*, edited by Jane Ford, Patricia Pulham, and Kim Edwards Keates, 122–42. New York: Routledge.

Demoor, Marysa. 2004. "Introduction." In *Marketing the Author: Authorial Personae, Narrative Selves and Self-Fashioning, 1880–1930*, 1–18. London: Palgrave Macmillan.

Ford, Jane. 2015. "Socialism, Capitalism and the Fiction of Lucas Malet: 'The Spirit of the Hive.'" *English Literature in Transition, 1880–1920* 58(4): 551–71.

Fraiman, Susan. 1993. *Unbecoming Women: British Women Writers and the Novel of Development.* New York: Columbia University Press.

Gagnier, Regenia. 2000. *The Insatiability of Human Wants: Economics and Aesthetics in Market Society.* Chicago: The University of Chicago Press.

Gillies, Mary Anne. 2007. *The Professional Literary Agent in Britain 1880–1920.* Toronto, Buffalo, and London: University of Toronto Press.

"Glimpses of New Books: Lucas Malet's Latest Story '*The Far Horizon*.'" 1907. *Town and Country*, 12 January, 47–48.

Lundberg, Patricia. 2003. *"An Inward Necessity": The Writer's Life of Lucas Malet*. New York: Peter Lang.

Malet, Lucas. 1906. *The Far Horizon*. New York. Dodd, Mead & Company.

———. 1910. *The Golden Galleon*. New York. George H. Doran Company.

Srebrnik, Patricia Thomas. 1995a. "Lucas Malet (Mary St. Leger Kingsley Harrison) (4 June 1852–27 October 1931)." *Late-Victorian and Edwardian British Novelists*, 177–85.

———. 1995b. "The re-subjection of 'Lucas Malet': Charles Kingsley's Daughter and the Response to Muscular Christianity." In *Muscular Christianity: Embodying the Victorian Age*, edited by Donald E. Hall, 194–214. Cambridge: Cambridge University Press.

Part 2

Dissident Women

4 Mad Dogs and English (New) Women

Grotesque Gender in *The Carissima*

Alexandra Gray

Lucas Malet's 1896 novel *The Carissima* announces its concerns with late nineteenth-century modernity—specifically, those surrounding the modern woman—in conspicuous fashion, both by reference to Alphonse Daudet's 1882 play *La Menteuse* (*The Liar*) and by the novel's subheading *A Modern Grotesque*. Daudet's three-act play, written with Léon Hennique, is a scathing portrayal of courtesans who are blamed for disrupting the stability of the home; the titular liar is an artist's mistress who is dishonest about the gifts she receives from other men. Malet's text opens with a quotation from *La Menteuse*, seemingly signalling the exploration of female grotesquery which is to come. According to Mikhail Bakhtin's definition of the grotesque, the body in exaggerated and degraded form both undermines and reinforces hierarchies of power. Bakhtin's grotesque is potentially subversive, having "not only a destructive, negative aspect, but also a regenerating one" (1984, 21); thus, he argues, scatological or degraded forms serve as potentially liberatory schema. Indeed, the grotesque features prominently in Malet's fiction, and was largely made permissible by aesthetic devices which allowed her to express *and* conceal such matters.[1]

Malet's use of the 'aesthetic' grotesque to subvert conventions is well documented, particularly her dramatisation of the morally regenerative potential of coming to terms with deformity in both *Little Peter: A Christmas Morality for Children of any Age* (1887) and *The History of Sir Richard Calmady* (1901).[2] If, as Kathleen A. Miller argues, Malet's *Calmady* values abnormality "as though it was a rare and artistic work of grotesquerie, but not a sign of degeneration" (2012, 194), then *The Carissima* operates in reverse fashion in its depiction of mental illness. Published five years prior to *Calmady*, *The Carrissima* was accused of being "rather merciless, gruesome, and pro-formdly [*sic*] pessimistic" and its primary narrator as "typical of the hardness and cruelty of the whole book" ("Recent Novels" 1896, 22). The text is certainly less straightforward in its deployment of the grotesque, complicating existing readings of Malet's work by disability studies scholars and literary critics alike. Of particular interest, for example, is the novel's recourse to both the Jamesian and Lewisite (masculine) gothic traditions to foreground the epistemological concerns haunting Victorian society at the end of the nineteenth century.[3] However, unlike Malet's ghostly heroine in *The Gateless Barrier* (1900)—whose disembodiment at the hands of deviant patriarchal forces exposes and denounces male tyranny—the supernatural serves an entirely different purpose in *The Carissima*, one which obfuscates the notion of Malet as a New Woman writer. Extending critical assessments by Talia Schaffer (2000, 202–4) and Catherine Delyfer (2011, 81–83), this essay explores the conceptual relations between grotesquery, femininity, mental illness, and modernity invited by the novel's unusual heroine. It situates this nexus of anxieties within the context of misunderstandings about Malet's 'feminism' on the one hand, and her problematic critique of the New Woman, on the other. An examination of these interrelated concerns supplements and reconsiders existing scholarly contributions on the subject of Malet's New Woman status, and it considers, for the first time, the resonances between *The Carissima* and Arthur Conan Doyle's *The Hound of the Baskervilles* (1902).

Malet's plot revolves around Englishman Constantine Leversedge, a man who, having made his fortune on the outskirts of the empire, arrives in Geneva to marry Charlotte Perry, his long-standing fiancée. Prior to his arrival, Leversedge has witnessed a grotesque spectacle of death on the South African Veldt—the murdered bodies of a camp, survived only by a dog last seen consuming the remains of a child. Owing to this traumatic experience, Leversedge suffers hallucinatory delusions during which he is haunted by a phantom dog: bloody, vicious, and with phosphorus yellow eyes. After learning of Leversedge's condition, Charlotte seeks to rid herself of her fiancé, first by attempting to seduce his friend and the (second-framed) narrator of the novel, Antony Hammond.[4] When she is rejected by Hammond, Charlotte plots to estrange herself from Leversedge following their wedding, after which she has become the sole legal beneficiary of his substantial fortune. With the help of the unscrupulous society journalist Percy Gerrard, Charlotte exploits her new husband's mental anxiety by invoking the phantom dog and by claiming that she shares the delusion, culminating in Leversedge's suicide by drowning. Narrating the events of Malet's novel is fellow hotel guest Hammond, a famous poet and aesthete, and the antagonist from Malet's 1888 novel *A Counsel of Perfection*.

Malet drew on and contributed to a *fin-de-siècle* literary tradition which featured demonic animals of various types. For example, in Bram Stoker's *Dracula* (1897) Count Dracula arrives in Whitby in the form of an enormous dog, and Arthur Conan Doyle had experimented with demonic animals in "The King of the Foxes" (1898) and "The Brazillian Cat" (1898) both of which had appeared after Malet's own offering. The phantom dog motif would be deployed to dramatic effect, and with more commercial and critical success, a few years after the publication of *The Carissima*, by Arthur Conan Doyle in *The Hound of the Baskervilles*.[5] Serialised in *The Strand Magazine* from 1901, the text featured many of the same narrative devices deployed in *The Carissima*—South African wealth, a 'supernatural' dog, a plot to steal an inheritance, and an insincere marital engagement—yet Conan Doyle's mystery was precipitated by male treachery, and solved by the deductive reasoning of one male character, and the scientific rigour of another.[6] Conversely, Malet's earlier tale of a similarly phosphoric demon dog, addresses the horrors of female duplicity and fails to solve them, resisting a conclusion that reinforces a masculine world order of the kind implicit in the safeguarding of Henry Baskerville's life and fortune. Indeed, in many ways *The Carissima* resists a straightforward reading of Charlotte Perry's horrifying subversion of gender expectations, a theme only vaguely suggested by Conan Doyle through Mrs Stapleton's forced complicity. Stapleton, who is, in fact, an imposter and next-in-line to the Baskerville fortune, forces his wife to pretend to be his sister, so that he can propose to another woman as part of his plan. Mrs Stapleton is excused because she is so poorly treated by her husband and because she tries to warn Baskerville of the threat. Charlotte Perry is, however, fully culpable for her actions and the originator of the plot to drive her fiancé to insanity in *The Carissima*.

It is perhaps partly for this reason that while Conan Doyle's 1902 novel edition of *The Hound of the Baskervilles* was applauded for its use of the hellhound as a narrative device, Malet's recourse to the same trope was less warmly received. Malet's phantom dog was accused of being "far from novel" and failing "to cause a shudder" in *The Times* (16 February 1897), and, like the other characters, the dog was both "tiresome" and "done to death," according to *The Standard* (8 January 1897). One of the few resoundingly positive appraisals of Malet's much-anticipated novel, by a reviewer as yet unaware of the author's gender, appeared in the *Pall Mall Gazette*. He writes that the dog "is good—it is ghastly—it is convincing" and that "Lucas Malet seems to have found *his* own manner" [emphasis added]. Tellingly, Malet was accused by a reviewer for *The Times* (16 February 1897) of appropriating her demon dog from one of her male contemporaries: Sheriden Le Fanu, whose short story "Green Tea" (1872) had featured a demonic monkey. Such accusations were never levelled at Conan Doyle despite his own use of a range of plot features found in Malet's 1896 dramatisation of a spectral canine not unlike the Baskerville hound. As Talia Schaffer argues in her contribution to this collection, the double standard that saw Malet's novels judged as poor examples of domestic realism yet praised her male contemporaries for their avant-gardism in treating the same subject matter, would be a major contributing factor in Malet's disappearance from the literary canon (179). Just as Malet's fictionalisation of the hellhound escaped the critical acclaim accorded to Conan Doyle, contemporary readings of Charlotte Perry also missed the mark because

Victorian critics underestimated a woman writer's ability to subvert the conventions of the nineteenth-century literary marketplace.

The grotesquerie of Malet's provocative subtitle ostensibly references Leversedge's phantom dog. However, it is the excessive, and by implication grotesque, cruelty of the female protagonist which underpins the novel's concerns with the *fin-de-siècle* body in (Bakhtin-esque) exaggerated or degraded form. In Charlotte Perry Malet explores the *fin-de-siècle* woman and the type of masculinity necessary to respond effectively to the dangers she personifies. Charlotte, in part, dramatises the reportedly "rapacious and unsexing appetites" (Heilmann 2004, 34) of the New Woman, yet also provides an antidote to the politically aware, morally resolute and self-sacrificing heroines of the New Woman novels with which *The Carissima* was competing in 1896.[7] Read in relation to Julia Kristeva's "Powers of Horror," the threat of the phantom dog, which, as I will argue, is incarnated in Malet's anti-heroine,

> emanate[s] from an exorbitant outside or inside, ejected beyond the scope of the possible, the tolerable, the thinkable. It lies there, quite close but it cannot be assimilated. It beseeches, worries, and fascinates desire, which nevertheless, does not let itself be seduced … Unflaggingly, like an inescapable boomerang, a vortex of summons and repulsion places the one haunted by it literally beside himself … It lies outside, beyond the set, and does not seem to agree to the latter's rules of the game. And yet, from its place of banishment, the abject does not cease challenging its master.
>
> (Kristeva 1982, 1–2)

Kristeva's linguistic choices resonate with the canine motif; the abject lies, beseeches, worries, unflaggingly haunts, is banished, and challenges its master. Conjuring beast-like imagery of a creature both servile and threatening, the abject is uncanny: known and unknown, seen and unseen, domestic and wild, evoking desire and disgust. Malet's phantom dog operates as a decentralising symbol of abjection, of the repressed desires and fears occasioned by a dissolution of gender boundaries, dramatised through the degraded colonial masculinity of one protagonist, and the subversive feminine stratagems of the other. Additionally, it allegorises the perceived problem of women's role in the changing *fin-de-siècle* publishing landscape—women writers were increasingly hard to ignore but not usually credited with the sort of genius exemplified by their male counterparts.

§

Charlotte Perry is complicatedly 'modern'; attractive to men because of the aesthetic veneer of innocence and simplicity she performs, she embodies both Victorian ideals *and* the threat of their dissolution. While not a typical New Woman figure (she does not aspire to education, work, or literary output) Charlotte is highly intelligent, artistically gifted, aesthetically minded, independent, and ambitious.[8] She represents many of the criticisms levelled at the New Woman, specifically her 'unfeminine' desire for financial gain and her unwillingness to accept marriage as a duty. Aestheticism offered women writers opportunities to address social issues in much the same way that New Woman novels did, and while not all female aesthete characters were New Women, there was often some overlap (Schaffer 2000, 10–15). Women who failed to exhibit the qualities associated with ideal femininity—passivity, disinterestedness, obedience, and maternal feeling—were accused of espousing modern views and were often rhetorically aligned with the New Woman. This was largely because the term 'New Woman' was an unstable referent emblematising any female threat to patriarchy, regardless from whom it originated, discursively eliding the aims of women with widely different political and social agendas.[9]

Charlotte is the product of her era, a woman without the attributes of the previous generation so clearly evidenced by her guileless and uncultured mother. Mrs Perry is "kindly" (6), with a "home-loving nature" (122); a "perfectly simple and a genuine being" (157) with an "insular voice," a "somewhat uncontrolled figure" (158), and solid adherence to her "domestic duties" (123). Meanwhile, Charlotte is "positively seductive" yet "a little displeasing," (75) "a past-master in the art of strategy," (78) "a person who listens and thinks acutely," (84) and a "*fin-de-siècle* Bacchante" (109).[10] She fears "contracting a marriage in which [love] must of necessity be absent" (82) and causes Hammond to "bow low before the genius of Charlotte Perry" because he has "not the wit to fathom" her (153). Like Henrietta Pereira, the *femme fatale* of Malet's 1916 novel *Damaris*—about whom Malet admitted "she has no soul" (qtd. in Lundberg 2003, 364)—Charlotte's femininity is both grotesque by virtue of the hyperbolic deviance and exaggerated purity she evinces, and abject as "beyond the scope of the possible, the tolerable, the thinkable" in the society in which she operates (Kristeva 1982, 2). Her duality is so pronounced, yet so oblique, that it can be neither understood (or "assimilated" to use Kristeva's term) nor combatted in a text which features only incomplete and unconvincing performances of masculinity.

Although depicted by Hammond as intelligent and difficult to read, clues as to Charlotte's mercenary and cruel nature, which remains partially obscured until the dramatic dénouement, are scattered throughout. She is "artificial and theatrical" (76), her simplicity a mere "virginal effect" (139), leading Hammond to question whether her tears are "merely a pose more elaborate, more realistically developed, than all former poses" (185). Adding to such suspicions are Charlotte's musical abilities, which leave a sinister impression. For instance, Hammond explains:

> What she played during the ensuing ten to fifteen minutes I do not know. I never heard it before; I am more than willing never to hear it again. I suppose it must have been a tarantella, but a tarantella conceived in a madhouse. It gave me a nightmarish impression of innumerable tormented shrieking, human figures whirling in a desperate and formless dance ... It was exciting, for it took one into the region of utter lawlessness; and that region is always exciting, however undesirable. This was decidedly exciting, but it was not quite nice. Miss Perry lent herself whole-heartedly to the spirit of the music. I trust I am far from being a prude, but there are limits, and she passed them. Her playing was not quite nice.
>
> (122)

Malet's use of the tarantella image draws on a history of work featuring the New Woman. In Henrick Ibsen's *A Doll's House* (1879) Nora dances the tarantella with wild abandon; in Mathilde Blind's prose poem *Tarantella* (1885), New Woman ideas and themes frequently appear; in George Egerton's "A Cross Line" from *Keynotes* (1893), Gypsy dreams of dancing to "wild music" with "swaying human souls" (2006, 9), and, as Ann Heilmann has explored, the tarantella emerges as a potent metaphor in the work of Sarah Grand (Heilmann 2004, 42–43). The image of bodies, not only wild with the exotic, syncopated frenzy of the dance, but also with madness, signals Malet's exploration of gender ambiguities and the fears occasioned by transgressive liminality. Such liminality is realised in the opposition of lawlessness and excitement, arousal and undesirability, exhilaration and desperation elicited by the performance. The eroticism of the piece is underscored both by the reference to conception and by the sexually vague impression of genderless "human figures" who are both "tormented" and dancing without form, their bodies suggestive of an orgy. While Percy Gerrard is mesmerised and aroused by the music, Hammond—in his use of the term "prude," notes the crossing of both social and sexual boundaries yet continues to evince a detached yet voyeuristic hauteur. Charlotte's sexuality, the transgressive desires which denote her unsuitability as a wife, contribute to her characterisation as both modern and grotesque in the eyes of the text's narrator-voyeur but also pique his observational interest and, implicitly, his desire.

Responsible for originating the term 'New Woman,' the social purity novelist Sarah Grand had codified what late nineteenth-century woman writers had been dramatising for some time in her famous article "The New Aspect of the Woman Question" (1894). Written two years before *The Carissima*, it advocated equal educational and marital rights for women, and characterised those who refused to conform to the roles prescribed by Victorian society as both 'new' and 'modern.' In addition to the demand for legal, social, and economic rights for women, Grand petitioned for a new type of masculinity, for a more fitting partner for the New Woman—a morally superior and sexually pure New Man who would help her face the changes in society brought about by her emancipation. Grand argued that the trouble "is not that women are too mannish, but because men grow ever more effeminate" lamenting that "manliness is at a premium now because there is so little of it" (275). Grand envisioned that "the man of the future will be better" since "we know his weakness and will be patient with him" (272–3), listing consistency, responsibility, respect, practical good sense, good manners, manliness, nobility, and a lack of conceit as requisite virtues.

For Grand, who was ideologically invested in colonialism, manliness was synonymous with physical strength, sexual potency, and self-reliance, attributes associated with the empire-building in which Malet's Leversedge has spent his life.[11] It is tempting to read Malet's characterisation of assertive, transgressive female figures and her scathing critique of Victorian social norms, including marriage, as typical of the New Woman agenda. However, Malet made clear in both "The Progress of Woman: In Literature" and "The Threatened Re-Subjection of Woman" that her sexual politics were far more complex than those of her (comparatively) pro-suffrage contemporaries. More ambivalent than Grand's, Malet's position on imperial forms of masculinity both reflects Victorian cultural anxieties and complicates *fin-de-siècle* stereotypes. Malet positions Charlotte's betrayal as a potential consequence of oversimplifying, and thus misreading, women's bodies and desires, and suggests that this is the real threat posed to forms of masculinity lauded by social purists like Grand. Tellingly, the archetypes of manhood so revered by social purists were those also most wholeheartedly endorsed by Malet's father Charles Kingsley, in his commitment to muscular Christianity as a solution to economic and social evils. Despite this, Malet's novel reveals the New Woman and the New Man to be unrealistic, volatile, and problematic constructions, warning about the instability of traditional and modern gender roles and questioning their usefulness. This essay will now demonstrate how, through privileged metaphors of the erotic and the bestial, Malet addresses late nineteenth-century concerns about gender norms, at times both lauding and condemning new forms of masculinity equally, if not more, than the modern femininity implicated as grotesque in the title of her novel.

§

None of Malet's male characters manage to perform normative masculinity effectively in *The Carissima*, nor are they capable of responding to Charlotte's subversion of traditional womanhood. Charlotte's father admires his daughter unfailingly and is "a voracious, adhesive little rat of a man" who "smiled upon [Hammond] ravenously" (20). Mr Perry cannot perceive his daughter's complex nature, and as such is manipulated by Charlotte like the other men in the novel. His vertiginous ambition, his voracity, as well as his "adhesive" and rat-like qualities, evoke his parasitic nature and signal mercenary motives for ensuring that Charlotte marries well. Meanwhile, Leversedge is "charming," "delightfully clean" with his beard "neatly trimmed" (4), and is a "quiet, steady, sensible fellow" (13). Hammond greatly respects his friend and presents him as a heroic and gentlemanly New-Man-ish figure. Despite this, he also emphasises Leversedge's frontierism and frames him as an animal. Leversedge, we are told, is "very long and lean and brown" and "furnished with a vocabulary floridly rich in abusive epithets applicable to South African society" (4). The source of his huge wealth is troublingly vague, leaving Hammond unable to explain "whether it consisted in exploiting the aborigines, digging for diamonds, pulling the tail feathers out of live ostriches, or undertaking dental operations on dead elephants" (4).

Not only is Leversedge an example of colonial prosperity—his lean, tanned body and colloquialisms indicative of the lifestyle required by his pursuits—but, speculations about his exploits indicate both rugged manliness and a lack of refinement. The activities specified are negatively encoded adaptations of working-class professions—usury, mining, butchery, and dentistry—indicative of both the vulgar physicality and accelerated social mobility implicit in forms of English colonial prosperity. So too is Hammond's later discussion of Leversedge's body which:

> Always seemed to imply the near neighbourhood of a horse ... Leversedge had just that hint of a stoop about the shoulders, indolent fashion of moving, and slightly distracted look across the eyes and brow which riding-men so frequently have. He had more legs, too, than are absolutely requisite in civilised society ... Pardon these details. Since it is necessary to the application of what follows that you should see the creature 'in his habit as he lived.'
>
> (4)

In his reference to Leversedge's horse-like frame, sluggish posture, and distracted look, Hammond sympathetically reads the effects of both physical work and emotional trauma on his friend's tired body. However, Hammond's characterisation of Leversedge as a creature infers an animalism in Malet's doomed hero which unsettles the narrator's subjectivity. Furthermore, the addition of an excess of legs, an oblique reference to Leversedge's genitalia, connotes the sexual potency of this particularly virile form of masculinity, an image further compounded by the choice of a horse with which to compare him. Malet's references to Leversedge's horse-like tendencies likely gesture towards Jonathan Swift's *Gulliver's Travels* (1726), in which the Houyhnhnms (the horse race) are more learned, philosophical, and civilised than the Yahoos, the humanoid race—although they have what could retrospectively be described as eugenicist tendencies and imperial ambition. After spending time in the country of the Houyhnhnms, Gulliver adopts a neighing kind of intonation and returns home only to find he prefers the company of his horses to human beings. Malet likely intended Leversedge as a Gulliverian figure, a man operating outside his native habitat in an uncertain world, having abandoned his faith in (wo)mankind by the end of his 'travels.'

According to Hammond, "a being half equine ... produces in me an annoying sense of the limitations of my opportunities" (4). While not as educated or refined as Hammond, Leversedge's sheer physicality, his embodiment of the ideals of muscular Christianity and masculine vitality so necessary to the Empire, threaten Hammond's claim to the social superiority conferred on those of his own leisurely profession and upper-class status. Leversedge embodies a catalogue of *fin-de-siècle* anxieties prompted by Darwinian theories, which envisioned man as the evolutionary end product of an animal progenitor. Referring to Darwin's *The Descent of Man* (1871), Cyndy Hendershot proposes that evolutionary theories threatened Victorian masculinity, forcing men to renegotiate their gender "within the context of Darwinian science" which "pointed to questions of gender and science that troubled stable identity" (98).[12] Evolutionary discourses inevitably gave rise to concerns about degeneration as men, purportedly and largely anecdotally, become increasingly feminised, while women gained unprecedented access to hitherto male-dominated spaces. Leversedge's manliness is brought to crisis by the intervention of the dog, a symptom of and synecdoche for, twin threats to the very foundations of English imperialism: the colonial other and the feminised abject.

Leversedge is not the only character whose masculinity is questioned and explored. Exemplary of effeminacy and degeneracy (in a far more pronounced fashion than Hammond) is Percy Gerrard, Charlotte's secret beau and her partner in the plot to unhinge her fiancé. Gerrard is unpopular with both Hammond and Leversedge for reasons neither can quite articulate but which both men connect to his profession as a journalist and decadent literati. He is thought to be conversationally brilliant, engaged in "wordy battle" (28) with Charlotte, with whom he pontificates on literary, religious, and artistic subjects. However, he is, as Hammond explains, "a scavenger of genius" (35), suggesting merely talentless exploitation of others. Much like the characterisation of both the eponymous subject of Malet's unpublished story "In Memoriam, Ernest D. Chesterfield," and Heber Pogson in her short story "The Birth of a Masterpiece" (1922), Hammond's description of Gerrard amounts to a critique of the decadent authors of Malet's period. This is most evident in an exchange during which Hammond explains that:

> In his youth [Gerrard] produced a very witty and improper novel, which everybody said was impossible to read, and everybody promptly read. It affected to be autobiographical. Now he has ceased to be immoral—at all events in print—having laid the golden maxim that public confession of the sins of others is, on the whole, an even more paying speculation than public confession of sins of your own. I am afraid he has ceased to be witty. That is a matter of regret.
>
> Leversedge looked hard at me.
>
> "Sounds a bit of a skunk, I think" he said.
>
> (35)

Much critical attention has been paid to the resonances between the work of Henry James and that of Lucas Malet: in particular the possibility that James 'borrowed' (largely unacknowledged) from Malet's novels (Schaffer 179–180). While James's late work betrays signs of the decadent strain deplored by Hammond, parallels between Gerrard and decadent authors such as Oscar Wilde and Joris-Karl Huysmans are equally possible. Aside from the similarities between Gerrard's witty, improper and "autobiographical" novel and those of these particular *fin-de-siècle* authors, Hammond alerts the reader to the decadence of both Gerrard's authorship and lifestyle. Gerrard's novel is "impossible to read" evoking the florid and impenetrable style affected by decadent novelists, and, likewise, scandalous enough to draw a wide, if condemnatory, readership.[13] The implication of Gerrard's immorality is resurrected effectively in Hammond's clear disgust at the crude dishonesty implied by his exposure of secrets for financial gain. However, like Leversedge, Percy Gerrard is described as animal—not the dynamic, equine, colonial animalism embodied by Malet's doomed hero, but a more unpleasant, if not necessarily less inhuman, variety. Hammond recounts:

> Just then I heard a distinct grunt. Various animals grunt; my knowledge of natural history, though by no means profound, carries me as far as that. But only one human being of my acquaintance produces—whether voluntarily or involuntarily I know not—that unengaging sound. A rather squat black person passed slowly down the farther side of the marble steps. "Percy Gerrard!" I exclaimed …
>
> (72)
>
> He was not a large man yet he had the iniquitous habit of slightly overflowing every chair in which he sat. To-night he overflowed more than usual, changing his position frequently, shading his eyes

> with the music score, glancing about him restlessly, grunting ... he rose with sloth-like slowness to his small square feet.
>
> (98–99)

While Gerrard is, like Leversedge, a creature, he is described in markedly more bestial terms which emphasise the abjection inherent in his degenerate masculinity. Like a pig, Gerrard is squat, black and grunting; like a sloth he is listless and idle; like an ill-bred pet, he fidgets and is uncomfortable to watch. These analogies reflect Hammond's claim that Gerrard is a scavenger, and Leversedge's assertions that he is "more or less of a skunk" whom "nature specially constructed ... with a view to a kicking" (96). Gerrard is a pest, and, failing to evince manliness instead conveys a sense of animal restlessness, of persistent movement and iniquitous corporeality. Gerrard's unacceptably corrupt masculinity is located in his unfit body, his fixation on worldly desires, and his complicity in the plot to disrupt Leversedge's masculinity for financial and sexual gain.

Hammond is also depicted as an aesthete, but his sexual desires are secondary to both his aestheticism and to the homosocial bonds which power his relationship with Leversedge. While the things he admires in Charlotte are aesthetic—her beauty, artificiality, and theatricality draw his attention and amuse him—these highly prized 'symptoms' of aestheticism both imply Charlotte's grotesquerie and undermine the sagacity of the aesthete figure. Despite being momentarily tempted by Charlotte, Hammond resists her charms, preferring to value her as an intriguing visual and psychological study, a technique deployed in Malet's earlier treatment of Antony Hammond in *A Counsel of Perfection*. Malet draws a distinction between the type of impotent, aesthetic masculinity affected by Hammond, and the baser and more degenerative drives of Percy Gerrard, whose inability to sublimate his desire for Charlotte drives him to commit social and moral crimes. More so even than in Leversedge's case, a *fin-de-siècle* crisis of masculinity is schematised through metaphors of animalism which reflect and reinforce the central (though arguably ironic) allegory of grotesque femininity at play in the novel. However, while Charlotte, Leversedge, and Gerrard are all subject to diegetic disapproval, Hammond does not remain unscathed.

Malet's male narrator is a Jamesian voyeur, piqued and entertained by the unfolding tragedy, scopically consuming the actors in the "Perry-Leversedge drama" (8) as *objets d'art*. James had frequently deployed the decadent *flaneur* figure as a character and/or narrator in his works, to which psychological studies of women were central. Such studies also supplied inspiration for New Woman writers such as Vernon Lee in both "Lady Tal" (1892) and *Miss Brown* (1884) and Constance Fenimore Woolson in "Miss Greif" (1880), who satirised James's scopic and literary appropriation of feminine genius. Malet's use of a flawed and unreliable narrator too concerned with the study of 'woman' draws on a distinctly proto-feminist tradition and possibly references James in the same way. Deploying the technique of frame narration, a "feminized strategy that undermines the tendency to believe the stereotypical 'observant' male narrator" (Lundberg 1998, 392), Malet questions the reliability and disinterestedness of Hammond's account. His representation as a largely unhelpful onlooker attests to Malet's ambivalence surrounding aestheticism, a narrative device she effectuates throughout, but an ideology she has cause to critique.[14] Neither Leversedge's muscular goodness, Gerrard's despicable plotting, nor Hammond's aesthetic detachment can answer to Charlotte's defiance of gender norms, revealing the futility of both traditional and idealised 'new' forms of masculinity. Malet suggests that by relying upon recognisable gendered archetypes, however new or transgressive, masculinity runs a dangerous gauntlet in which madness, degeneration, suicide, and sexual apathy are the inevitable consequences of a feminine threat.

§

Despite Leversedge's clear physical strength, the weight of his colonial exploits has taken its toll; his mind has become unhinged by his encounter with the horrors lurking at the fringes of the Victorian imperial project. Leversedge calls his traumatic experience "the Thing-too-Much," drawing on a well-known Victorian social and medical discourse of hysteria formulated through Freudian symptoms such as hallucination, repression, and intrusive memories.[15] Of his encounters with the phantom dog he tells Hammond:

> I am ashamed, downright ashamed of myself. I can't hold my tongue—I want to talk about it. I want to tell somebody. I am as full of my own symptoms and sensations as some hysterical girl. I can't keep them to myself. Oh! It's humiliating; I tell you it's degrading to one's manhood.
>
> (48)

Leversedge adheres to the rules governing homosocial relations by downplaying and subordinating his emotional responses and maintaining a stoic silence; he also describes the emasculating effect of his desire to narrate his own trauma. Freud and Breuer's *Studies in Hysteria* had been published a year prior to *The Carissima* and its case studies—in which talking functioned as a therapeutic response to trauma—would have been well known to those of Malet's educated milieu.[16] Leversedge directly associates his compulsion to recount his trauma with the femininity implied by psychoanalysis and with a specifically female malady.

The degradation of manhood of which Leversedge complains is further compounded by Hammond's depiction of his escalating madness. Upon first witnessing Leversedge mid-hallucination, Hammond observes that "his mouth was slightly open, while his lips curled back queerly from his teeth. It may sound ridiculous, but I could almost swear his hair bristled" (13). Redoubling his reading of Leversedge's equine features and excess of legs, Hammond's observation situates his friend's escalating anxieties as bestial—reflective of savagery, and thus associated with the uncivilised world from which he has recently arrived. The image of bared teeth and bristling fur blurs the ontological boundary between Leversedge and the demon dog since the dog "places the one haunted by it literally beside himself" (Kristeva 1982, 2) and calls into question any sense of a unified, cohesive identity or subjectivity.

Leversedge is haunted by both his desire for the increasingly aloof and unattainable Charlotte, and by the disgusting dog whose presence symbolises both his own fantasies and the (bodily) horrors of imperialism. The dog appears at the intervals during which Leversedge transacts his relationship with Charlotte, so that the "vortex of summons and repulsion" (Kristeva 1982, 2) which characterises their difficult relationship is emblematised by the dog. For example, the first reference to the Thing-too-Much is followed by a swift interruption in dialogue, during which Leversedge's intense discussion of the grotesque is interjected with "Oh! I say ... Here comes Charlotte" (22). The tragicomic effect of this juxtaposition, what Hammond sarcastically underplays as a "contrast" (22), not only establishes Charlotte as the perceived salve to Leversedge's anxieties but simultaneously incriminates her as the trauma, the Thing-too-Much. So too does the suggested equivalence between the dog's consumption of an infant at the South African camp and Charlotte's pointed lack of maternal or caregiving qualities, a parallel that reinforces her characterisation as beyond the scope of the possible, the tolerable, the thinkable.

When Leversedge first confesses to having seen the phantom dog, he is some way into his renewed courtship of Charlotte. He explains how:

> The beast has taken a fancy to my bedroom, unfortunately. Last night, as soon as I put the candles out, I saw the eyes down by the side of the bed and they made a rush. I heaved a book at them which I had been reading. It was *Vanity Fair.* I'm awfully fond of *Vanity Fair.* Poor little Becky, I always wanted to give her five thousand a year to 'be good on'. Oh dear me!—Well, they wriggled down again; the beast was knocked backwards to the floor, you understand. But in a minute it made another rush, and came up across the counterpane, and settled itself against the pillow, those eyes staring bang into mine.
>
> (50–51)

Later, he tells Hammond "I have been spending a happy night with my faithful dog ... Nine hours of uninterrupted enjoyment" (189). Several things are notable about these excerpts: the action takes place in the bedroom—the site of sexual activity promised by Leversedge's impending nuptials and the intimate space in which his body is most vulnerable; the unsettling and uncanny familiarity with which the dog takes its place in bed alongside its victim; the encoded eroticism of "uninterrupted enjoyment"; and, finally, Leversedge's pronounced sympathy for Thackeray's Becky Sharp, a recalcitrant sinner who commits (implied) adultery for financial gain. These clues frame Leversedge's encounter with the dog as one of both desire and disgust, a combination which reflects the duality of Charlotte Perry as both the faithful domestic pet of his desires and the demonic bitch that haunts him. Leversedge struggles to recognise that Charlotte is both the Victorian angel and the demon which threatens his happiness; her true nature as impossible, intolerable, and unthinkable is revealed only by a careful consideration of the phantom dog, an equivalence which Leversedge fails to comprehend but which becomes apparent to the reader as the novel progresses.

The dog appears again while Charlotte is playing her tarantella, at which point the eroticism and depravity lurking behind her carefully constructed mask is momentarily revealed. Leversedge's reaction to the tarantella metaphorises latent yet unconsciously acknowledged fears about his fiancée's monstrosity. Hammond describes how during the performance:

> Suddenly a cry—it was exceedingly dreadful, it turned me cold and sick—broke in through the rhythm of the music, and Leversedge rushed past me across the room. The train of Charlotte Perry's dress lay out pale over the floor; and he kicked it, stamped on it, trampled it under foot. The music stopped with a harsh discord, and, without rising, the girl turned half round on the music tool, stretching out her hands as though to save herself and push him from her.
>
> (112)

Metaphors for marriage and sexuality abound in this extract. The train of Charlotte's pale dress—designed to traverse the aisle during the wedding ceremony—is stamped upon, connoting an interruption of innocence and a distinctly libidinal metaphor for such loss. In attempting to stop the phantom dog from spoiling the dress of his fiancée, Leversedge succeeds in violently soiling it, in a bodily disruption to the rhythmic movements of the sordid music. Charlotte's response to such advances is to push her betrothed from her, to protect against his madness, specifically, to resist the invasion of her bodily space and his assault on the very fabric which protects her body from his view.

Leversedge's anguished cry, his vocal release of (sexual) torment and audible assault on the overt, public eroticism of the music, accompanies his physical assault on the dress—a paradox in so much as Leversedge's actions protest the unwanted penetrative practices of the dog as he replicates them.

The appearance of the dog coincides with Charlotte's sexually charged playing and the unspoken plot to rob Leversedge of his impending rights to her body, an appearance which is later repeated at the scene of the wedding celebrations. Hammond questions:

> Was not Constantine Leversedge making love, his soul delivered from the grotesque and ghastly dream of the diabolic dog? And was not Charlotte, née Perry, listening, her soul delivered from dreams hardly less grotesque and ghastly—from false standards of taste, of fashion, from false refinements, false intellectualities, from a silly pursuit of decadent eccentricities? Was she not beginning to comprehend what an exquisite, yet very simple solution—notwithstanding the prurient purities of contemporary feminine novelists and reformers—true-love offers to the much-vexed question of the sexes?
>
> (230)

Here Charlotte and the dog are merged through ironic metaphorical slippage. Hammond's rhetorical questioning gestures to the ambiguity of Charlotte's intentions whilst alerting the reader to the ways in which she parallels the "ghastly dream" and the "diabolic dog." Indeed, the falseness of Charlotte's taste, fashion, refinement, intellect, and her decadent eccentricities have been implied throughout, allowing Hammond's rhetoric to undercut any ambiguity about Charlotte's sins. Once again, the swift movement between discussion of the dog and the bride, and the use of the interrogative to undermine certainty establishes a strong thematic relationship between transgressive 'modern' femininity and the grotesque.

Eventually, Hammond's questions are answered. Charlotte and Gerrard participate in an elaborate ruse, bringing a dog to the wedding reception to disturb Leversedge's sanity, and the suggestively sexual language returns when the desired effect is produced:

> The girl did not look at him; she continued in the same rigid attitude, her arms still flung out across the table amid the wreck of the supper; her fingers doubling and undoubling convulsively—the only sign she gave of her agitation. And Leversedge laid his hand on her bare arm just below the elbow. It was rather ghastly to think how her muscles working like that, right under his fingers, must have affected him ....
>
> (272)

At the site of an uneaten feast—an allegorical tableau of sexual restraint and unfulfilled desires—Charlotte is frigid with anxiety, both pleased and worried by Leversedge's unmanning, and the scene of her discovery is likened to sexual aversion. Whilst she clenches her convulsive fingers, she resists physical contact, becoming rigid and flinching at her husband's touch. Meanwhile, Charlotte addresses Hammond in the language of matrimony, reproaching his refusal of her advances earlier in the novel, telling him:

> You were right in your estimate of me. I am cheap, flimsy, insincere—an actress. My learning is mere cram, my talents mere imitation. I am a sham—colourless, characterless, a mere reflection of other people's thoughts, fashions, affectations ... But you were relentless; you forced me back on myself; you dragged aside the veil with which I tried to conceal my nothingness ....
>
> (276)

Reference to the veil is suggestive of both exoticism and Christian marital tradition; the dragging aside of an item of dress designed to connote purity, to conceal the bride's "nothingness," as part of the wedding ceremony conveys Charlotte's duality as both the pure bride and sullied, demonic woman. The violence of the scene she describes, the forcing back and the dragging of the veil, is suggestive of rape, and Charlotte's references to acting, as well as her cheap, flimsy nature draws on a deep cultural connection between the actress and the fallen woman in Victorian art and literature (Davies 1991; Powell 1997; Marshall 1998).[17] Despite this, Malet's text does not depict Charlotte as sexually compromised, and Charlotte's self-criticism reflects what the novel demonstrates overall—that *fin-de-siècle* female subjectivity was far more complicated than the choice between New and Old, modern and traditional, pure and impure.

In Charlotte Perry, Malet constructs a dangerous *femme fatale*, a woman whose success at manipulation relies upon the deeply engrained, yet superficial, expectations of femininity fashioned and enforced by Victorian social mores. However, she does so through the unreliable dialogic performance of Hammond, a narrator who is problematically framed by an additional layer of gender-ambiguous and writerly narration. In using the same technique adopted by many of her New Woman contemporaries, Malet subverts masculine authorial and discursive authority whilst simultaneously lampooning the hollow aestheticism of the dilettantish *fin-de-siècle flaneur.* Although Charlotte's cruelty is monstrous, her modernity aligned (through the dog) both with imperial horror and female (sexual) deviance, Malet's male characters are also branded as animal, their own grotesquely exaggerated physiognomies presented as uncivilised and bestial.

Malet disrupts the discourse of social purity lauded by New Woman commentators like Grand, critiquing the impossible fantasy of the 'New Man.' She addresses gender stereotypes, arguing the dangers of inflexible categories which demand particular kinds of performance. Ultimately, the most successful of the novel's characters is Charlotte, who becomes wealthy, ditches Gerrard and marries again. Her ability to negotiate, subvert, and challenge Victorian ideologies of the eternal feminine make her grotesque, yet also make her the only character fit for the society she inhabits; Charlotte's monstrosity has, as Bakhtin argues of the grotesque "not only a destructive, negative aspect, but also a regenerating one" (21). Faced with the irretrievability of his manliness, Leversedge commits suicide; Percy Gerrard is jilted; and Hammond wallows in a state of ascetic (and aesthetic) asexuality, having failed to marry Lydia Casteen, the only woman he has ever loved. Malet came in for criticism in her lifetime for what other female authors saw as outdated opinions on marriage and motherhood. Her essay "The Threatened Re-Subjection of Woman" had provoked the ire of New Woman novelist Mona Caird, who decried that "Lucas Malet comes forward, not to defend her sex—and, be it noted, humanity—from the primitive barbarism here threatened, but to fasten yet another stone around the neck of the drowning" (1905, 110). Yet such readings of Malet's reputedly disappointing 'feminism' fail to account satisfactorily for the inconsistencies exemplified by fictional accounts of transgressive women like Charlotte Perry who succeed against all odds.

In the words of one highly critical but rather astute contemporary reviewer, readers of the novel remained "not at all sure that Lucas Malet means us even to disapprove of the Carissima" (1896, 841). Although Charlotte fails as an Angel in the House and bastion of moral purity, she successfully navigates a world which restricts women's potential and denies them the same opportunities as men. Such an achievement makes her an unlikeable character, but, I argue, no more so than the morally pure but endlessly self-defeating heroines constructed by New Woman novelists (Caird included) publishing around the same time. Malet's tale seems to suggest, in opposition to Leversedge's claim early in the text that "nobody's afraid of what they can strangle" (12), that women who can recognise and exploit nineteenth-century social dictates, may find a way to beat the system altogether.

Notes

1 See Schaffer (2000) for discussion of Malet's concern with both disability and aestheticism.

2 See Walker Gore (2014) who describes the grotesque body as "the antidote to those forms of progress Malet judges to be essentially secularist and thus unsound" (372). See also Bourrier (2014), O'Connell (2012), Miller (2012) and Schaffer (2000).

3 See Lundberg (1998) for detailed discussion of the ways in which the supernatural elements in Malet's work reflect and distort the masculine gothicism of both James and Lewis.
4 *The Carissima* is a frame narration, beginning with an unnamed and gender-ambiguous narrator who asks Hammond to tell them a story about "the modern young woman" (3).
5 *The Carissima* was not a bestseller. It ran to two editions in 1896 (one an American edition) and was never reprinted. It received mostly unfavourable reviews. As Patricia Lorimer Lundberg notes, the *Athenaeum* was "almost alone among [positive] reviews" (2003, 187). *The Hound of the Baskervilles* was an unprecedented success for *The Strand* in serialised form, running to seven printings to meet demand—it is estimated to have increased the magazine's circulation by 30,000 copies (McDonald 1997, 157).
6 W.W. Robson notes in his introduction to the 1993 Oxford edition of the text that the feminisation of the animal in "The Brazilian Cat" lends the text an erotic undercurrent missing from *The Hound of the Baskervilles* (Conan Doyle 2009, vi).
7 For example: Sarah Grand's Morningquest trilogy (1888–1897), Mona Caird's *The Wing of Azrael* (1889) and *The Daughters of Danaus* (1894), Ella Hepworth Dixon's *The Story of a Modern Woman* (1894) and Victoria Cross's *The Woman Who Didn't* (1894).
8 Lundberg makes a case for Charlotte as an example of the New Woman (1998, 392), but Charlotte's lack of interest in women's advancement (although she is clearly interested in her own) and/or politics complicates this assumption.
9 Most critics of New Woman writing agree that the term is largely a journalistic construct, applied to a variety of women with divergent political and literary agendas. See Richardson (2016, 150–67), Ledger (1997) and Heilmann (2004) for discussion of the instability of the term 'New Woman.'
10 Worshipers of the Roman God Bacchus: the god of wine, winemaking, harvest, fertility, ritual madness, theatre, and religious ecstasy. These associations reinforce a reading of Charlotte as a modern woman, particularly given the (largely overstated) association between the New Woman and the decadent movement.
11 See Richardson (2008) for detailed discussion of Grand's interest in eugenics and imperialism.
12 Hendershot discusses Sheridan Le Fanu's "Green Tea" (1869), in which the male protagonist is haunted by a phantom monkey. There are some interesting parallels between these texts, although Malet's use of the phantom dog seems positioned as a more explicit critique of gender norms than Le Fanu's tale.
13 Perhaps the most infamous example is Joris-Karl Huysmans's *A Rebours* (1884) a text which revels in the impenetrability of its verbose style, as it celebrates the decadence of its central character.
14 See Schaffer's discussion of Malet's aesthetic style to communicate her suspicions about aestheticism (2000, 197–216).
15 Freud would later adapt his work on hysterical neurosis, expanding his study of trauma in work with shell-shocked victims of trauma after the First World War. See Freud's "Introduction to Psycho-Analysis and the War Neurosis" (1919).
16 The preliminary paper upon which *Studies in Hysteria* had been founded was published in the *Neurologisches Centralblatt* journal in 1894 (after having been delivered as a lecture in 1893) and was entitled "On the Psychical Mechanism of Hysterical Phenomena." Malet had a keen interest in Freud's

work (noted by Lundberg 2003, 45) and references to Freud appear in *The Survivors* (Malet 1923, 162).

17 It is also possible that Malet here references Bertha from George Eliot's *The Lifted Veil* (1859) in which the *femme fatale*'s coldness and manipulation are revealed too late for the naïve male protagonist. Charlotte and Bertha are remarkably similar in the apparent impenetrability of their respective characters or motivations.

Works Cited

Bakhtin, Mikhail. 1984. *Rabelais and His World*, trans. by Hélène Iswolsky. Bloomington: Indiana University Press.

Blind, Mathilde. 1885. *Tarantella: A Romance*. London: T Fisher Unwin.

Bourrier, Karen. 2014. "Orthopaedic Disability and the Nineteenth-Century Novel." *Nineteenth-Century Contexts: An Interdisciplinary Journal* 36(1): 1–7.

Caird, Mona. 1905. "The Duel of the Sexes—A Comment." *The Fortnightly Review* 78(463): 109–22.

Carter, Boyd. 1940. "Alphonse Daudet: In Memorium 1840–1940." *The French Review* 14(1): 21–25.

Conan Doyle, Arthur. 2009. *The Hound of the Baskervilles*. Oxford: Oxford University Press.

Darwin, Charles. 2004. *The Descent of Man: Selection in Relation to Sex*. London: Penguin.

Daudet, Alphonse, and Leon Hennique. 1893. *La Menteuse*. Paris: E. Flammarion.

Davies, Tracey C. 1991. *Actresses as Working Women: Their Social Identity in Victorian Culture*. London: Routledge.

Delyfer, Catherine. 2011. *Art and Womanhood in Fin-de-Siècle Writing: The Fiction of Lucas Malet, 1880–1931*. London: Pickering & Chatto.

Egerton, George. 2006. *Keynotes and Discords*. London: Continuum.

Eliot, George. 1999. *The Lifted Veil and Brother Jacob*. Oxford: Oxford University Press.

Ford, Jane. 2015. "Socialism, Capitalism and the Fiction of Lucas Malet: 'The Spirit of the Hive.'" *English Literature in Transition* 58(4): 551–71.

Freud, Sigmund. 2001. *The Standard Edition of the Complete Psychological Works of Sigmund Freud: Vol. 17*. London: Vintage.

Gore, Clare Walker. 2014. "Noble Lives: Writing Disability and Masculinity in the Late Nineteenth Century." *Nineteenth-Century Contexts* 36(4): 363–75.

Grand, Sarah. 1894. "The New Aspect of the Woman Question." *The North American Review* 158(44): 270–76.

Gray, Alexandra. 2017. *Self-Harm in New Woman Writing*. Edinburgh: Edinburgh University Press.

Heilmann, Ann. 2004. *New Woman Strategies: Sarah Grand, Olive Schreiner, Mona Caird*. Manchester: Manchester University Press.

Hendershot, Cindy. 1998. *The Animal Within: Masculinity and the Gothic*. Ann Arbour: University of Michigan Press.

Ibsen, Henrick. 2008. "A Doll's House." In *Four Major Plays*, 1–88. Oxford: Oxford University Press.

Kristeva, Julia. 1982. *Powers of Horror: An Essay on Abjection*, trans. by Leon S Roudiez. New York: Columbia University Press.

Ledger, Sally. 1997. *The New Woman: Fiction & Feminism at the Fin De Siécle.* Manchester: Manchester University Press.

Lundberg, Patricia Lorimer. 1998. "Dialogic Fiction of the Supernatural: 'Lucas Malet.'" *English Literature in Transition* 41(4): 389–407.

———. 2003. *'An Inward Necessity': The Writer's Life of Lucas Malet.* Oxford: Peter Lang.

Malet, Lucas. 1896. *The Carissima: A Modern Grotesque.* London: Methuen & Co.

———. 1905. "The Threatened Re-Subjection of Woman." *Fortnightly Review* 77(461): 806–19.

———. 1923. *The Survivors.* New York: Dodd, Mead & Co.

———. "In Memoriam, Ernest D. Chesterfield." L. Tom Perry Special Collections, Harold B. Lee Library, Brigham Young University, Utah. MSS 8149, n.p.

Marshall, Gail. 1998. *Actresses on the Victorian Stage: Feminine Performance and the Galatea Myth.* Cambridge: Cambridge University Press.

McDonald, Peter D. 1997. *British Literary Culture and Publishing Practice 1880–19.* Cambridge: Cambridge University Press.

Miller, Kathleen A. 2012. "'Your loving is unlike any other': Romance and the Disabled Body in the Gothic Fiction of Edith Nesbit and Lucas Malet." In *Writing Women of the Fin de Siècle: Authors of Change*, edited by Adrienne. E. Gavin and Carolyn de la W. Oulton, 193–203. London: Palgrave.

O'Connell, Rachel. 2012. "That Cruel Spectacle: The Extraordinary Body Eroticized in Lucas Malet's *the History of Sir Richard Calmady.*" In *Sex and Disability*, edited by Anna Mollow and Robert McRuer, 108–22. Durham: Duke University Press.

Powell, Kerry. 1997. *Women and the Victorian Theatre.* Cambridge: Cambridge University Press.

"Recent Novels." 1896. *The Spectator*, 22.

"Review of *The Carissima.*" 1896. *Blackwood's Edinburgh Magazine*, 160, 838–41.

Richardson, Angelique. 2008. *Love and Eugenics in the Late Nineteenth Century: Rational Reproduction and the New Woman.* 2nd ed. Oxford: Oxford University Press.

———. 2016. "Who *Was* the New Woman?" In *Late Victorian into Modern*, edited by Laura Marcus, Michèle Mendelssohn, and Kristen E. Shepherd-Barr, 150–67. Oxford: Oxford University Press.

Schaffer, Talia. 2000. *The Forgotten Female Aesthetes: Literary Culture in Late-Victorian England.* Charlottesville: University of Virginia Press.

Srebrnik, Patricia. 1994. "The Re-Subjection of Lucas Malet: Charles Kingsley's Daughter and the Response to Muscular Christianity." In *Muscular Christianity*, edited by Donald E. Hall, 194–214. Cambridge: Cambridge University Press.

5 Cosmopolitan Romance and Feminist Aestheticism in *Adrian Savage*

Catherine Delyfer

This essay reads *Adrian Savage* as a late aestheticist political novel, whose primary aim is to explore forms of female discontent, dissidence, and self-realisation at the dawn of the twentieth century. Indeed, despite its title, this novel is less about the suave bicultural eponymous protagonist, than about the diverse female characters he encounters who shape, refine, and permanently alter his views on gender relations. Not unlike Laurence Rivers, a character who, in *The Gateless Barrier* (1900), travels from the United States to England to learn about early-Victorian patriarchal tyranny, Adrian Savage navigates between twentieth-century France and England. He becomes deeply involved in two cultures, two romantic plots, and two narratives of femininity. As he repeatedly crosses the Channel to fulfil his obligations to the paternal, English side of his family, Adrian develops into a keen analyst of the sexual politics of Protestant England versus Catholic France, ultimately becoming a spokesperson for the British feminist cause. Like Dickens's *A Tale of Two Cities* (1859), this novel's bifocal structure undergirds a serious political warning about the state of Britain at a time when the British women's movement was becoming radicalised and fiercely militant.[1]

While there is no question that *Adrian Savage* is a political novel, one would be wrong to assume that it falls easily into the categories of either New Woman novel or suffrage fiction. Preoccupied as it is with the Parisian art world, nonnormative lifestyles, and aestheticist portraits; with beauty, desire, and individualism; and with various forms of pictorial, literary, and musical creativity, this novel can more accurately be described as a post-Victorian aestheticist novel which binds together politics and art. In fact, as a journal editor and a respected critic of art and literature, Adrian sees women's cause as intrinsically linked to the cause of art, thus drawing the reader's attention to a gendered politics of the aesthetic. Half psychological novel, half feminist pamphlet, *Adrian Savage* contrasts French and English artistic traditions and cultural discourses by considering the value of Renaissance painting, the pitfalls of idealism, the insights of decadent art, and the poignancy of naturalist drama, in order to explore contemporary sexual politics.

A "new tale of two cities"[2]

Lucas Malet's tenth published novel opens on a playful, mildly derisive, portrait of the eponymous protagonist, followed by the theatrical depiction of "cosmopolitan twentieth-century Paris" (Malet 1911, 8) and the beginnings of a conventional romance between the dashing Adrian Savage and the witty, and recently widowed, Gabrielle St. Leger.[3] Throughout the novel, the omniscient narrative voice remains mostly humorous and, at times, detached or incisive. Each chapter is headed by a title which comments ironically on its contents, thus flaunting a literary tradition which owes much to Henry Fielding and George Meredith.[4] To contemporary readers such as Catherine Oothout, the novel's quick, spirited tone and direct, realist manner appeared "modern ..., vivacious, well contrasted and balanced ... fresh" (qtd. in Lundberg 2003, 332).

The prosperous heir and son of a talented French poetess and a successful English physician established in Paris, Adrian combines his parents' best qualities: he is a promising young man of artistic, scientific, and practical talents. Now at twenty-nine years old, having fallen in love with the lovely widow of his old friend Horace St. Leger, the well-favoured Adrian is keen to embark on a romantic quest to woo and win Gabrielle: a woman whom he naively views as a mysterious and inaccessible Mona Lisa or, alternatively, as a lovely Sleeping Beauty that he wishes to awaken and marry. The novel, however, opens as he is forced to bid the lady of his dreams goodbye, for he has just been summoned to England to act as coexecutor of his deceased English cousin's last will and advisor to his two daughters, Joanna and Margaret Smyrthwaite.

At first, the narrator's swift, confident banter may suggest that the novel is little more than an Edwardian marriage plot with a French flair, or a modern fairy tale romance—the last chapter is entitled "Wherein Adrian Savage Succeeds in Awakening *La Belle of Bois Dormant*" (447). A contemporary advertisement from *Publishers' Weekly* commented that the final union between Adrian and Gabrielle constituted a happy dénouement and that *in fine* "All works out well" ("Weekly Record of New Publications" 1911, 1477). Yet in the Maletian corpus, such an ending is suspiciously uncharacteristic, considering the overwhelming majority of protagonists who reject or escape wedlock, or whose marriages turn out to be disastrous, nonnormative, or scandalous.[5] Moreover, this interpretation completely ignores the novel's embedded tale of dark eroticism and wild despair. It similarly fails to address Malet's art of bilocation and the duality, or self-dividedness, which lies at the core of the narrative.

Indeed *Adrian Savage*, like Dickens's *A Tale of Two Cities,* alternates between sections set either in France or England, with a view to provoking cultural distance, critical awareness, and historical perspective.[6] The first four chapters depicting the scintillating, art-loving, "feminine" (111) Parisian scene offer a vivid contrast with the second half of Part I, which is set in the parochial, materialist, and patriarchal middle-class community of Stourmouth, in the countryside of the English South East. While Part II and Part IV return us to Paris, Part III is devoted entirely to the novel's English subplot, and the final section, Part V, reaches its tragic climax in England before bringing the story back to Paris for its conclusion. The novel's dual focus allows Malet to expose the arid, hypocritical, and predatory nature of English society and to set it against a depiction of French Bohemianism. Self-righteous, utilitarian, Protestant England is shown to be more deeply immoral, ruthless, and sinister than hedonist Paris. For example, Joanna Smyrthwaite's dissolute brother Robert is saved from suicide by the artist René Dax in Paris, only to be murdered as soon as he returns to his native land and Stourmouth solicitor Joseph Challoner puts an end to his affair with Gwynnie Spencer with the same sadistic determination he used to show hunting rabbits as a boy.

But what strikes Adrian the most is that "Protestant English-speaking peoples" seem characterised by a tendency towards

> [a] democratic, scientific, unsparing self-knowledge, physical and mental, on the one hand, and a narrow, sectarian, self-sufficiency, on the other; a morbidly cold-blooded acknowledgment of fact and application of means to ends, in which neither poetry nor religion had any determining part. The artist in [Adrian] protested hotly. For really a world so ordered did not look enticing in the very least! (91)

The effects of such a stern culture, Adrian feels, are especially devastating for British women. In addition to leading inartistic lives, they are subjected to the tyranny of "the sour, pedantic, man-imagined deity of some Protestant sect" (411), on the one hand, and to the middle-class Englishman, on the other:

> All Englishmen are pedants, even in their games, even in their sport. They have been called a nation of shopkeepers. They might with equal truth be called a nation of schoolmasters; not because they desire to impart knowledge, but because they crave to exercise power. ... Truly, they are very disagreeable sons, husbands and fathers those middle-class Britons [absorbed as they are in] their own selfish pleasures, their clubs, their playing fields, their interminable football, and cricket, and golf ... Her countrymen's relation to [the Englishwoman] is so inartistic, so utilitarian, so without delicate humor. (156)

Consequently, Adrian interprets his English female cousin's joyless scrupulousness, excessive intellectualism, and strained sense of morality as sure signs of internalised oppression, starved sensuousness, and existential despair. Further, she makes him realise how very fortunate he and Gabrielle are to have been born in France, away from the blighting influences of "Luther, the burly renegade German monk" and "Calvin, the parchment-dry, middle-class Picard lawyer" (157). Indeed, he argues that, when Luther and Calvin

> conspired to depose Our Blessed Lady from her rightful throne in heaven, they, incidentally, went far to depose woman from her rightful throne here upon earth. So that, small wonder, having no eternal, universal Mother, whose aid and patronage she can invoke in hours of perplexity and distress, the modern, non-Catholic woman is constrained to rush around in prison-vans, or any other unlovely public vehicle which may come in handy, invoking the aid of parliamentary suffrage and kindred dreary mechanical forms of protection against the tedious tyrannies of arrogant, sullen, selfish, slow-witted, birch-rod-wielding, pedagogic man.
>
> (157)

In Malet's fiction, such views concerning the Catholic cult of Mary are not unusual.[7] Other female Victorian authors raised in the Protestant tradition, such as Anna Jameson, George Eliot, Elizabeth Barrett Browning, Christina Rossetti, or Margaret Oliphant had also used similar arguments. As Kimberly Van Esveld Adams has shown, these authors developed a proto-feminist "politics of Mary," using the Catholic Madonna as a political symbol, a source of female empowerment, a figure of gender equity, as well as a model of female intellectual and spiritual self-reliance. In the above quotation, Adrian is following in the footsteps of these women writers, when he argues that Calvin and Luther are indirectly responsible for the rise of the British suffragist movement: once Englishwomen were deprived of the "protection" of Mary, suffragism became the only form of resistance available to them against the "tyrannies … of man." In addition, Adrian links the Protestant rejection of the Madonna to a rejection of beauty, sensuality, and art ("unlovely public vehicle," "dreary mechanical forms of protection").

By contrast, France is envisioned by Adrian as both inherently feminist *and* artistic. Not without some humour, Malet has him claim that "though we [Frenchmen] may have tolerated, even invented, Revolution, we have at least withstood that most time-serving and inartistic compromise, Reformation" (157). And, although he admits he is not a practicing Catholic, Adrian congratulates himself for living under a Catholic god. Not only does Adrian consider Him as the "supreme artist," but He is also the "maker of man's flesh as well as of his spirit," a god "divinely reasonable and divinely human" (411–2), that is, a divinity who fosters aesthetic, intellectual, and sensuous self-realisation. According to Adrian, in a Catholic culture such as France, all men are of necessity "Feminists, every man-jack of us" (158), whereas in England, the treatment of women leaves much to be desired.

Even though the casualties in Malet's English narrative are not as numerous as in Dickens's revolutionary France, it is hardly surprising that *Adrian Savage* involves two failed suicide attempts, one attempted murder, one homicide, and culminates in Joanna Smyrthwaite's self-poisoning. Moreover, like Dickens's historical novel, *Adrian Savage*'s climax hinges on a dramatic dénouement which involves the self-chosen death of one individual as corollary to the happiness of the novel's main couple, thus radically calling into question the notion of a happy ending.

Joanna

As we follow Adrian on his English journey of initiation, Joanna Smyrthwaite's engrossing story and eventual death shift the novel's centre of gravity from the French to the English plot. So much so that some contemporary readers, such as Margaret Froude or Rhoda Broughton, remarked that the book might have been better entitled *Joanna* (Lundberg 2003, 338). In the English segments of the novel, the powerful drama of oppressed womanhood, psychological violence, and repressed sexuality in which Adrian becomes entwined is described with absorbing detail and a poignant realism reminiscent of Emily Brontë's *Wuthering Heights.*[8] Not unlike Brontë, Malet opts for a double narrative framework by inserting several fragments from Joanna's private diary as part of her novel (chapters V and VI in Part I, chapter IV in Part III and chapters I and VII in Part V). The author's use of autobiografiction is significant.[9] Indeed, the various "passages from Joanna Smyrthwaite's Locked Book" (61) increasingly impact the main plot in part V, when they are read by Adrian. The disruption is such that it temporarily interrupts the marriage plot and jeopardises its resolution.

The fact that Joanna's embedded text surpasses the narrative in interest and intensity illustrates the power of female life-writing as a compelling act of self-fashioning and defiance as well as a literary act ("I sat and read the journal from cover to cover. Having once begun, I could not leave off" (464), Adrian explains to Gabrielle). Importantly, the last segment of Joanna's diary functions as a long and detailed suicide note left to Adrian. Whereas predictably, Joanna's English family is busy trying to conceal her death as accidental, Adrian is forced to confront the minute reality of Joanna's lived experience. As Margaret Higonnet has argued, "[t]o take one's life is to force others to read one's death" (Higonnet 1986, 68). Here *reading* Joanna's death implies acknowledging her tragic destiny as a victim of paternal "cannibalism" (77); her heroism as "a modern Antigone" (94) rebelling against her father's ignoble treatment of her brother; and her loss of religious faith as a rational Dissenter. It also implies recognition of the irresistible, but unrequited, erotic attraction Joanna feels for Adrian, and exploration of the connections between gender, sexuality, faith, and the suicidal impulse. As Joanna's Unitarian faith declines, it is replaced by her blind (but misguided) faith in Adrian's love, on which she now completely depends for her election and her justification, until she eventually realises her mistake and decides to abandon herself in "the arms of the lover who has never failed man or woman yet—in the arms of Death" (424).

Adrian's experience of reading Joanna's diary is described as life-changing. It purges him of any masculine self-complacency and alienates him from himself:

> I wanted to escape. I wanted to get away from every person I knew, whom I had ever seen. Above all I wanted to get away from myself; but I was obliged to take myself along with me. And I found myself a dreadful companion. I hated myself.
>
> (464)

Ultimately, instead of dismissing female suicide as a sign of waywardness or temporary insanity, this novel proposes to read Joanna's suicide as a perfectly rational and logical choice in a society which ignores female desire and affords no place for strong, intelligent women.[10] Joanna's self-chosen death is thus represented in all its "stoicism" and "dignity" (465) as an assertive act of free will which reveals a crisis in social norms and values.[11]

In this context, Joanna's gift of her writing to Adrian is significant, insofar as it signals the emergence of a singular, dissident, authentic female voice and the possibility for a wider recognition of female agency as well as female distress. "I want you to know me as I really am" (424), Joanna writes to Adrian at the end of her diary. Although she is at first described as "a diarist absolutely innocent of any thought or wish of eventual print," Joanna nevertheless reflects on the "act of writing" (75). She cherishes it as "exclusively, inviolably her own" (64), takes refuge in it as in a "drug" (64) and engages in it with the passion and feverish excitement of an addict. The narrative twist by which Joanna leaves the last volume of her diary to her cousin as a legacy is therefore an invitation for him to read it, of course, but also to make it public. Indeed, as editor of a "leading bimonthly review" which has become a "powerful factor in contemporary criticism and literary output" (7), Adrian's main occupation is to select material for publication. In fact, the narrator repeatedly emphasises that he is a discerning critic, who assesses artistic, literary and intellectual merit regardless of the morality or immorality of the artist or the subject tackled. Additionally, Adrian is curious about women's writing and female subjectivity, but doubts that modern literature has adequately represented

> woman's mind, woman's outlook, in itself, divorced from her relation to man. ... Woman in her relation to man was a stale enough, obvious enough, story. But in her relation to her fellow-woman, in her relation to herself—had not this tripped even the cleverest novelists and dramatists of his own sex?
>
> (92)

Interestingly, Adrian himself is a writer with a keen interest in "psychology" (6), which he incidentally shares with his Edwardian namesake, the prominent psychiatrist Dr George Savage (1842–1921).[12] Gabrielle goes as far as to call Adrian a "professional psychologist" (17). The reader is thus encouraged to speculate that Joanna's story will be published and possibly contribute to a more sympathetic understanding of English feminism, or at least a more lucid approach to female suicide than was usually the case in the sensationalist press, medical or police reports, and works of fiction.

The Threat of Women's "Re-Subjection"

As the English and the French plots become more entwined and protagonists cross and recross the Channel, the easy binary oppositions between French and English womanhood, however, begin to dissolve and important similarities also emerge. Love triangles form on both sides (Adrian-René-Gabrielle, Margaret-Gwynnie-Joseph, Adrian-Joanna-Gabrielle) and, significantly, the English plot and the French plot similarly end with a marriage (Adrian and Gabrielle in France, Margaret and Joseph in England). On both sides of the Channel too the heroines experience or come close to experiencing death: Joanna kills herself and Gabrielle is being pressured by the Parisian painter René Dax to commit suicide out of love for him and his art. Additionally, Malet creates a multitude of mirror effects which operate not only at the narrative level but also at the level of characterisation. Many examples could be given. Joanna and Margaret are twin sisters, even though their physical appearances, temperaments, and destinies are starkly contrasted. Because of her unusual (masculine) looks, Joanna is said to resemble her brother—to the point that Robert's grotesque caricature by René Dax is at first taken for a portrait of Joanna. As for René Dax, he is not only Adrian's childhood friend but, when he decides to appropriate/vampirise Gabrielle, also his perverse alter-ego and his rival. Last but not least, Gabrielle and Joanna, though radically dissimilar, are linked by a strong feminine bond, a kind of sisterhood. As Adrian observes, despite "their differences of circumstances, endowment, and experience," they are "still essentially nearer to each other, more capable of mutual sympathy and understanding in the deep places of their nature, than he, with all his acute sensibility and dramatic insight, could ever be to either of them!" (92). His estimation turns out to be correct since, following the gothic tradition, both female characters are shown to be haunted by the ghosts of patriarchy, by the vivid memory of their subjection to masculine desire: even after the deaths of their husband and father respectively, the two women equally struggle to assert themselves.[13] Clearly, in spite of the opposing connotations which attach to their names, their stories are not simplistically binary.[14] In fact, when Adrian visits René Dax's art studio in Paris (chapter VI part II), he is met simultaneously with a portrait of Gabrielle and sketches of Joanna, as if to draw his (and the reader's) attention to the fact that the two women embody two facets of the same reality.

Malet's Anglo-French narrative thus complicates its representation of womanhood by highlighting continuities between England and France, as well as between women's past and present lives. Intergenerational insights into the sorrows of the aging pianist Miss Beauchamp and Gabrielle's mother Madame Vernois (in France), or Joanna's late mother Mrs Smyrthwaite and the middle-aged widow Mrs Spencer (in England), shed light on the new directions taken by the younger female generation of Margaret Smyrthwaite (the pretty opportunist), Marion Chase (the frivolous New Woman), and Zélie de Gand (the immoral French political activist). Moreover, by reading together Joanna's tragic (ugly) embodiment of Victorian womanhood and the more hopeful (radiant) Gabrielle, Malet retraces women's history, from oppression to the early stages of emancipation, thus exploring the roots and ferment of "awakening militant feminism" (18).

Although in a letter to M.P. Willcocks, dated 14 November 1911, Malet rejoiced that "Joanna—my poor, poor Joanna—belongs I trust to the *past*—even under the repressive English system. … I am glad to observe no budding Joannas among the younger generation" (qtd. in Lundberg 2003, 339), she was also acutely aware of possible regressions. Six years earlier, in an essay published in the *Fortnightly Review* entitled "The Threatened Re-Subjection of Woman," Malet vehemently protested against U.S. President Theodore Roosevelt's public address advocating a return to traditional gender roles. Clearly, Malet feared a reactionary turn in global gender politics:

> President Roosevelt preaches the American nation a sermon involving very wide issues—issues so wide, indeed, that they affect the office and status of women in civilized communities all the world over and of every rank. "The prime duty of the man," he tells us, "is to work, to be the bread-winner. The prime duty of the woman is to be the

> mother, the housewife. All questions of tariff and finance sink into insignificance when compared with the tremendous, the vital importance of trying so to shape conditions that these two duties of the man and of the woman can be fulfilled under reasonably favourable circumstances." This is a return to first principles with a vengeance. It is also the seriously considered pronouncement of the popularly elected ruler of the most progressive nation of the world, in the first decade of the twentieth century ... Is it possible to set back the hands of the clock, and eradicate tendencies which have been enthusiastically fostered during two generations in England, and are now in active development in various Continental countries? Is it possible to place woman again, in respect of her ideals and her romance, in the position of our great-grandmothers ... depriving her of advantages in education, in the tenure of property, in social and civic freedom, and, indirectly, of usefulness to the State, which she has so laboriously and, let it be added, so courageously acquired? ... [M]arriage, housewifery, the permanent subordination of the woman to the claims of the husband, the family and the household, this is rank heresy—heresy, moreover, seasoned with insult. ... [T]he demand for self-abnegation on the part of a large section of our feminine population would be a very heavy one in thus setting back the hands of the clock.
>
> (Malet 1905, 806–7)

This was a controversial essay, which was criticised, and sometimes misinterpreted, by suffragists such as Agnes Grove, partially because of Malet's scepticism concerning the impact of the women's movement on certain social classes and partly because of her celebration of the modern middle-class woman as "ambitious," "impatient of authority," "sexless," "nomadic," and "increasingly unmaternal" (Malet 1905, 815).[15] Yet, as this excerpt makes clear, there is no question that Malet was a staunch supporter of women's rights and felt some alarm that they might be jeopardised, thus setting back "the hands of the clock" of female emancipation.

In her 1911 novel, Malet kept the disturbing possibility of such a regression present in her readers' minds. Almost as a warning, the novel's gothic subtext persists, lying dormant in the male protagonist's family name. Though the caring, sensitive, and sympathetic Adrian seems the reverse of "Savage" and, in fact, as we have seen, fully supports what he calls "the revolt of the Englishwoman" (156), his surname reminds the reader always to be wary and on her guard.

Aesthetic Feminism

After the First World War, Harold Williams's influential study *Modern English Writers* described *Adrian Savage* as a novel "belonging to the feminist movement" (Williams 1918, 440). Yet earlier reviewers had been more nuanced in their appraisal. The *New York Times Book Review* argued, perhaps more accurately, that feminism in *Adrian Savage* is "weighed and found wanting" ("A Dream Face and a Tragedy" 1911, 655).

Indeed, it is hard to ignore the French protagonists' final distancing from militant feminism, both when Adrian and Miss Beauchamp assert that "[f]eminism has next to no legitimate excuse for existence here [in Paris]" (163) and when Gabrielle eventually "surrender[s]" to Adrian's marriage proposal, instead of embracing the cause of the activist Zélie de Gand. In the end, though she longs for power and freedom, Gabrielle does not follow those whom Adrian petulantly calls

> agitators and extremists, Feminists, Futurists, and such-like pestilent persons—enemies of marriage and of the family, of moral and spiritual authority, of all sane canons of art, music and literature, reckless anarchists in thought and purpose if not, through defective courage, in actual deed.
>
> (169)

So what kind of feminist novel is *Adrian Savage*? Was M. P. Willcocks right when she claimed, in her review in the November 1911 issue of *The Bookman*, that ultimately "both [Gabrielle and Joanna] are left unsatisfied—though one goes to death and the other to a lover. Only the man has his will" (qtd. in Lundberg 2003, 337)?

In the novel, the feminist anti-marriage activist Zélie de Gand is only mentioned three times and never seen. Summarily described by Adrian as "that much-discussed, plausible, very astute and clever, also very much discredited arrivist [*sic*] and novelist," (169) she seems to stand for vaguely distasteful, aggressive, excessive, "unsavory" aspects of militant feminism (163). Zélie belongs to René Dax's circle of shady, disreputable friends, and it is through Dax's help that she gains access to Gabrielle. As the plot unveils Dax's sinister obsession with Gabrielle, it becomes evident that Gabrielle's involvement with Zélie too might be more destructive than liberating. In fact, Zélie's strategy in trying to rally Gabrielle to her cause is presented from the beginning by Miss Beauchamp as entirely self-serving:

> She is crazy to recover lost ground, to get herself and her clique re-instated. Madame St. Leger's beauty, brains and her reputation—so absolutely unsullied and above suspicion—represent an immense asset to any cause she may embrace.
>
> (163)

In choosing "Zélie de Gand" as her character's name, Malet may have had in mind the scandalous Irish New Woman novelist and social purity activist "Sarah Grand" (Frances Elizabeth Bellenden Clarke McFall, 1854–1943), who wrote daring books on female individualism and the limitations of marriage. In such novels as *The Heavenly Twins* (1893) or *The Beth Book* (1897), Grand had prioritised women's individual freedom within, and sometimes over, marriage in plots where male protagonists were shown to be either dissipated, abusive, manipulative, or dishonest. But Zélie de Gand's political tactics are also almost certainly an allusion on Malet's part to the tensions and party politics which dominated the women's movement in the early twentieth century. Against these veiled references to turn-of-the-century debates about the Woman Question, marriage, suffrage, and politics, Malet, however, proposes a different, less binary, type of feminism. One, I would argue, which is inflected by her passionate engagement with the values of aestheticism, and which celebrates individual choice, the transformative power of art, the life of the senses, and emotional, physical, and intellectual self-development. Malet's contribution to *fin-de-siècle* feminism is specifically aestheticist.

Following the example of Théophile Gautier, Walter Pater, and Oscar Wilde, Adrian is an aesthete who gains insight into people, life, politics, and religion through the prism of art. Even though his business acumen and practical abilities are commended among his English relatives, it is his knowledge of painting, literature, and music which enables his fine appreciation of the more complex aspects of Miss Beauchamp's, Gabrielle's, or Joanna's personalities. For example, his deep empathy with Miss Beauchamp is strengthened through his hearing her play the piano in her private salon. His knowledge of Henrik Ibsen's drama and Edvard Grieg's music mediates, illuminates, and sharpens his understanding of Joanna's experience and environment. The area around Stourmouth is assessed as "arrestingly northern in character, the spirit of it questioning, introspective, coldly complex, yet primitive and elfin, reminding [Adrian] of Grieg's Occasional Music to the haunting parable-poem of Peer Gynt" (90). While Joanna herself is revealed to have distinct aestheticist tastes—when she allows herself to indulge in the "tumult of her own sensations" by attending Wagner's operas with a fervour akin to "religious sentiment" (210–1)—she is an ill-fated, repressed female aesthete, and Adrian rightly refers to her mentally as "the Ibsen woman." She bears a striking resemblance to the Norwegian playwright's "penetrating and disheartening" female characters "which, heretofore, had so perplexed him by their distance from any moral and racial conditions with which he was familiar" (91).

By contrast, Gabrielle is depicted as an embodied, sensuous Renaissance woman, someone whose "nature was too rich—let it be added, too normal and wholesome—for the senses not to play their part in the shaping of her destiny" (451). Throughout the novel, she is called "la Belle Gabrielle," a phrase which was used as a nickname for Gabrielle d'Estrées, Henri IV's favourite mistress, a *femme fatale* who almost became queen of France, and whose celebrated beauty, intelligence, and modesty were recorded in several well-known sixteenth-century French paintings. However, Adrian also perceives in Gabrielle a more self-contained, mysterious, specifically Paterian type of Renaissance womanhood. He observes "the subtle likeness which … she [bears], in the proportions of her face and molding of it, to Leonardo's world-famous 'Mona Lisa' in the Salon Carré of the Louvre," and he is sensitive to the "strange recondite quality of her beauty, and the challenge it offer[s]" (11). Further, she startles him by looking at him with her "eye-lids … half-closed," "sideways without turning her head … it was Mona Lisa in a most mischievous humor." (17) Like Leonardo's *Gioconda* and Walter Pater's "Lady Lisa," Gabrielle remains enigmatic and elusive—a fact which is humorously highlighted via the paratext, when Malet informs the reader in her "Prefatory Note" about the sensational disappearance of Leonardo's painting from the Louvre in August 1911 (the painting was only returned in 1913, when the thief was identified). In a way, Malet's own *Mona Lisa* also exceeds her representations: she is meant to remain forever ungraspable, aloof, changing, and free—perhaps for this reason, Gabrielle's viewpoint is seldom expressed in the narrative.

Depicted as an independent-minded female aesthete, whose "soul and senses are constantly and actively interpenetrative, [and] instinctively responded to the spiritual influences which reside in places and even in material objects" (292), Gabrielle enjoys acting as patron of the arts, delights in her new-found freedom, and does not hesitate to defy social conventions. Her positive, liberating, life-enhancing aestheticism, however, is starkly contrasted with René Dax's exploitative, destructive, and exclusively masculine decadent aestheticism.

Not unlike Montagu Rivers, the misogynist dandy of *The Gateless Barrier* (1900), Dax has fitted his apartment with dark hangings and black blinds which block off the bright sun and natural daylight, giving Gabrielle the impression that "the atmosphere was stagnant, listless and dead" (293). With its Japanese bric-à-brac, its pet lemur, and its central glass fish tank, which contains lazy goldfish, "dull-hued tortoises with skinny necks and slimy carapaces" and "black-blotched, orange-bellied, crested tritons" (166), Dax's studio is also reminiscent of Jean des Esseintes's interior in J.K. Huysmans's *A Rebours* (1884). Throughout the novel, Dax himself is depicted as a reptilian creature, whose stunted, diminutive stature likens him to a "Tadpole" (Adrian's favourite nickname for his friend) or to a "homunculus" (165). He is a Beardsleyian dwarf, "all brain—all head, rather, since his tired little face seemed to also have dwindled and to occupy the most restricted space permissible in proportion to the whole" (294). Far from making him harmless, as Gabrielle initially believes, Dax's "puny person" and "lowness of stature" are oblique references to *fin-de-siècle* tropes of degeneration, insanity, and criminal psychology which recall Robert Louis Stevenson's description of the murderous Mr Hyde. In her characterisation of Dax as a fascinating but mentally unstable genius Malet is also, finally, indebted to Wilkie Collins's Misserimus Dexter in *The Law and the Lady* (1875).

When she visits Dax's *atelier*, Gabrielle therefore instinctively concludes that this is "the strangest and, perhaps, most repellent human habitation she had ever yet set foot in," one which reveals "a section of that exclusively man's world, in which woman's part is at once fugitive and not a little suspect" (292–3). Gabrielle's impression of suddenly confronting a hostile masculinist culture is further reinforced as she notes the phallic presence of "swords, rapiers, scimitars, daggers, and other such uncomfortably cutting, ripping, and stabbing tools" (295) above the mantelpiece. Thus it is not without "a shudder of disgust" and much resentment that Gabrielle discovers a "nearly life-size red chalk drawing set on an easel in the center of the studio" which represents her and her dear little daughter Bette. The drawing, which has been made without her knowledge, is used by Dax to soothe his exhausted nerves: night after night, the painter explains, the pictured Gabrielle "step[s] off the paper," crosses the room, bends over him to alleviate his suffering and, Madonna-like, bring him peace and comfort (296).

Crucially, it is through René Dax's illicit portrait of Gabrielle as "Madonna of the Future" that Adrian takes the full measure of Gabrielle's radical elusiveness and complete autonomy. Here again, feminism and Mariolatry intersect, as this painting revisits the Leonardesque rendition of the theme of Madonna and Child, in order to represent Gabrielle with her daughter on her arm, triumphantly going "forth from things habitual and familiar in obedience to the call ... of the new and tremendous age" (385) with her eyes "turned toward the future and the strange unrestful wind—the wind of Modernity—which blows from out the future, ... upon her face" (171). Clearly, Dax's picture is a compelling allegory of radiant new womanhood and the new generation of daughters it has brought into the world.

However, unlike the maniacal Dax, who succumbs to his obsession with Gabrielle as a universal, "deified" mother—ultimately attempting to kill himself and Gabrielle, in order to secure her for eternity—Adrian shows his ability to see Gabrielle as a woman, rather than as a mother, and moreover as a woman "divorced from her relation to man" (108). Just as he is profoundly changed through reading Joanna's writing, he is altered too after seeing Gabrielle's portrait: both works enable him to see these women as they are in themselves and for themselves.

By the novel's end, Adrian is not the only transformed character. Gabrielle's outlook too is altered after her brush with death. In the final stages of the novel, when Gabrielle rejects Zélie de Gand's militant feminism and accepts Adrian's marriage proposal, she does so neither out of "compulsion," regard for social conventions, nor out of "pity" for Adrian (469). Rather, on the one hand, Joanna's story as told by Adrian has convinced her that he (unlike Dax) is a fellow feminist and free thinker. On the other hand, Gabrielle is willing to succumb to the irresistible power of "Eros" (450) because she now views Zélie's feminism as narrow-minded. As the narrator points out, she

> had coquetted with Feminism, it is true; but such appeals and opportunities as Feminism has to offer the senses are not of an order wholesome natures can accept ... in her existing attitude, an exclusively intellectual fanaticism ... no longer could control or satisfy her. Against it her ironic and critical humor rebelled, making sport of it. ... *la belle Gabrielle* would inevitably seek satisfaction, scope for her young energies, for her unimpaired joy of living, elsewhere.
>
> (451)

In other words, after resisting Dax's death wish, Gabrielle eventually musters "the courage of [her] emotions" (168) and realises that "nature [i.e. life, love, and erotic desire] is too strong" for her (469). Just as Adrian had earlier decided that he could not sacrifice himself and give up Gabrielle for the sake of saving Joanna from misery, Gabrielle eventually decides that rejecting Adrian for the sake of following Zélie de Gand's objectives would be tantamount to self-abnegation.

Not unlike E.M. Forster's Italian novel *A Room with A View* (1908) or H.G. Wells's *Ann Veronica* (1909), *Adrian Savage* suggests that female (or male) self-sacrifice—whether in the name of conventions, moral duty, or political agendas—is of limited value, even possibly criminal, if it goes against individual liberty, the aesthetic sense, and the driving force of desire. It is not that Malet's novel argues that women should choose marriage *over* feminism. Such a ridiculous interpretation would contradict the rest of Malet's oeuvre and negate the examples set by such memorable fictional figures as Mary Crookenden (*The Wages of Sin*), Honoria St. Quentin (*The History of Sir Richard Calmady*), or Lydia Aylwin (*The Survivors*). Rather, Malet's aesthetic feminism in this novel consists of proposing multiple female points of view, including Joanna's conviction that a life without passion is not worth living and Gabrielle's realisation that women should not necessarily reject marriage, in the name of feminism conceived in narrow terms, if and when marriage fosters individual self-realisation.[16] As Talia Schaffer has observed, the politics and gender ideologies of female aesthetes such as Lucas Malet are often complex and ambiguous, for they coincide neither with those of New Women writers nor with those of the traditionalists. But by offering alternative feminine/feminist ideals and working outside of binary discourses, Malet's novel enables the construction of modern male and female subjects who are contradictory and struggling, being both subversive and conformist, defiant and powerless, rebellious and genteel. Malet's Anglo-French diptych should therefore be read as a political, feminist fiction which addresses the complexity of gendered experiences at the turn of the century without trying to offer conclusive lessons or missions. Although, in many ways, Malet herself led the life of a New Woman, she knew full well that her objectives as a novelist and a female aesthete were not those of an activist.[17] In her letter written on 14 November 1911 to M. P. Mallock about *Adrian Savage*, she explained

> Yes, I halt between two opinions, because I write merely of what is, not what should be or may be. I never pretend to prophecy. We are not far enough on the road of the great woman revolution ... to do more than note surrounding phenomena. Ten, twenty years hence, it may be possible to have a clear and reasoned opinion. At present no, not for the artist. For the partisan, the active reformer, it is different.
>
> (qtd. in Lundberg 2003, 339)

***

Notes

1 The Women's Social Political Union was founded in 1903 after Emmeline and Christabel Pankhurst split from the nonmilitant National Union of Women's Suffrage Societies led by Millicent Garrett Fawcett. Disappointed at the lack of success of the NUWSS's moderate tactics of persuasion, the Pankhursts adopted a more aggressive stance, illustrated by their slogan "Deeds, not words." After the rejection of the Conciliation Bills of 1910 and 1911, the members of the WSPU became fiercely militant, smashing shop windows, cutting telephone lines, chaining themselves to railings, burning unoccupied homes and churches, or bombing empty public buildings. In opposition to the continuing and repeated imprisonment of many of their members, the WSPU also introduced the prison hunger strike.

2 Patricia Lorimer Lundberg mentions that this was the title of a review of *Adrian Savage* in *The Bookman* (Lundberg 2003, 334).

3 *Mrs Lorimer* (1882), Malet's first published novel, also focuses on the romance between a lovely young widow and an artistic young man, but the marriage plot is subverted and the novel ends with Elizabeth Lorimer's death.

4 For example, "Wherein a very modern young man tells a time-honored tale with but small encouragement" (Chapter II, Part I), "Pistols or Politeness—for Two" (Chapter VII, Part III), or "In which a strong man adopts a very simple method of clearing his own path of thorns" (Chapter VIII, Part V).

5 The main protagonist's marriage is presented as a distinct possibility but is ultimately averted, for example, in *Mrs Lorimer* (1882), *A Counsel of*

Perfection (1888), *The Wages of Sin* (1891), *The Far Horizon* (1906), and *The Survivors* (1923). Marriage turns out to be disastrous, nonnormative, or both, for the heroes and anti-heroes of *Colonel Enderby's Wife* (1885), *The Gateless Barrier* (1900), *The History of Sir Richard Calmady* (1901), *Damaris* (1916), *Deadham Hard* (1919), and *The Survivors* (1923).

6 On Malet's admiration for Dickens, and particularly *A Tale of Two Cities*, see Lundberg (2003, 345–51).

7 Malet's Catholicism should be understood in part as a rejection of her father Charles Kingsley's masculinist Anglicanism and Muscular Christianity. Catholic imagery is used in Malet's fiction as early as 1882. She reflected on the cult of the Madonna and its politics in her first novel, *Mrs Lorimer* (1882), and continued to explore its ramifications, for example, in her conversion novel, *The Far Horizon* (1906) or, in a darker satiric vein, in *The Survivors* (1923). See Chapters 1 and 4 in Delyfer (2011, 2016, 122–42).

8 In his review for the *Times Literary Supplement*, Sir Claud Schuster praised the novel's "Brontësque grandeur" (Schuster 1911, 385).

9 On the use of fictional diaries in the Victorian novel, see Delafield (2016); on the use of autobiografiction in the late-Victorian, modernist, and postmodernist periods, see Saunders (2010).

10 These are interpretations which, according to Emma Liggins (2001, 5–17), were common in Victorian and Edwardian fiction, and remain valid in the case of Robert Smyrthwaite's and René Dax's suicide attempts. Andrew Merriman, the manager of the Smyrthwaite mills, who is in love with Joanna Smyrthwaite and once hoped to marry her, asserts that "in this family, if Miss Smyrthwaite had been born a boy it would have been better for the name and for the business." (88)

11 For a comprehensive overview of suicide as a literary trope, see Laird (2011).

12 In the late-nineteenth and early-twentieth centuries, Sir George Savage held a prominent position in the field of psychiatry. He appeared in *Vanity Fair*'s "Men of the Day" series in 1912 and was considered an authority on insanity and hysteria. He treated Virginia Woolf for over a decade and is lampooned in *Mrs Dalloway* (1925) as Sir William Bradshaw.

13 In chapter III, Gabrielle's heart sinks when she momentarily believes that her husband is back from the dead, playing with her little daughter Bette (33). In chapter V, a weak Joanna sees a movement on the bed where the corpse of her father lies, "as though some one was trying to crawl from underneath the sheet" (71).

14 "Smyrthwaite" evokes the smothering environment Joanna lives in, while "St. Leger" suggests holiness, insouciance, freedom, and lightness in French.

15 Lady Agnes Grove wrote a critical essay in response to Malet's article, entitled "'The Threatened Re-Subjection of Woman': A *Reply to Lucas Malet*," which was published in the *Fortnightly Review* (Grove 1905, 123–28).

16 Although biographical interpretations lie outside the scope of this essay, one may surmise that Malet had personal reasons to think more positively about love and marriage in *Adrian Savage* than in any of her other fiction. In the "Prefatory Note" the author insists that the novel should always be "impersonal" and that the characters portrayed in *Adrian Savage* are entirely her own invention and should not be thought of as real people. However, she also provocatively gives her French female protagonist her own family name (St. Leger) and the first name of her adoptive cousin/daughter (Gabrielle), to whom the novel is dedicated.

17 In *The Forgotten Female Aesthetes*, Talia Schaffer reminds us that Malet's early training as a painter at the Slade School and her conversion to Catholicism shaped her life as an aesthete and that, as a writer, her carefully crafted prose aligns her with other novelists from the school of art for art's sake (Schaffer 2000, 199–200). However, Schaffer also points out that after 1891, when Malet separated from her husband, William Harrison, she started leading the life of a New Woman, insofar as she was "a member of the literary avant-garde who wrote about sex more openly than any other novelist of the period, lived alone in reprehensibly immoral France, wore cosmetics, and praised Zola." Despite her ambivalence towards New Women, Malet wrote several articles defending women's writing and insisting that women's viewpoint was as valid as men's (Schaffer 2000, 15–16).

Works Cited

"A Dream Face and a Tragedy: 'Soul Projection' the Motif of Lucas Malet's New Novel 'Adrian Savage.'"1911. *New York Times*. 22 October, 655.

Delafield, Catherine. 2016. *Women's Diaries as Narrative in the Nineteenth-Century Novel.* Farnham: Ashgate.

Delyfer, Catherine. 2011. *Art and Womanhood in Fin-de-Siècle Writing: The Fiction of Lucas Malet 1880–1931.* London: Pickering and Chatto.

———. 2016. "The Aesthete, the Banker, and the Saint: Economies of Gift and Desire in Lucas Malet's *The Far Horizon* (1906)." In *Economies of Desire at the Fin-de-Siècle: Libidinal Lives*, edited by Jane Ford, Patricia Pulham, and Kim Edwards Keates, 122–42. London: Routledge.

Grove, Agnes. 1905. "'The Threatened Re-Subjection of Woman': A Reply to Lucas Malet." *Fortnightly Review* 78(463): 123–28.

Higonnet, Margaret. 1986. "Speaking Silences: Women's Suicide." In *The Female Body in Western Culture*, edited by Susan Rubin Suleiman, 68–83. Cambridge: Harvard University Press.

Laird, Holly A. 2011. "Between the (Disciplinary) Acts: Modernist Suicidology." *Modernism/Modernity* 18(3): 525–50.

Liggins, Emma. 2001. "Her Resolution to Die: 'Wayward Women' and Constructions of Suicide in Wilkie Collins's Crime Fiction." *Wilkie Collins Society Journal* 4: 5–17.

Lundberg, Patricia Lorimer. 2003. *An Inward Necessity": The Writer's Life of Lucas Malet.* New York: Peter Lang.

Malet, Lucas. 1895. *The Wages of Sin.* London: Swan Sonnenschein & Co.

———. 1900. *The Gateless Barrier.* New York: Dodd, Mead.

———. 1905. "The Threatened Re-Subjection of Woman." *Fortnightly Review* 83: 806–19.

———. 1911. *Adrian Savage: A Novel.* New York and London: Harper & Brothers Publishers.

———. 1923. *The Survivors.* London: Cassell & Co.

———. 2003. *The History of Sir Richard Calmady*, edited by Talia Schaffer. Birmingham: University of Birmingham Press.

Saunders, Max. 2010. *Self-Impression: Life-Writing, Autobiografiction, and the Forms of Modern Literature.* Oxford: Oxford University Press.

Schaffer, Talia. 2000. *The Forgotten Female Aesthetes: Literary Culture in Late-Victorian England.* Charlottesville: University Press of Virginia.

Schuster, Claud. 1911. "Adrian Savage." *The Times Literary Supplement*, 12 October, 385.

VanEsveld Adams, Kimberly. 2001. *Our Lady of Victorian Feminism: The Madonna in the Work of Anna Jameson, Margaret Fuller, and George Eliot.* Athens: Ohio University Press.

Williams, Harold. 1918. *Modern English Writers: Being a Study of Imaginative Literature 1890–1914.* London: Sidgwick and Jackson.

"Weekly Record of New Publications." 1911. *Publisher's Weekly*, 14 October, 1472–86.

6 The Authorial Ambition of *Deadham Hard*

Reimagining Womanhood, Profession, and Desire

Crescent Rainwater

> The visible, tangible attributes of the man—as man—presented themselves in fine relief, delighting [Damaris], stirring her heretofore dormant senses, begetting in her needs and desires undreamed of until now.
>
> (Malet 1919, 331)[1]

Lucas Malet's ambitious novel *Deadham Hard: A Romance* (1919) is the sequel to *Damaris* (1916): a novel set in imperial India in 1864, that tells the story of a motherless English girl's upbringing in a community beset by sexual jealousy. As a sequel, however, *Deadham Hard* does not follow a predictable pattern that reveals how its protagonist, Damaris Verity, develops first as an adolescent and then as a young woman who is ready to take her place in the marriage market. Instead, this far-from-ordinary sequel breaks new ground in the ways in which it talks about one woman's determination to pursue a profession as well as asserting her sexual desires. As the narrative unfolds, we learn that Damaris Verity, who is coming of age in the late 1870s and is the heir to her father's estate, decides that the only way to satisfy her personal goals is to take up the "writing of books" as her "vocation" (215). But as we eventually discover, this decision spurs a further realisation that the only means through which she can succeed as a writer is to confront the "mysterious and haunting question of sex" (491) and embrace her own desires.

In this chapter, I begin by looking at Damaris's destiny as a literary author in relation to the detailed family history that preoccupies the opening pages of the novel. I want to discuss the somewhat unexpected methods Malet employs in order to realise not only Damaris's professional ambitions but also her development of an independent selfhood. In particular, the opening chapters do not hint that authorship will be Damaris's calling. More to the point, these introductory sections scarcely make it plain that she is the protagonist of the novel. Here, I show that *Deadham Hard's* structure is strategic for the following reason: in the process of leading us to see Damaris's desire to become an author, we discover that Malet is involved in a crucial rewriting of conventional aspects of the nineteenth-century English novel. Part of my argument is to demonstrate that *Deadham Hard* defamiliarises features of both the inheritance plot and the marriage plot that are so common in works we generally associate with Victorian realism. Instead, Malet's narrative draws on the considerable resources of the aesthetic romance (with which Malet had been in dialogue from the beginning of her long career) in order to rethink the personal and professional opportunities for a young independent woman. Damaris's striving for autonomy is noticeably set at a time prior to the popularisation of the professional New Woman author in several well-known feminist novels from the *fin de siècle*. This slightly earlier cultural moment allows Malet to produce a history about a mid-Victorian woman's struggle to realise her independent selfhood prior to the more visible advancements that began to take place in women's lives in the final decades of the nineteenth century.

The 1870s are significant for Malet in relation to decisive shifts that took place in fiction. The aesthetic romances of Ouida (the professional name of Marie Louise Ramé) were at the height of their popularity and are particularly relevant here. Ouida's daring novels employ lush language to describe the decadent lifestyles of her flamboyant male and female characters, and her extravagant prose was admired by Malet, as well as such notable figures as Oscar Wilde and Max Beerbohm.[2] It is no accident that it is in Ouida's aesthetic romance *Othmar* (1885) that we discover a character also named Damaris, although she is a figure whose destiny is the complete reverse of Malet's Damaris in *Deadham Hard*. Ouida's Damaris, who is called "a great heiress in her own little way" (Ouida 1885, V.1: 111), falls in love with Othmar, a married man, but she never expresses to him her individual desires, which in private she makes clear when she admits, "I would give my body and my soul to him if he wished for them" (Ouida 1885, V.3: 229). Her denial of her own longings is so complete that she permanently silences herself by taking her own life. The fact that Malet rewrites the plot of female desire found in *Othmar*, however, is not to say that *Deadham Hard* constitutes an unbending critique of Ouida's fiction. To the contrary, in her 1919 novel Malet shows, through her beautifully textured prose, how elements of Ouida's romance provide the representative resources for Malet's romance plot. Malet, however, enables her own Damaris to affirm her passions and become "mistress of her powers, [and] self-realized" (Malet 1919, 433). To be sure, Damaris Verity's sexual awakening is hardly idealised. We will see that the life events of Malet's protagonist reveal that the opportunities for both intimacy and professional success remain especially scarce. Nonetheless, Damaris's decision to pursue a career as an author and embrace her sexual nature constitute an important claim about the legitimacy of female agency that was still relevant to ongoing debates about women's autonomy at the time of *Deadham Hard*'s publication.

Deadham Hard: The Verity Family Chronicle

In order to understand the unexpected narrative structure of *Deadham Hard*, it is important to recount salient details from the opening pages, which will be followed by an overview of the novel's main action. Malet's narrative begins with an account of the ways in which the house at Deadham Hard, a fictional town located in Hampshire that also gives its name to the estate, came into the hands of the Verity family. We learn that Thomas Clarkson Verity purchased the house "in the closing decade of the eighteenth century" (3), which suggests that this is not an *established* ancestral home. Instead, it was acquired at the time of the French Revolution, a period of political upheaval that undermined the *ancien régime*: "the goodly child Democracy was veritably ... in the act of being born among men" (5). That this transformational historical moment is crucial to the family history becomes clear when we learn that Thomas, a humanist, had enthusiastically "hurried off to Paris after the opening of the National Assembly and fall of the Bastille" (5). The spectacle of the guillotine and the possible threat to his own life sent Thomas fleeing back to England, bitterly disillusioned. His relief upon his return was so great that he bought the house at Deadham Hard, whose sea-wall was the first thing he saw when he set foot again in his beloved country. From the beginning, then, the narrative makes it clear that Deadham Hard symbolises refuge from political tumult. We discover that Thomas, who never married, left Deadham Hard to his nephew Charles, Damaris's father. Charles, who was a Commissioner stationed in India and Afghanistan, finds in Deadham Hard the respite he craves from his own experience of political unrest (especially the Sepoy Rebellion of 1857), just as Thomas did before him.

Why, we might wonder, does a narrative that ultimately focuses on a young woman's personal development expend energy on introducing this detailed history? In what follows, I argue that Malet's 1919 novel is making many striking claims about women's independence, claims that emerge largely through the narrative structure rather than overt polemic. By beginning with a chronicle of the family's genealogy, *Deadham Hard* sets in motion Malet's quiet interrogation of the perpetuation of patriarchal structures at home, in England's empire, and, what is more, in the form of fiction itself. Here, Robert Miles's discussion of the "philosophical romance"—a term he adopts from Hugh Murray's *The Morality of Fiction* (1805)—is useful in illuminating the larger structural organisation of Malet's novel. Miles defines the philosophical romance as "an aesthetic space, charged with the historic mission of making the ideological visible as ideology" (Miles 2001, 191). Catherine Delyfer has found this an apposite term for discussing Malet's bestselling novel of 1901, *The History of Sir Richard Calmady*, arguing that "Malet's narrative treatment of [the titular protagonist's] maimed body and damaged subjectivity performs a commentary on the status of disability while also testing the limitations of our ideological configurations, cultural definitions and artistic representations" (Delyfer 2011, 109). *Deadham Hard* produces a comparable type of cultural commentary, but in this instance Malet's interest is in the status of women in society. By setting up a structure in which plot developments familiar to novels about Victorian women are designed to be turned on their heads, her novel strikingly reveals the damaging restrictions inherent in these narrative blueprints for female behaviour. Furthermore, Miles's assertion that the philosophical romance is a genre that "exfoliates out of the germ of challenged legitimacy" (Miles 2001, 192) concentrates attention on *Deadham Hard*'s interest in precisely that: contesting traditional notions of legitimacy. At the most literal level, we have an estate that belongs to a father with one legitimate child (Damaris). Yet we also soon discover that Charles Verity has fathered an illegitimate son, with whom he has no relationship. On his deathbed, Charles designates his male offspring as the next in line after Damaris.

Especially important in this discussion of inheritance are women's relations with property. The Married Women's Property Act of 1870 is not mentioned at all in the novel. This is a fiction that foregrounds male ownership and features an illegitimate son but indicates that property ownership will ultimately fall to a woman. It addresses a very sensitive political issue, since the 1870 act allowed women to inherit property, but the doctrine of coverture would not be abolished until 1882. These concerns regarding lawful inheritance underlie deeper questions that emerge from the narrative about the relationship between gender and agency—namely, what it means to be a woman protagonist, what it means to be a woman who elects to have professional work, and what it means to be a woman who accepts and expresses her erotic desires.

One of the most striking ways that Malet reimagines narrative form in order to challenge assumptions about gender and agency is by structuring *Deadham Hard*, initially, around a male protagonist: Damaris's cousin Tom. Tom Verity is Thomas Clarkson Verity's great-great nephew, who comes to Deadham Hard to stay with his uncle Charles and cousin Damaris before moving to Bombay to assume an imperial post. With several chapters detailing his visit, the reader is led to believe that Tom's imperial adventures will be the focus of the narrative. As one reviewer complained in the *Dial*, "The construction … has a tendency to lead down blind alleys. Tom Verity, who enters the second chapter with all the attendant circumstance of a hero, holds the scene for fifty pages and then drops out" ("Notes of New Books" 1919, 350).

This expectation is reinforced by the closing lines of the narrative in the first of the novel's four "Books." A local ferryman says to Tom, "[I] [w]ish you a pleasant voyage and a rare good picking up of honours and glories, and gold and silver likewise, there across the seas and oceans where you're a-going to" (63).[3] It is fair to say that when *Deadham Hard* was first published in September 1919—not even a whole year after the horrific events of the First World War had come to an end—these glories of empire may have seemed to suggest that one of the arcs of history had been from empire to the First World War. Vincent Sherry asserts that

> [g]iven the massive scale of casualties in this first mass war, no degree of Victorian optimism could turn the Allied 'victory' in November 1918 into a new writ of legitimacy or restored warrant of authority for British interests of any far-reaching kind.
>
> (Sherry 2007, 112)

Malet's readers in 1919 would no longer have taken for granted Tom's notion in the 1870s that he is going to India as a "natural ruler" (13).

The narrative shift enacted in the second "Book," which supplants Tom with Damaris as the central figure, addresses concerns about the legitimacy of Britain's empire, though from an unexpected direction. The transition in protagonists replaces a history of empire documenting men's public lives with a private history of what it meant to be an Englishwoman possessing aspirations beyond domesticity. In this way, Britain's patriarchal system, one that underpins the ideology of empire by claiming that only certain people are qualified to exercise agency, is undermined on its own soil by a woman who asserts her rights to autonomy, professional work, and sexual expression. What is more, the narrative of a woman's interior development is implicitly granted the same level of importance as the male adventure plot that it replaces.

Damaris first comes into view in relation to her cousin's visit, and although we are not yet aware that she will be the protagonist, it is clear that Deadham Hard has very little to offer a young woman who is both intelligent and attractive. We learn that Damaris, whose mother died in childbirth, lived with her father in India until the age of six, and thereafter was educated at a boarding school in Paris. Her first encounters with Deadham Hard were on summer vacations when her Aunt Felicia would bring her back to England. This information reveals that, until recently, Damaris had only a distant connection with the estate. Furthermore, she still feels a profound tie to India, explaining, "[a]ll my caring for people, all my thinking, begins there" (38). Her isolation in the family home becomes evident when we learn that she has no intimate companions except her father, with whom she has an unusually close relationship. Little wonder that the visit from her cousin Tom marks a significant change in her routine; as the narrator notes, "[h]er world, before his advent, was other than that in which she now dwelt" (74). Tom attempts to flirt with Damaris, and the narrative teases the reader with the possibility that this might be a cousinship plot such as we find in Margaret Oliphant's *Miss*

Marjoribanks (1866). We soon perceive, however, that Damaris is sufficiently self-possessed to respond critically to Tom's gallant overtures. Tom, too, realises that in his interaction with her "he had not been at all a success" (58).

Little by little, the narrative discloses that Damaris's family situation is a bit more intricate and sensitive than she had previously realised. One day, she decides to venture by herself to a nearby sandbar where she makes a startling discovery: she learns about her half-brother Darcy Faircloth—a very attractive, and highly successful merchant sea captain. Her father's illicit liaison with Darcy's mother Lesbia, the owner of a public house who at the time was married to a much older man, at first greatly disturbs Damaris. This episode is significant, for it helps bring to the surface Damaris's own sexual desire. The narrator records how deeply Damaris is affected by learning of her father's history: "[i]t came too close, laying rough hands not only upon the deepest of her love and reverence for her father, but upon that still mysterious depth of her own nature, namely her apprehension of passion and of sex" (179). At the same time, though, Damaris delights in learning that she has a half-brother, a relative who expands her family circle, and for this reason she fosters an affectionate relationship with him.

Despite this development, the plot still suggests that Damaris's life remains unpromising. She and her father travel to Paris, accompanied by his best friend, Colonel Carteret, who has acted as a confidante to Damaris her whole life, and now also finds himself attracted to her. Carteret remains silent about his feelings, however, deeming them inappropriate in a man in his late forties. Damaris's social opportunities remain restricted to their small party, in spite of the change of scene. The only unanticipated aspect of this episode occurs when Damaris is reunited with Henrietta, an Englishwoman who—as recorded in detail in *Damaris*—inspired an intense passion in Charles Verity. And it is not only in Charles that Henrietta aroused fervent yearning. As a child in India, Damaris herself loved Henrietta to the point of obsession. Henrietta, a woman "almost extravagantly finished and feminine" (219), sees Damaris as an ideal catch for her husband's cousin, Marshall Wace, and she does all in her power to spark a romance. Here, then, the narrative suggests, is another incident that might go toward consolidating a marriage plot. However, the narrator's mocking tone in regard to Wace—his manner is described as "a subtle cross between the theatrical and the parsonic" (229)—indicates that he is not a promising partner. Furthermore, Damaris shows much greater interest in assisting her father with writing a history book than in this new beau. It is through this work as her father's secretary and the intimate acquaintance that she acquires with the "written word" (491) that Damaris begins to imagine a future in which she takes up authorship as her "vocation" (215). Alongside the discovery of her literary ambition, Damaris becomes aware of her erotic responsiveness to Carteret; but she is confused to realise that she has entered the "mystical empire . . . of sex as sex" (302). When Carteret returns to England, Damaris gratefully suspends her exploration of her feelings. Even if Damaris has found in Carteret a man who calls forth her passion (unlike Tom or Wace), it remains unclear whether this encounter will result in wedded union.

All of the episodes I have discussed occupy the first three-quarters of the novel. The final "Book" takes a completely different turn. Once Damaris comes back to Deadham Hard, she embarks on a series of steps to assert her individuality. This process begins in church when a new parish priest confronts the congregation to which Damaris belongs. He delivers a moralistic sermon that condemns the town's secret sins. This includes his denunciation of "[a]dulterous father, bastard son" (403), in which Damaris recognises "those whose honour was dearest to her, whom she boundlessly loved" (403). Since the vicar's words incense her, Damaris takes the risk of claiming Darcy as her blood relation in front of the other churchgoers. The community, angered by this outsider's sanctimonious hectoring, turns up in a show of support for her—making it clear that she is not to be stained by the taint of illegitimacy. Damaris, now having acted in bold independence, rises to several more challenges before the novel concludes. I briefly outline the novel's final action here, but later in my discussion I will consider the most transformational of these episodes in detail. After a short stay with Carteret, Charles returns to Deadham Hard and has a heart attack, dying a few days later. Following her loss, Damaris constructs a new direction for her life: she resolves to be a writer and embraces her sexuality. Almost immediately afterward, she encounters Carteret and discloses that he is the object of her erotic longings. Damaris cannot see that this sexual choice is extremely limited for a woman with her beauty, intelligence, and position as a property owner, and *Deadham Hard* ends before we know whether Damaris will take the implicitly unsuitable Carteret's hand in marriage.

Erotic Womanhood and Literary Femininity

As I have pointed out in my summary of the major events in *Deadham Hard*, Damaris appears for a short while to be a potential partner for her cousin. Once Tom leaves for India, however, the narrator depicts her for the first time in a style that suggests the centrality of her character:

> Damaris Verity, resting in a wicker deck-chair in the shade of the great ilex trees, found herself alone, free to follow her own vagrant thoughts, perceptions, imaginations without human let or hindrance. Free to dream undisturbed and interrogate both Nature and her own much wondering soul.
>
> (67)

Here, we see that Damaris's freedom takes a different form to that of her cousin. Rather than the ability to travel to India like Tom, as a woman, her freedom consists of being in control of her own thoughts. Moreover, she elevates both her "soul" and "Nature" as subjects worthy of her "interrogation." This is a pivotal moment. The transition to Damaris's "own vagrant thoughts" (67)—ones that implicitly stray from the path that others assume she should follow—suspends the potential marriage plot and inaugurates a narrative of female interiority and sexual awakening.

It becomes clear that in her personal life, even before she is consciously aware of her sexual nature, that Damaris is already attracted to fictions that explore dissident forms of desire. In a scene that is the catalyst for Damaris's erotic awakening, Malet not only draws explicit attention to the relationship between women's lives and fictional forms, but she also indicates some of the specific Victorian novels that *Deadham Hard* is reimagining. On a day that Damaris finds herself alone in the house, she chooses to enjoy her solitude in reading. We learn about Damaris's literary preferences, with the narrator interjecting a tone of mock disapproval, remarking that it is "undeniable" that she found "'Vathek,' more to her taste than 'Amy Herbert'; and, if the truth must be told, 'The Decameron,' and 'Tristram Shandy' more satisfying to her imagination than 'The Heir of Redcliffe' [*sic*] or 'The Daisy Chain'" (101–2). These allusions show that Damaris does not enjoy the works that her former governess, Theresa Bilson, admiringly considers as designed for "the greater preservation of female innocence" (101). The fictions in question are Elizabeth Sewell's *Amy Herbert* (1844), along with Charlotte M. Yonge's *The Heir of Redclyffe* (1853) and *The Daisy Chain* (1856). Both Sewell and Yonge were extremely popular mid-nineteenth-century authors whose realist novels reflect their dedication to Protestant ideals of virtuous womanhood. The inclusion of Yonge's *The Heir of Redclyffe* is not surprising, not least because this inheritance plot (with its undeserving male heir) "had a reception such as has been given to no other book in our language" (Cruse 1935, 50). The narrator's faux-embarrassment over the fictions Damaris prefers is derived from the nature of the more shocking content discovered in the favoured texts: the bold sexual tales of Boccaccio's *Decameron,* Lawrence Sterne's eccentric *Tristram Shandy* (1759–67), and the gothic romanticism of William Beckford's *Vathek* (1786). That Damaris is delighted by the liberties permissible in narratives of male adventure and finds no enjoyment in marriage plots such as those in *Amy Herbert*, *The Daisy Chain*, and *The Heir of Redclyffe* clearly indicates her personal desire for a destiny other than the one customarily prescribed for marriageable girls of her age.

This scene of reading marks a further turning point that leads to the circumstances of Damaris's emerging eroticism. It is on this occasion, noticeably, that her longing for India influences her selection of literary material, as the narrator notes, "[o]n this particular morning Damaris elected to explore to the Near East, in the vehicle of Eöthen's virile and luminous prose" (102). Here we discover that Damaris is drawn to English writer and historian Alexander Kinglake's extremely popular travel narrative, *Eöthen*, published anonymously in 1844. Reading *Eöthen* puts Damaris in a contemplative state; the narrator records that "[Damaris's] present mood sent her down to the shore to satisfy, or rather further stimulate, her nostalgia for the East by gazing out to sea" (104). These words remind us of Damaris's dislocation in rural Hampshire and profound attachment to colonial India. In a striking passage the narrator reveals the cause of Damaris's restless mood:

> the inward tumult of her awakening womanhood, and still more, perhaps, the tumult of awakening talent which had not as yet found its appointed means of expression. She was driven hither and thither by the push of her individuality to disengage itself from adventitious surroundings and circumstances, and realise its independent existence.
>
> (104)

As this passage clearly shows, Damaris is in the process of becoming a woman capable of exercising her autonomy, and we see that her sexual maturity and cultivation of talent are the core developments that will enable her to actualise her selfhood. Reading about the East spurs Damaris's tumultuous awakening, which in turn initiates her desire to gaze out to sea. This indicates that her exposure to non-European culture is key to Damaris's desire for opportunities beyond the restrictions of traditional English middle-class femininity.

The immediate step that Damaris takes in response to her tumultuous feelings is her solitary trip to the sandbar that, as we have seen, brings about the meeting with her half-brother Darcy, and further encourages her consciousness of desire. Once this initiation occurs, the narrative repeatedly draws attention to Damaris's growing sensitivity to erotic feelings. The detailed accounts of Damaris's sensations bring to mind such earlier narratives of sexual development as Kate Chopin's groundbreaking and controversial novel *The Awakening* (1899). Damaris shares with Edna Pontellier, the protagonist of Chopin's novel, an attraction to the water's edge, a motif that is important in representing the way that both of these women protagonists want to be freed from sexual limitations.[4] Malet's narration of Damaris's blossoming womanhood also makes a significant departure from such earlier accounts by revealing, with almost uncomfortable indirectness, that before she is even conscious of it she is already highly erotic, especially in relation to individuals for whom sexual feeling is unsanctioned: her father, her half-brother, and an older woman (Henrietta). This is one of the key ways that Malet rewrites the plot of the Victorian young woman: Damaris never embodies ideal purity and innocence.

At first, Damaris's unconscious sexuality is evident in her closeness with her father, to whom she makes breathtaking declarations of devotion, and whose reciprocated displays of physical affection are unusually intimate for a father and daughter. The narrator explains that if "the affection given appeared to trench on exaggeration, the affection returned was of kindred quality, fervid, self-realized, absorbing, and absorbed" (42). Once she meets her half-brother, Damaris's eroticism quickly extends to Darcy. The two interact in a manner highly unusual for siblings, not only admiring each other's appearance but also experiencing physical sensations one would expect to find in a romance plot, such as her odd reaction to "[t]aking stock" of Darcy: "Damaris's colour rose, her pulse quickened" (189). The use of rich aesthetic language makes the passion in these interactions palpable, but nothing is ever stated, only suggested through elaborate description.[5] The narrator, however, never represents these incestuous erotic attachments in a censorial manner. Moreover, these unsanctioned passions are instrumental in deflecting more orthodox, yet questionable, romantic interest. For example, the moment Damaris realises that Wace wants to seek her hand in marriage, she reassures her father that her emotions are undivided, responding to his query of whether she is in love with anyone by saying, "[o]nly with you, dearest" (364). Similarly, Carteret is deeply wounded when Damaris tells him that her love for her half-brother Darcy is superior to romance: "It belongs to something much more beautifully part of oneself" (292).

Furthermore, Damaris's unusual relationship with Darcy not only brings about her awareness of sexuality but is one of the primary means by which she comes to accept her father's illicit past and her own erotic desires. The principle reason for this shift in Damaris's thinking about her father's history is that Darcy is both a symbol of, and an advocate for, what we might call a morality of beauty, an ideology found in British aestheticism. Kathy Alexis Psomiades discusses how in art for art's sake there exists "an alternative moral system in which all that is beautiful is both good and pure: [the aesthetic body's] beauty is thus part of a pro-sex polemic" (Psomiades 1997, 72). When the greatly surprised Damaris asks Darcy about the union between his mother and their father saying, "wasn't it wrong?" (123), his response is to articulate this alternative moral system by excusing their liaison on the basis of their beauty: "They were young, and—mayn't we allow—they were beautiful ... They met and, God help them, they loved" (123). He then draws attention to how much he, the product of their union, delights in being alive: "I love life—love it too well to torment myself much about the manner of my coming by it" (124). This point is poignantly rendered, being delivered by a man who is himself so lovely that he is a symbol of the beauty of sex: when he first appears in the narrative he is said to be "notably, even astonishingly good-looking" (47). Damaris, whom we are told multiple times is "in love with beauty" (93), aligns herself, over time, with this alternative morality that beautifies sex.

While Damaris's relationship with father and half-brother represent one form of eroticism, Damaris's attraction to Henrietta Pereira adds a different dimension to the catalogue of Damaris's unorthodox passions. In Malet's earlier novel, *Damaris*, we find the details of the romance between woman and child that took place in India, in which, as a little girl, our protagonist suffered so greatly from being separated from Henrietta that she fell ill, almost to the point of death. Now, as a young woman encountering Henrietta in Paris, Damaris again feels deeply attracted: "Wasn't her darling Henrietta a being altogether captivating and unique? . . . Henrietta enthralled her eyes, enthralled her affection" (223). Henrietta's appeal, as we learn, is derived from her "charming" (219) superficiality: she is a person "in which all irregularities and originalities of Nature had suffered obliteration by the action of art" (219).

In Malet's characterisation of Henrietta, we find yet another direct engagement with Ouida's *Othmar*: Henrietta is clearly patterned after Othmar's wife, the Princess Nadine Napraxine. Nadine is Ouida's consummate female aesthete—a woman skilled in artifice, and a genius in manipulating others with her delicious sexual charm. In *Othmar*, Nadine represents the *femme fatale* in contrast to Damaris's role as the guileless maiden. In this way, the two women represent the familiar virgin/whore paradigm that was so pervasive in Victorian representations of female sexuality. In Malet's rewriting of *Othmar*, it is necessary for Damaris to reject the harmful model of self-serving sexuality that she finds in Henrietta and the artificial form of agency that Henrietta acquires through her manipulation of men. At the same time, Damaris Verity must claim her erotic longings, denouncing the passivity and preservation of purity that ended the life of her namesake in Ouida's novel.

Damaris's erotic development is a frequent focus of the narrative, but her "awakening talent" does not begin to move in any particular direction until she, her father, and Carteret travel to Paris. Once they are in France, Charles begins work on a project that draws on his experience as a Commissioner in the British Raj: he writes a "history of the reign of Shere Ali" (205). Damaris acts as an amanuensis to her father: the narrator notes that her work consists of writing from "dictation, verifying names and dates, [and] checking references and quotations" (214). Damaris's role as secretary to a male intellect aligns her plot with that of other Victorian novels that feature women whose talents are subjugated by men, such as—to give a well-known example—Dorothea Brooke's arduous transcription of her pompous husband Edward Casaubon's tiresome work, *The Key to All Mythologies*, in George Eliot's *Middlemarch* (1871).[6] For both Dorothea and Damaris, it is necessary to be freed from their respective duties in order for each woman to develop independence. Although after Casaubon's death Dorothea's intelligence is not directed into a professional project of her own, in the wake of her father's demise Damaris will put her literary training toward her own vocational pursuits. For as we discover, assisting her father has a profound effect on the ways in which Damaris starts to imagine a future for herself. The narrator notes, "Ambition prodded her on.—For mightn't she aspire to do it too, some day? Mightn't, granted patience and application, the writing of books prove to be her business, her vocation?" (214–5). Just as Damaris will inherit her father's property and replace him as the owner of the estate, so too will she inherit the skill of writing, and at the novel's close it seems she is destined to become an author. Damaris's apprenticeship shows that she is acquiring a kind of agency that we are meant to see as associated with a man's world, but which by way of her awakening womanhood she will possess and wield distinctly as a woman. Damaris's desire to have a profession, moreover, constitutes another disruption to the marriage plot, for although she is surrounded by young men who hover around her at fashionable parties, she does not fantasise about romantic possibilities and nuptial bliss. Instead, she imagines a life of professional creative work. Indeed, she is so occupied with her ambition that she fails to recognise that Wace is courting her.

Damaris's eager devotion to assisting her father in fashioning beautiful prose—and thus allowing her "awakening talent" to develop—is not matched by an equally energetic abandonment to experiencing her erotic desires. The first time that she becomes fully conscious of her responsiveness to Carteret's demonstrations of passion she realises that any personal indulgence in sexuality is likely to endanger her autonomy. We witness her loss of self-control when, following Carteret's gift of an extravagant string of pearls, she first recognises her attraction to him. In a long scene that narrates her turbulent emotions, the reader witnesses her transition from exultation to confusion:

> this riot of the blood and heady rapture, this conflict of shame and triumph in which the animal part of one has so loud a word to say—she didn't like it ... Neither did she like herself in relation to it—like this unknown, storm-swept Damaris.
>
> (331)

Here, we see that Damaris does not enjoy feeling overcome with strong desire because her sense of self is overpowered. Damaris's halting progress towards choosing to embrace her sexuality, then, is due in part to her fear that experiencing her longings will undermine her increasingly daring assertions of independence. I make this point in order to emphasise not only the gravity of Damaris's conflict with her sexual nature, but also to set up my discussion about how this tension is manifested in *Deadham Hard*'s conclusion, in which the immediate result of expressing her passion is to cede some of her agency to Carteret.[7]

"[N]o longer a passive but an active agent": Damaris's Independent Womanhood

Before Damaris begins the decisive chain of self-assertions that will lead to her declaration of desire, the narrative suggests an altogether different possibility for her destiny, one that proposes an unprecedented outcome for an Englishwoman in the 1870s. Once Charles and Damaris have returned to what she experiences as the "stagnant" (376) atmosphere of Deadham Hard, Charles receives an invitation to return to India as "Lieutenant-Governor of an Indian presidency" (446). This post would allow for Damaris not only to go with him, but also provide the unusual opportunity for her to have a role in the government. As she reflects, she would be among "the handful of elect persons who count in [India's] social, political and administrative life" (447). This unlooked-for opportunity would allow her to be an independent woman and provide her with a ready-made profession. Scarcely have father and daughter agreed that they mean to accept the offer than Charles has a heart attack and only lives for a few more days. It is possible to read this plot reversal as a missed opportunity for Damaris's liberation from the many layers of restriction that she will continue to battle by staying in England. That Damaris must remain in Hampshire, then, makes her self-motivated desire for personal and professional transformation all the more remarkable.

In the wake of her father's death, Damaris becomes the mistress of Deadham Hard, and it is here, under the weight of disappointment at losing her opportunity for a new life—and even more so the grief of losing her father—that she nevertheless finds the means to assert her independence. Determined to assume her new position as mistress, Damaris goes out into nature in order to process her mourning in a deliberate effort to "begin again" (500). She reflects that she needs to take responsibility over her domestic establishment, but she also longs for more to do than simply run the house. The narrator records Damaris's reflection: "[h]er life had been full, it must find fresh purpose, fresh interest and occupation, in a word, be refilled" (491). It is at this juncture that the excitement she had earlier felt at the prospect of authorship reasserts itself: "[l]iterature allured her. She dreamed of wonderful tellings, dreamed of the engrossing joys of the written word" (491). That it has taken Damaris so long to arrive at this point following her initial attraction to authorship indicates how critical it was that she be freed from her father's authority in order to pursue individual action.

Becoming a writer, however, will hardly be a seamless process for Damaris. With her renewed interest in pursuing a literary vocation comes the blunt recognition that she is not equipped for authorship. This revelation occurs when she muses about what kind of fiction she will write, asking herself, "in what form—poetry, essay, history, novel?—The extreme limitation of her own knowledge, or rather the immensity of her own ignorance, confronted her" (491). Here, she becomes aware that the area of her life that requires her greatest increase in knowledge is "the mysterious and haunting question of sex" (491). The narrative therefore makes a striking claim about female authorship: in order to succeed, the woman writer must act on her eroticism. In this regard, Malet further rewrites Eliot's plot in *Middlemarch*. For if, as David Kurnick asserts, "the erotic is the ground of Dorothea's exclusion from insight" (Kurnick 2007, 584), Malet reconfigures this relationship and imagines female desire as the means through which Damaris must acquire the knowledge that she lacks. Moreover, as Damaris muses, she must accept her erotic longings in order to have the chance to "play an individual part in the beautiful, terrible earthly scene" (492). Sexual experience is thus shown to have an instrumental purpose, one that facilitates maturity of insight and personal growth, even while making it clear that this wished-for encounter may prove painful and involve risks for a young woman.

Furthermore, counter to the expectations that surrounded marriageable young women of Damaris's generation—as Regenia Gagnier reminds us, "the official Victorian view of female sexuality was that it did not exist except for purposes of procreation" (Gagnier 1986, 157)—the narrative demonstrates that Damaris's sexuality has no connection with any inborn yearning to bear children and enjoy motherhood. Instead, Damaris's erotic passions serve self-expressive and creative purposes, and it is even suggested that they will assist her in meeting her professional goals. Here, we have a formulation about sexuality and art that is once again aligned with aestheticism. Gagnier has written about the way in which "art for art's sake was allied with a defense of sex for sex's sake, or non-reproductive sex" (Gagnier 1999, 284). In Malet's formulation, we have something like sex for art's sake: a championing of creative productivity that is enabled first by the experience of pleasure. Malet's narrative makes professional success dependent upon experiencing erotic satisfaction, thereby revealing that the two are necessary corollaries.

The narrator explains why Damaris's success is intertwined with her sexuality, as we can see in the language that describes the young woman's return to Deadham Hard: "[a]nother Damaris came home to the Damaris who had set forth—a Damaris rested, refreshed, invigorated, no longer a passive but an active agent" (493). And once she enters her property, she is immediately confronted by all of its symbolic meaning:

> The house was stronger than she. But—but—only stronger, surely, if she consented to turn craven and give way to it?—Whereupon

> she consciously, of set purpose, defied the house, denied its right to browbeat thus and enslave her.
>
> (493–4)

This passage dramatises a struggle for power with the house in which Damaris faces the menacing potential of patriarchal subjugation that threatens to overpower her in spite of the fact that she is now the owner. Damaris is refusing, as the title of this romance implies, this hard deadening of her subjectivity. Just as Damaris took the place of the 'hero' Tom Verity as the focus of the narrative, she now also takes the place of her father as the mistress of the Hard not only in name, but also as its "active agent."

Even though Damaris's defiance is a significant triumph, she must at once face another challenge, for upon entering the house she discovers that Henrietta has recently been there. Damaris's interior dialogue makes clear the gravity of the situation: "wasn't she confronted with another battle—a worse one than that with the house, namely, a battle with her long-ago baby-love, and her father's love too—Henrietta" (498). The purpose of Henrietta's visit, as we learn from Damaris's discussion with her Aunt Felicia, was to insinuate that Damaris is in debt to the love-struck Wace, and marriage is the only form of adequate recompense. Henrietta's scheming clearly attempts to force Damaris into a marriage in which she would occupy a familiar role as a literary Victorian maiden who feels gratitude for a man's attentions, and even a sense of obligation for his feelings toward her. We find such a scene in one of Damaris's cast-off novels: *The Daisy Chain*, where Meta Rivers, "Charlotte Yonge's ideal woman in every respect" (Dennis 1988, ix), realises that she might be a man's "best beloved," and it causes her to feel "warmth and gratitude" (Yonge 1988, 563). Such a conditioned response obviously erases the woman as an "active agent," making her simply a grateful vessel for the man to pour his feelings into. Damaris, however, will not become the obliging maiden in Henrietta's plot, and she utterly denounces Henrietta's renewed attempts, saying to her aunt in a voice that is "gravely proud": "my attitude is unchanged … I didn't want to marry Marshall Wace then … I don't want to marry him or have him care for me one bit more now" (498). Furthermore, Damaris makes it clear that she fully understands—and repudiates—Henrietta and her self-serving sexuality, describing her as "soulless, finished, and exquisitely artificial to her finger-tips" (494).

Still, in the light of this decisive victory the novel's final pages offer something of a conundrum for the reader. Damaris boldly takes action on her resolve to experience the world of sex and that very afternoon expresses her desire to Carteret. While this is an audacious move, the fact that Damaris's erotic choice is her father's best friend—a man almost three decades older than herself and something of a father figure—does not resonate with the same level of defiant autonomy as her other acts of agency.[8] Patricia Lorimer Lundberg, in one of the few scholarly discussions of *Deadham Hard,* laments this conclusion, asserting that such an ending exposes Malet to the criticism that she "lived a life wider and more significant than that she affords her protagonists" (Lundberg 2003, 374). Anna Catherine Priebe takes a similar view, reading the closing passages as a plain indication that Damaris has chosen "the comparative safety of marriage with Colonel Carteret" (Priebe 2003, 73). Indubitably, the ending displays the conventionality that Lundberg and Priebe mourn. But this scene requires some further unpacking. Carteret initiates a mutual confession of attraction by declaring, "I love you" (502). After a substantial explanation about the development of his feelings, he discloses that he has been tormented by "[t]he seven devils of desire," and then declares, "of which you knew nothing, bless you" (503). Damaris, who has been silent, now cuts him off and counters, "I'm not sure that I do know nothing" (503).

Damaris's unexpected rebuttal of Carteret's assumption about her innocence of sexual matters is powerful and accords with her final words to him, that it is "beautiful" to have him "for quite [her] own" (503). Damaris's dissident eroticism (in relation to her father, her brother, and Henrietta) has been superseded by what promises to be a conventional heterosexual alliance. It is, though, worth bearing in mind that this episode wraps up very quickly, with no opportunity for the narrator to comment upon the prospect of this union any further. Without guidance from the narrator, it remains difficult to determine what tone the scene is striking in relation to the events that have come before. The reader is left to decide whether one is to sense complacency in the union with Carteret, or, at a minimum, be regretful that the ostensibly charming and attractive fiancé is undeniably the best partner that the novel offers. In the end, we are left in suspense, not entirely sure what the future might hold for an unconventional young woman who has tried to lend personal and professional authority to her longings. It remains unknown whether Carteret's hellish "seven devils of desire" will satisfy or destroy this young literary author and female heir who has finally emerged as the sexually assertive protagonist of *Deadham Hard.*

Notes

My thanks to Jane Ford and Alexandra Gray for their generous feedback on early drafts of this essay, and to Joseph Bristow for his insightful comments and support.

1 All subsequent references to Lucas Malet's *Deadham Hard* (1919) will be given as page numbers in the text.

2 Malet singles Ouida out as one of the most important British women novelists in "The Progress of Woman: in Literature" (1888). Malet calls her a "genius" (299) and praises her for rejecting the pressure to perpetuate the ideal of domestic womanhood, writing: "Ouida, by her refusal to circumscribe

her art by '[what was thought] desirable' for artificially-innocent and modest young ladies from eighteen to eight-and-forty, has unquestionably helped to give [the works of modern English artists] a shove down towards the horizon" (299).

3 Readers familiar with *Damaris* would know that, in spite of that novel's title, the narrative was in fact more about Charles's exploits in India than his very young daughter. These readers would thus be set up to also expect *Deadham Hard*'s plot to focus on foreign conquest.

4 Joseph Allen Boone has argued that female passion is repeatedly represented in terms of moving water in "narratives of female sexual awakening ... at the beginning of the twentieth century" (64). Boone argues that while many of these texts can be found in the modernist canon, there are also several "whose ostensibly realistic formats are nonetheless subtly, and profoundly, infused with the rhythms and reverberations that evoke the power of libidinal activity and unconscious desire to shape not only human subjectivity but external 'reality'" (5). In this motif, then, we see one of the ways in which *Deadham Hard* rewrites Victorian plots while contributing to a literary development typically associated with high modernism.

5 Talia Schaffer has written about the ways in which Malet's gorgeous language enabled her to represent deformity, incestuous passion, lesbian romance, and shocking scenes of eroticism in her bestselling novel *The History of Sir Richard Calmady* (1901). See Schaffer (1999).

6 Throughout her career, Malet rewrote the plot of the female amanuensis a number of times. In her 1888 novel, *A Counsel of Perfection,* Lydia Casteen is secretary to her father and gives up the possibility of marriage to care for him instead. Her erotic desires are awoken, and although she comes to recognise her limitations, she does not overcome them. Lundberg asserts that Lydia "epitomizes repressed desire" (Lundberg 2003, 120). In *Adrian Savage* (1911), Malet's portrait of Joanna Smyrthwaite is perhaps her most bleak imagining of this figure, since Joanna, freed by her father's death from the necessity of suppressing her own needs, pursues her sexual desire for her cousin Adrian, only to take her own life when her feelings are not reciprocated.

7 The dilemma of finding and losing oneself in sexual passion is one that Malet had explored in previous novels, and a celibate friendship had more than once been the favoured solution. See, for example, the glorification of the pure friendship between Dominic and Poppy in *The Far Horizon* (1906).

8 It is possible to see in this arrangement an echo of Malet's own unhappy marriage to William Harrison (1840–1897), who was the close friend and former curate of her father, the Anglican divine Charles Kingsley. Harrison was older than her by twelve years.

Works Cited

Boone, Joseph Allen. 1998. *Libidinal Currents: Sexuality and the Shaping of Modernism.* Chicago, IL: University of Chicago Press.

Cruse, Amy. 1935. *The Victorians and Their Books.* London: George Allen and Unwin Ltd.

Delyfer, Catherine. 2011. *Art and Womanhood in Fin-de-Siècle Writing: The Fiction of Lucas Malet, 1880–1931.* London: Pickering and Chatto.

Dennis, Barbara. 1988. "Introduction" to Charlotte M. Yonge. *The Daisy Chain.* London: Virago.

Gagnier, Regenia. 1986. *Idylls of the Marketplace: Oscar Wilde and the Victorian Public.* Stanford, CA: Stanford University Press.

———. 1999. "Productive Bodies, Pleasured Bodies: On Victorian Aesthetics." In *Women and British Aestheticism*, edited by Talia Schaffer and Kathy Alexis Psomaides, 270–89. Charlottesville: University Press of Virginia.

Kurnick, David. 2007. "An Erotics of Detachment: *Middlemarch* and Novel-Reading as Critical Practice." *ELH* 74(3): 583–608.

Lundberg, Patricia Lorimer. 2003. *An Inward Necessity: The Writer's Life of Lucas Malet.* New York: Peter Lang.

Malet, Lucas. 1888. "The Progress of Woman: In Literature." *The Universal Review* 2(7): 295–301.

———. 1919. *Deadham Hard: A Romance.* New York: Dodd, Mead and Co.

Miles, Robert. 2001. "What is a Romantic Novel?" *Novel: A Forum on Fiction* 34(2): 180–201.

"Notes on New Books." 1919. *The Dial* 67(801): 350.

Ouida. *Othmar.* Vol. I. 1885. London: Chatto and Windus.

———. *Othmar.* Vol. III. 1885. London: Chatto and Windus.

Priebe, Anna Catherine. 2003. "'May I disturb you?': British Women Writers, Imperial Identities, and the Late Imperial Period, 1880–1940." PhD diss, University of Cincinnati. http://gateway.proquest.com/openurl?url_ver=Z39.882004&res_dat=xri:pqdiss&rft_val_fmt=info:ofi/fmt:kev:mtx:dissertation&rft_dat=xri:pqdiss:3093391 (accessed January 19, 2018).

Psomiades, Kathy Alexis. 1997. *Beauty's Body: Femininity and Representation in British Aestheticism.* Stanford, CA: Stanford University Press.

Schaffer, Talia. 1999. "Connoisseurship and Concealment in *Sir Richard Calmady:* Lucas Malet's Strategic Aestheticism." In *Women and British Aestheticism*, edited by Talia Schaffer and Kathy Alexis Psomaides, 44–62. Charlottesville: University Press of Virginia.

Sherry, Vincent. 2007. "T. S. Eliot, Late Empire, and Decadence." In *Modernism and Colonialism*, edited by Richard Begam and Michael Valdez Moses, 111–35. Durham, NC: Duke University Press.

Yonge, Charlotte M. 1988. *The Daisy Chain.* London: Virago.

Part 3

Malet and Her Contemporaries

7 Reorienting the Bildungsroman

Progress Narratives, Queerness, and Disability in *The History of Sir Richard Calmady* and *Jude the Obscure*

Jill R. Ehnenn

> But I am not as other men are. I am a creature by myself, a unique development as much outside the normal social, as I am outside the normal physical law. ... And so if I do queer things, things off the conventional lines, who will be surprised?
>
> (Malet 2003, 170)

This essay examines intersecting discourses of disability and queerness in context of Victorian narratives about progress in general and progress vis-à-vis legacies and heritability in particular. The popular genre of the bildungsroman or, novel of education, provided the Victorians with progress narratives that reinforced their dreams for industrial and imperial expansion. By the 1890s, however, Britain saw fierce debates over eradicating primogeniture, reports of many 'unfit' men serving in the Second Boer War forced the country to acknowledge its weakening national legacy, and modern eugenics emerged, promising to counter *fin-de-siècle* 'degeneration' and restore the nation's strength. In the context of such anxieties about failed inheritances and about ensuring the forward motion of individuals, families, and the nation, I examine two *fin-de-siècle* bildungsromane whose protagonists' development are shaped by inherited curses: Lucas Malet's *The History of Sir Richard Calmady* (1901) and Thomas Hardy's *Jude the Obscure* (1895).[1] Following Sara Ahmed's *Queer Phenomenology*, I am interested in how these novels orient their protagonists in the world—characters who reside at or near the limits of intelligibility. My essay asks how do queerness and disability operate in these texts, making certain kinds of lives and movement possible while foreclosing others? What does such an inquiry contribute to thinking about genre's relationship to national narratives, to considering the role of queerness and disability vis-à-vis literary and cultural history, and to thinking about intersections of queerness and disability in crip perspectives, today?

This essay demonstrates how, in these unique bildungsromane, the inherited curse does not reinforce but instead works against a genre otherwise characterised by impulses to enforce normalcy through compulsory able-bodiedness and compulsory heterosexuality. While the outcomes of each of the curses are 'real,' these inherited curses, ironically, also illustrate that "the very idea that bodies 'have' a natural orientation is exposed as fantasy in the necessity of the enforcement of that orientation, or its maintenance as a social requirement for intelligible subjectivity" (Ahmed 2006, 85). Thus, the curses in *Calmady* and *Jude* offer unlikely opportunities to challenge conventional narratives—in their time and ours—about queerness and disability.

Progress: Nation and Fiction

Victorian England's obsession with progress has been widely noted. Captains of industry hoped the Industrial Revolution would advance England's wealth and strength, and they used the Great and subsequent Exhibitions to display England's manufacturing prowess. Progress also meant expansion, and by the end of the century the sun never set on Britain's sprawling empire. In the sciences, from geology, to thermodynamics, to evolution, narratives emerged of an ever-dynamic planet, a story increasingly slanted and popularised with promises that change meant improvement.[2] Societies were established to better the status of women, the education of the masses, and the aesthetic sensibility, and thereby the morality, of the working classes.[3] The new fields of sexology and psychology also provided compelling and influential developmental narratives.

These progress narratives, especially by century's end, convey a sense of urgency. Perhaps, given increasing secularisation, these Victorian progress narratives replaced for many the Christian narratives of every man's 'pilgrim's progress' that had provided direction in a fallen world and uncertain present. Certainly, despite the ubiquity of discourse invoking progress, many late Victorians worried Britain might *not* be progressing: critiques of industry's pollution and capitalism's corruption, anxiety that Britain would collapse like the Roman Empire before it, and fears that humans, both individually and as a society, could devolve or, in Max Nordau's parlance, "degenerate" (Nordau 1895), raised the stakes for the notion of progress.[4]

In *fin-de-siècle* discourses, anxieties about progress converge with anxieties regarding legacies and heritability. During this time, Lord Chancellor Farrer Herschell was twice defeated in hotly debated attempts to eradicate primogeniture in the case of intestate properties in his Law of Inheritance Amendment Bill. Had the bill passed it would have brought England's inheritance laws up to date with most other Western countries; it failed by a thin margin.[5] Also, in these years, Britain reluctantly acknowledged its weakening national legacy in reports revealing that over forty percent of Second Boer War soldiers were untrained and physically unfit. In addition to widespread panic-mongering brought about by press coverage, the public also got caught up in a bitter and highly publicised debate between investigative journalist W.T. Stead, who opposed the war, and author and physician Arthur Conan Doyle, who supported it. Paula Krebs (2004) observes, the "fight about the nature of the Victorian solider appears to have less to do with their positions on the Boer War than with their relations to turn-of-the-century notions of masculinity, Darwinism, and social progress" (83). And of course, the *fin de siècle* soon gave rise to beliefs that England's legacy could be strengthened by eugenics.

Intimately related to Victorian anxieties over national progress, legacy, and heritability were questions regarding individual progress: how do we learn who we are, who we should become, and how? More apropos to the discussion I will develop here, how do we explore these questions as *embodied* subjects? And what of social norms—how similar to one another can or should we be, and how different? These issues of personal development are questions for any age, but for the Victorians they were particularly pressing, and resonant with larger questions of national progress. They are also central questions for queer and disability studies.

Personal progress and social norms (and more implicitly, the relationship between these concepts and embodiment) are precisely the issues explored by the bildungsroman, or novel of education/development, which rose in the nineteenth century and established the novel as the most influential literary form of the period. As numerous critics agree,

> this form [contains] a plot so stylized that it becomes archetypal. … The hero of the Bildungsroman is usually an orphan, (though he may only be spiritually orphaned): he is personally gifted but of an ambiguous, or at any rate, not entirely secure social position; in the course of the novel he undergoes initiation, moving from innocence to experience, often from a simple rural life to a more sophisticated urban one. He falls in love, usually more than once (usually the stereotype would be one false love and one true).
>
> (G. Robert Stange qtd. in Giordano 1972, 582–3)

In the bildungsroman, the hero's journey to maturity brings success, but he is "devastated by a reversal of fortune; from this suffering he learns the moral or social truth that makes it possible for him to rise and live again" (Stange qtd. in Giordano 1972, 583). Notably, by the bildungsroman's conclusion, the hero's status is less than before his fall, and generally, less than the gifts s/he displayed as a child would imply.[6]

From *David Copperfield* to *Portrait of the Artist as a Young Man*, and from *Jane Eyre* to *Harry Potter*, this most influential of novelistic forms performs important cultural work in its role as a progress narrative. As most scholars of the genre observe, the bildungsroman's goal is not to turn the promising young protagonist into an outstanding adult; rather, the goal is development for social assimilation; to that end, often the reader observes the hero reaching the happy ending by ultimately settling in love and/or vocation. The goal of the Victorian bildungsroman in particular, like so many other nineteenth-century discourses, is to accomplish what Lennard Davis terms "enforcing normalcy" (Davis 1995). Thus, I would argue, following Jerome Buckley (1974), that the bildungsroman's seeming focus on agency and personal efforts are mere diversion. It is primarily a didactic genre; accordingly, readers ought not contemplate the protagonist's actions as ends in themselves. Rather, readers are, ultimately, to contemplate their own personal development, within strict parameters.

In so doing, the bildungsroman trains readers to recognise difference—behavioural and physical—in the main and supporting characters. Victorian supporting characters are often marked by behavioural quirks and physical difference, deviate from sex-gender norms, and embody, as Martha Stoddard Holmes and David Mitchell and Sharon Snyder observe, well-worn codes to signify equations between body and soul, such as the evil hunchback, the pure maiden wasting from illness, and the chronically ill, desexualised adult male.[7] As Mitchell and Snyder (1997) argue, such literary rhetoric functions as narrative prosthesis, with differently bodied supporting characters not present as fully developed subjects, but as plot devices that move the story or protagonist forward, create diversions or delays, or otherwise affect the novel's pacing.

Although nonnormate[8] secondary characters in the bildungsroman function as narrative prosthesis and/or metaphor; notably, the genre often figures a hero's oddness as potential, as in Jane Eyre's "unfeminine" strong will and passion. Eventually, however, strangeness in the protagonist must be reined in, even completely erased. Thus ultimately, the bildungsroman teaches its protagonists and its readers to see difference in order to develop, better overcome it, and thereby, better assimilate. In this manner, the bildungsroman reinforces existing social ideals.

If the bildungsroman's work is to model personal development, what of protagonists who are not wholly intelligible as subjects—who reside, as Judith Butler describes, at the "limits of intelligibility"? How does the world of the novel, which both reflects and affects the "real" world, determine how such subjects move through time and space? Per Merleau-Ponty, if "the body is no longer merely *an object in the world* ...; it is our *point of view on the world*" (1964, 5), what can we learn about representations of such subjects? Following Sara Ahmed's work on queer phenomenology, here I am interested in how the bildungsroman orients such characters—those at or near the limit of intelligibility. In the novel of development, what literary devices and what kinds of potentially "real" events make certain kinds of movement possible while foreclosing others? Who and what can such subjects direct their energies against?

There are numerous ways of addressing these questions, but here I've chosen to examine *The History of Sir Richard Calmady* and *Jude the Obscure* because these novels feature characters that could be said to reside at the limits of intelligibility, yet are notable in three useful ways. First, the nonnormate subject is not merely a secondary character who functions as a narrative prosthesis but the protagonist, which is surprising. Second, the protagonist's development is problematised by his difference, which is *not* surprising, but nonetheless is interesting since (*contra* Mitchell and Snyder) it is remarkable that Victorian nonnormate subjects have a *bildung* at all. Third, the protagonists' differences are attributed, at least in part, to a curse. As I will show, considering how these curses are experienced and negotiated has, significantly, queer, crip implications for the concept of personal development, especially in context of late-Victorian fascinations with progress narratives and the era's tension-filled discourses regarding legacy construed as heritability.

Curses, Perverts, and Dwarves

The History of Sir Richard Calmady and *Jude the Obscure* were widely read in their time. They are long and complex, so the glosses that follow aim to highlight the *bildung* of each nonnormate protagonist vis-à-vis each novel's curse. The eponymous protagonist of *The History of Sir Richard Calmady* is born to Katherine, an aristocratic widow. Richard is beautiful and brilliant, but with impaired mobility and stature because his feet are where his knees would be. His father's family has been cursed for centuries, when an ancestor impregnated but refused to marry his forester's daughter, and the child was killed by its father's carriage wheels, which severed its body just above the knee. The bereaved mother "cursed the man who had brought this ruin upon her and his descendant … declaring … no owner of Brockhurst" should live to old age until a "fatherless babe" is born with "a foot that will never know stocking or shoe" (Malet 2003, 19).

Katherine loves the disabled boy fiercely for his dead father's sake and attempts to shelter him, but, as Richard matures, he becomes increasingly uncomfortable with his difference. All medical interventions fail until learning to ride gives him mobility and independence. He succeeds at Oxford and Katherine facilitates his engagement to a neighbour, Lady Constance, who, repulsed by his nonnormate body, jilts him. In contrast, his cousin, Helen, fetishises his body and repeatedly attempts to seduce him. Richard discovers he has a voracious sexual appetite and pursues a "Rake's Progress," learning that women find his body both powerfully despicable and desirable. Ultimately, in an act of erotic displacement for incestuous desires toward his mother, he sleeps with Helen. Haunted by his actions and the family curse, Richard succumbs to self-loathing and returns to the care of his mother and another cousin, Honoria, a New Woman who has long had homoerotic feelings for Katherine. Honoria and Richard are drawn together by a newfound desire to help others and reject their privileged lifestyle. They enter a chaste marriage, adopt a child, and establish a home for men injured in industrial accidents. The novel closes with Honoria, Richard, and Katherine happily living together in a relationship erotically charged with lesbian and incestuous desires.

Scholarly interpretations of Malet's text rightly observe, in Richard, a refutation of her father's Muscular Christianity; they also note Richard is like a woman because his disability confines him in the domestic sphere (Srebrnik 1994, 200). Many also read Richard as a displacement of lesbian desire, both in the novel's representation of sexual freedom during his rake's progress, and more queerly, in his relationship with Honoria in which they, sexologically speaking, create a couple of perfect inverts (Srebrnik 1994, 203). In Talia Schaffer's introduction to her edition of the novel, she astutely demonstrates that Malet strategically employs the style and language of aestheticism in order to distract the reader from scandalous textual elements, including lesbian desire, fellatio, sex with prostitutes, and the "monstrous" excesses of the text's various bodies (Malet 2003, xv). More recently, Rachel O'Connell examines Richard as a sympathetic character and employs Rosemarie Garland Thomson's work on staring, to consider how *Calmady* sustains "the strange intimacy between reader and extraordinary body" (O'Connell 2012, 111). My reading of Malet's novel draws upon these foundations and also critiques recent analyses by Catherine Delyfer and Kathleen Miller who each interpret *Calmady* from a disability studies perspective in relation to conventions associated with the gothic.

In a novel published six years prior to *Calmady*, the reader meets Thomas Hardy's Jude Fawley, a sensitive, working-class orphan. His schoolmaster, Mr. Phillotson, encourages in Jude intellectual habits no one else appreciates. Loneliness and alienation seem to be Jude's destiny; even in youth his aunt mysteriously portends that the Fawleys seem cursed in marriage: "don't you ever marry. 'Tisn't for the Fawleys to take that step any more" (Hardy 2008, 8). Jude uneasily matures, and, too bookish for sustained work or friendship, aspires to attend the novel's version of Oxford: Christminster. Jude's plans derail when he marries Arabella, who seduces him, faking pregnancy. Miserable, Jude botches a suicide attempt, Arabella heads to Australia, and Jude moves to Christminster to work on the university's buildings as a stonemason while unsuccessfully trying to gain admission to them as a student. Jude also meets his cousin Sue, a New Woman whose intellectual interests and religious scepticism match his own. They become reacquainted with Phillotson and Sue trains at his school.

Ironically, Sue and Phillotson marry shortly after Jude realises he loves her; the marriage is an unhappy one, marked by Sue's sexual revulsion for her husband. Jude increasingly drowns his sorrows in liquor and Arabella returns with a child, "Little Father Time," whom she deposits with Jude. Both Jude and Sue get divorces and, realising they are soulmates, embark upon a mutual romance whose intense happiness is marred by poverty, their refusal to marry, and social disapprobation regarding their growing family. Little Father Time hangs his siblings and himself, leaving a note, "Done because we are too menny" (325). Sue suffers a breakdown and renounces her atheism, declaring God has punished her for divorcing Phillotson. She remarries Phillotson, and in a final self-obliterating act, submits to his sexual attentions, living the rest of her life as a shadow of her former self. Meanwhile, Arabella tricks Jude, in his drunken misery, into remarrying her. At the novel's end, Jude sees Sue, who declares she still loves but cannot be with him. He remembers his aunt's warning that his family's marriages were cursed, and how, in youth, he identified with rooks in a field who, "seemed, like himself, to be living in a world that did not want them" (9). Jude then passively invites the chill that eventually kills him, by spending the night in the freezing rain.

Critics often consider this bildungsroman alongside others with multiple protagonists; when viewed from Sue's perspective, it is a conventional (if dark) example of the genre. However, reading the novel through Jude, as I do here, is more complicated. Some critics consider his passive suicide as contemporary readers would have: a horrific act and evidence of complete failure. Others, including myself, view it through the pagan conventions Jude himself would have embraced: "Jude's act of self-destruction may be seen as an heroic affirmation of his personal being" (Giordano 1984, 30). Many critics argue that the novel contributes to New Woman critiques of traditional marriage and femininity, and some scholarship addresses mental illness in Hardy's novels by examining alcoholism in *The Mayor of Casterbridge* or *Jude's* Sue Bridehead in the context of Victorian notions of neurasthenia. However, to date, no one has suggested a queer and/or disability studies perspective would yield useful insights. Nonetheless, reading *Jude* here alongside *Calmady*, a contemporaneous bildungsroman frequently analysed within queer/crip frameworks, highlights similarities between the two novels that, taken together, make possible my arguments that these unique texts ultimately subvert late-Victorian discourses of progress, normalcy, sexuality, and disability.[9]

These bildungsromane could invite multiple comments regarding an embodied subject's development, but from here I will focus, from a phenomenological perspective informed by Sara Ahmed, on the curse inherited by the novels' protagonists. I begin by observing that these curses are firmly entangled with the protagonists' relationships to compulsory able-bodiedness and compulsory reproductive heterosexuality. Richard's family curse results in his nonnormate body. Subsequently, he feels his unthinkable, unrepresentable desires for love and progeny render him less than human: "my fate is fixed, you know. … I am condemned to live a cow's life and die a cow's death" (Malet 2003, 202), and less than a man, "I wanted a wife because I wanted a son—a—son to prove to me the entirety of my own manhood" (245). Further, the 'monstrousness' of sexual desire for a disabled person, such as Helen's intimacies with Richard, is rendered perverse. The novel obfuscates such 'perversions' with aesthetic language: in the infamous fellatio scene, "her hands grasped the two arms of Richard's chair" but the focus throughout is on her gown, "a garment of such color as that which the waves of the Adriatic might have clothed the rosy limbs of new-born Aphrodite, as she rose from the cool translucent sea deeps" (180).

In *Calmady* it is clear that Richard's education, development, sexuality, and sense of otherness are intensely affected by his embodied differences, which the novel directly attributes to the family curse. In comparison, in *Jude* fate and economic hardship combine with "My two Arch Enemies—my weakness for womankind, and my impulse to strong liquor" to cause Jude's alienation and difficult *bildung* (Hardy 2008, 342). The Victorians would have categorised these "Arch Enemies" as moral insanity, melancholia, and monomania of the emotions and/or will. *Jude* depicts these psychological impairments as indirectly related to, although not completely the result of, the Fawley penchant for tragic marriages, an inescapable inherited trait. For instance, after Jude's marriage to Arabella shows signs of failure, his aunt reminds him that his parents' and his father's sister's marriages ended tragically and warns:

> The Fawleys were not made for wedlock. There's sommat in our blood that won't take kindly to the notion of being bound to do what we do readily enough if we're not bound. That's why you ought to have hearkened to me, and not ha' married.
>
> (Hardy 2008, 106)

When we consider this legacy not as coincidence or bad luck, but as an ill-omen or curse, Jude's misfortune and otherness become legible in relation to *Calmady*, as well as many other Victorian novels that, together, weave a series of anxious discourses about legacies and heritability.[10]

As in *Calmady*, *Jude's* curse problematises the protagonist's relationship to compulsory reproductive heterosexuality and compulsory able-bodiedness. Doomed in marriage, the Fawley curse alienates Jude from the only social institution that sanctions sexuality. Consequently, his sexual desires become pathologised as "erotolepsy" (Hardy 2008, 92). Hardy coined this term to denote a more reckless and intense form of sexual desire than erotomania (excess of sexual appetite), which the Victorians considered a form of insanity. Notably, Victorian psychological theory, following Jean-Etienne Esquirol—and drawing a strict distinction between nymphomania/satyriasis—considered a physical malady to be rooted in the reproductive organs, versus erotomania, which was considered a mental malady. Since erotomania, a subtype of monomania, was characterised by obsessive and disruptive thought patterns but not necessarily action, Hardy's deployment of "erotolepsy" seems to emphasise that Jude's compulsion to keep sleeping with Arabella (and Sue) indicates a more severe kind of disability.[11] Also, as an indirect result of the Fawley marriage curse, Jude's personal ethics lead him to a kind of queer heterosexuality (for his day) as a marriage resister, while his embodied reality includes alcoholism and depression.[12]

Beyond the narrative outcomes of the curse, we can also examine the cultural work of the texts' curses vis-à-vis discourses of disability and sexuality. As previously mentioned, the curse results in both Richard and Jude's nonnormate body-minds, yet each are embodied subjects who do not merely function as narrative prostheses. They each have a *bildung*, one that follows the genre's archetypal plot trajectory. Especially given the inherently pedagogical impulse of the genre, we can now consider whether the curse functions to reinforce or to subvert dominant discursive representations of compulsory able-bodiedness and compulsory reproductive heterosexuality.

To begin to address this issue, we should remember that traditionally, in folklore and subsequent literature, a curse is performative. Somebody says to another, "I curse you," and in the utterance, the curse comes into being. But this is not the case in *Jude* and *Calmady*. Instead, the curse is inherited; there is no moment of utterance personally directed at the protagonist. So, what is the difference between a curse performed and one inherited? Here it might help to remember Butler's theories of citationality, or the idea that gender norms (like curses) are "inherited." Butler shows that there is no fixed ontological status of gender that pre-exists the subject, only repetition which becomes naturalised over time. Like gender, the curse is not a fixed substance, but nonetheless it has powerful effects. Put another way, "the normative can be considered an effect of the repetition of bodily actions over time, which produces what we can call the bodily horizon, a space for action, which puts some objects and not others in reach" (Ahmed 2006, 66).

In these bildungsromane, the curse places certain things out of the protagonists' reach, for instance able-bodiedness and 'normal' sexuality. The fact that Jude will never have a happy marriage is intertwined with his alcoholism and "erotolepsy." He drinks to excess, often humiliating or otherwise harming himself; both times Sue returns to Phillotson and Jude can't resist his erotoleptic compulsions toward Arabella (Hardy 176, 365). Similarly, Sir Richard cannot walk or ride down the street without being stared at and often is "the subject of brutal comment" (Malet 2003, 115). *Calmady* makes clear Richard cannot expect a woman to love him and continue his line, and thus Lady Constance does not live up to her name and calls off the marriage their parents worked so hard to arrange (235).

While folktale curses often function as punishment, these inherited curses can be read as one effect of the repetition of norms: to exclude. They are symbolic cautionary tales about what happens to people who try to go through life disobeying the rules. But this is hardly the entire lesson to be gleaned from these novels. These texts engage disability and sexuality in a much more complex manner than first meets the eye.

One way to view the curse is how it calls attention to the progress narrative that protagonists are expected to follow—what Ahmed calls being "oriented toward the line" (2006, 16). As iterated in these bildungsromane, those cursed experience the hugely negative consequences of not following the narrative, not toeing the line. As Ahmed shows in *Queer Phenomenology*, society orients us along certain directions, and as I have been arguing, one goal of the bildungsroman is to reinforce this. Ahmed writes, "To become subject under the law one is subject to the law that decides what forms lives must take in order to count lives worth living" (84). As its negative, the curse is juxtaposed *contra* the form that is supposed to make life worth living. For instance, when Jude is deprived of Sue's love he drowns his sorrows in a tavern, "convinced that he was at bottom a vicious character, of whom it was hopeless to expect anything" (Hardy 2008, 113). Richard, too, sometimes feels hopeless with his lot: "I find it's beastly difficult to care a hang about your soul, one way or another, when you clearly perceive your body making you the laughing stock of half the people" (Malet 2003, 126). Here we see the curse calling attention to "normal goals" and emphasising their importance, especially if they exclude you.

The flip side of this first view of the curse is that Hardy and Malet also illustrate that the exclusionary curse is sometimes experienced as a relief or respite. In Hardy's tale, the family curse denies Jude a happy marriage, but Jude's failure with Arabella also grants him freedom to escape the stifling married life that has kept him from his beloved books. Soon thereafter, he meets Sue, and although he cannot marry her, he knows she will be everything to him Arabella is not: "a kindly star, an elevating power, a companion in Anglican worship, a tender friend" (Hardy 2008, 84). The curse makes this possible. Malet's Richard, too, ultimately finds relief through his family curse. The class-privileged, self-absorbed, and aimless Richard, by the novel's end, finds a fulfilling vocation through a socialist shift in perspective that results in a sense of universal brotherhood when he decides "by the fact of his deformity he was emancipated from the delusions of his class" (371). So, from this first point of view, the curse calls attention to normalcy and its exclusionary path, but also provides a critique of that path that could not have been possible were the protagonist currently on it.

Another reading of the curse is as a second, albeit abject, line, or narrative that the cursed protagonist is compelled to follow. Because Jude cannot marry Sue, and because they cannot "follow an occupation in which personal circumstances don't count" (Hardy 2008, 295), their personal and professional opportunities are limited and they are forced to adopt a "shifting, almost nomadic life" (298). Although he is not poor, in a low moment, Richard similarly equates the result of the curse—"his maimed body"—with "maimed chances and opportunities" (Malet 2003, 163). Yet, both Hardy and Malet demonstrate, as Ahmed would articulate over a century later, "The negated life still gets us somewhere, through the very turn toward others who are also seen as outside the contours of a good life" (Ahmed 2006, 105). Jude has a painful existence, but there are periods of contentment and pleasure. His life with Sue may be vilified, (and these may be the events Hardy most often chronicles) but it includes the few precious moments of authentic feeling in both their lives:

> That the two were happy—between their times of sadness—was indubitable. And when the unexpected apparition of Jude's child in the house had shown itself to be no such disturbing event as it had looked, but one that brought into their lives a new and tender interest of an ennobling and unselfish kind, it rather helped than injured their happiness.
>
> (Hardy 2008, 278)

Richard finds solace, acceptance and growth with sailors, courtesans, and his infamously adulterous cousin Helen. He vows to his mother:

> I'm going to have all that my money and position, and even this vile deformity … can bring me of pleasure and notoriety. I am going to lay hold of life with these terribly strong arms of mine … I mean to tear the very vitals out of living; to tear knowledge, excitement, intoxication, out of it, making them, by right of conquest, my own.

> I will compel existence to yield me all that it yields other men, and more. … I am not stupid. I shall not follow the beaten track.
>
> (Malet 2003, 252)

In both of these examples we see that another path, no matter how demonised or cursed, is still a path.

Which brings us to a related, third, perspective on the curse: in these novels, in addition to the imperatives one must follow (for Ahmed, being oriented to the line), we also see examples of what Kathryn Bond Stockton calls "the queer child growing sideways" (Stockton 2009) as the hero tries to avoid the curse. For Hardy and Malet, the nonnormate body gives rise to other possibilities: other images of embodiment and lived lives—embodied subjects with a unique position in and perspective on the world. As Gillian Beer observes, Jude and Sue see themselves as

> precursors of a New World order, but their children die, leaving them aberrant, without succession, and therefore 'monstrous' in the sense that can carry no cultural or physical mutations into the future and must live out their lives merely at odds with the present.
>
> (Beer 2000, 257)

But they know what they are and what they are doing. Sue proclaims, "Perhaps the world is not illuminated enough for such experiments as ours!" (Hardy 2008, 341). Likewise, even in the depths of Jude's depression, he asserts that his existence might be different were the world different, *which it someday might be*:

> I perceive there is something wrong somewhere in our social formulas; what it is can only be discovered by men or women with greater insight than mine,—if indeed they ever discover it—at least in our time … and who can tell a man what shall be after him under the sun.
>
> (Hardy 2008, 317)

Note here that despite Jude and Sue's despair, their dream of the future includes people like themselves living the 'cursed' life they have been trying to live. This aspect of *Jude* anticipates in some ways what Alison Kafer, in *Feminist Queer Crip*, calls for as a "politics of crip futurity" (Kafer 2013, 3). While some might argue that *Jude*'s ending implies his life cannot be lived, I instead read his death, in context of the above passages, as illustrating that his life cannot be lived *now*. In the above passage, Jude provides an image of crip futurity that does not turn away from suffering and instead points toward a further future where disabled lives are recognisable, intelligible, and considered lives worth living—lives that neither require able-bodiedness nor erase queerness.

Similarly, in *Calmady,* Malet struggles with both muscular Christianity and compulsory heterosexuality. Through Helen and Honoria, Malet dreams of a place for the New Woman and through Richard, Malet advocates radical action. Early in the novel, Richard warns:

> But I am not as other men are. I am a creature by myself, a unique development as much outside the normal social, as I am outside the normal physical law. … And so if I do queer things, things off the conventional lines, who will be surprised?
>
> (Malet 2003, 170)

By the end of the novel, Richard has expanded the notion of family into a community of caring: "not on the lines of a charitable institution, which must inevitably be a rather mechanical, step-mother kind of arrangement at best, but on the lines of family affection, of personal friendship" (389). Although Miller argues that by the novel's purportedly chaste ending, Richard's "bodily difference is ignored, hidden, and denied a healthy sexuality" (Miller 2012, 201), I think it's important not to ignore how, to again use Stockton's words, Richard provides an example of how perverts are diverts—those who extend themselves or linger over places that are not purely reproductive (Stockton 2009, 25). Richard, Helen, and Honoria's striking example of queer, crip, interdependent living anticipates important discussions among critical disability theorists such as Eva Kittay and Martha Nussbaum, and resonates strongly with today's conversations in both queer and disability studies about the important role of queer kinship[13] and nontraditional family structures.[14]

Growing sideways is precisely what *most* Victorian progress narratives work hard to foreclose. In particular, most bildungsromane enforce the straight, the direct, the able, and the (re)productive, and thus prevent, by shutting down, other modes of being and other social arrangements. Yet this is not necessarily so with Hardy and Malet, despite their novels' otherwise seeming grimness. Thus, I want to conclude by saying that, within these bildungsromane, the curse does not reinforce, but instead works against this genre that is otherwise characterised by the impulse to enforce normalcy. The curse reveals that, *contra* what more traditional bildungsromane would teach the reader, there is more than one possibility: more than one narrative and more than one kind of progress. In Darwinian terms, these bodies are highly adaptive, though not teleologically, nor in a manner consistent with the emerging social Darwinism of the era. As Malet herself wrote to her brother-in-law after reading Darwin:

> If we begin with spirit and with morals, one seems to end in despair, everything is so hopelessly dark, mysterious, unsatisfactory,

> unprovable. But if you begin with the idea of a single cell containing life countless ages ago, and see where it has worked up to by now, one gets a glimpse of the possibility of everlasting progression. Anyway, *living* is tremendously interesting; and it doesn't really much matter how things turn out eventually if they will only go on interesting one.
>
> (Lucas Malet to Clifford Harrison, qtd. in Lundberg 2003, 96)

As such, these inherited curses show, to use Ahmed's words, "The very idea that bodies 'have' a natural orientation is exposed as fantasy in the necessity of the enforcement of that orientation, or its maintenance as a social requirement for intelligible subjectivity" (Ahmed 2006, 85).

These late nineteenth-century representations of curses portending alternative or, to quote Malet, *interesting* possibilities are very curious. In contrast to late-Victorian anxieties about failed inheritances, degenerating heritable traits, and anxieties about ensuring forward motion of individuals, families, and the nation, *Jude* and *Calmady* can be read as reconceptualising the function of disability and sexuality in the bildungsroman—they provide a vision of life that Gillian Beer describes (regarding *Jude)* as "devious and resourceful, constantly reassembling about new possibilities which lie just off the path of the obliterative energies of the event" (246). Although Catherine Delyfer comes to a similar conclusion about *Calmady*, stating, "Malet asks the reader to recognise the fecundity and revolutionary potential of the extraordinary body of the 'monster' as the vessel of the radically new, the vehicle of the future" (Delyfer 2010, 92), she does so while keeping the novel firmly situated within the framework of gothic conventions. So too, Kathleen A. Miller argues that Malet "eroticizes, romanticizes, and values the bodily 'difference' of her protagonist ... as though it were a rare and artistic work of grotesquerie, but not a sign of degeneration" (Miller 2012, 193). Delyfer's and Miller's readings suggest that authors like Malet (and Hardy) are making a bid to accept the outcast and no longer "brand difference as inferior" (Delyfer 2010, 93)—to make a place at the table for the monster. What I am suggesting here, by instead using the framework of the bildungsroman, is subtly but definitively broader in its implications.

Here I have argued for a reading of *The History of Sir Richard Calmady* and *Jude the Obscure* as bildungsromane vis-à-vis Victorian investments in progress narratives; and I have also suggested that we focus our investigation upon the novels' use of their protagonists' orientations or points of view in the world as always already shaped by a curse that effectively changes the world for them. My purpose has not been to assess the extent to which the novels include Jude and Richard within a system that has previously excluded them; rather, my objective has been to highlight ways that Malet and Hardy critique the very systems of compulsory reproductive heterosexuality and compulsory able-bodiedness, teleological assimilation, and enforced normalcy, itself. These bildungsromane become then, not merely narratives of individuals who are different; rather they provide a queer, crip suggestion of a different kind of progress, the possibility of a different kind of future.

§

Acknowledgments

This chapter was conceived during the 2010 National Humanities Center seminar on *Reading Jude the Obscure*; I owe an enormous debt of gratitude to the intellectual generosity of seminar leader Kate Flint and all the wonderful seminar participants. Many thanks also to Kim Q. Hall and Sushmita Chatterjee for their feedback and support as this paper later found its current form. Finally, I am grateful to the editors of *The Journal of Literary and Cultural Disability Studies* for kindly providing permission to reprint this essay with minor revisions.

Notes

1 In *Calmady*, the text explicitly presents a physical impairment as part of a family curse. In *Jude* the text is more implicit about representing a family's marriages as cursed.
2 Darwin biographer Janet Browne reminds us that although we may today view natural selection as a progress narrative, this was not Darwin's intent in the *first* edition of *On the Origin of Species*: "Darwin did not allow his organisms any future goal, any teleology pulling them forwards ... He differed from Lamarck ... in that he eschewed any "doctrine of necessary progression" and "inner striving toward perfection" (61). Herbert Spencer coined the 1864 teleological phrase "survival of the fittest," which at Alfred Russel Wallace's insistence, Darwin substituted for the phrase he had been using, "descent with modification." Over time, Darwin's ideas (and popular understandings of them) took on a more teleological imperative.
3 See Maltz (2005) and Cleere (2014).
4 Cf. Nordau (1895).
5 Cf. Cecil (1895) and Jamoussi (2011).
6 Cf. Buckley (1974); Ellis (1999); Moretti (1987) and Summerfield and Downward (2010).
7 For examples of hunchbacks see *The Old Curiosity Shop*'s Quilp and *Our Mutual Friend*'s Silas Wegg. For examples of the pure, wasting maiden see *The Old Curiosity Shop's* Little Nell and *Jane Eyre*'s Helen Burns. For examples of desexualised adult men see *A Portrait of a Lady*'s Ralph Touchett; *John Halifax, Gentleman*'s Phineas Fletcher; and *Nicholas Nickleby*'s Smike.
8 Here I use Rosemarie Garland Thomson's useful term to delineate a range of body-minds outside "the social figure through which people can represent themselves as definitive human beings" (Garland Thomson 1997, 8) including but not limited to those the Victorians would have labelled "freaks."

9 Another reason for analysing *Jude* and *Calmady* together is Talia Schaffer's convincing work illustrating that by the time Hardy wrote *Jude,* he was certainly quite familiar with, and in fact owed a great debt to, Malet. Schaffer calls *Jude the Obscure* a "a kind of demonic twin" of Malet's 1891 novel, *The Wages of Sin* (Schaffer 1996, 279). It is beyond the scope of this essay (and would be redundant) to explore *Wages* here, but for more on the fascinating relationship between *Jude* and *Wages* see Schaffer (1996).

10 Cf. Lord George Gaunt in Thackeray's *Vanity Fair,* Yonge's *The Heir of Redclyffe,* Collins's *The Moonstone,* Caird's *The Wings of Azrael,* Doyle's *The Hound of the Baskervilles,* and Hardy's legend of the ill-omened d'Urbeville coach in *Tess.*

11 On Victorian erotomania see Berrios and Kennedy (2002) and Goodman (2012). And although not historically apropos to *Jude,* Lennard Davis (1995) provides a useful present-day meditation on the topic. Berrios, E. G. and N. Kennedy. (2002). *"Erotomania: A Conceptual History." History of Psychiatry.* 13: 381–400.

12 Norbert Lennartz (2014) analyses alcoholism in several Hardy novels, including *Jude.* On Victorian alcoholism as a form of mental illness, see McCandless (1984); and Valverde (1998).

13 Cf. "Is Kinship Always Already Heterosexual" in Butler (2004) and Eng (2010).

14 Cf. Bérubé (1996) and Adams (2014).

Works Cited

Adams, Rachel. 2014. *Raising Henry: A Memoir of Motherhood, Disability and Discovery.* New Haven, CT: Yale University Press.

Ahmed, Sara. 2006. *Queer Phenomenology: Orientations, Objects, Others.* Durham, NC: Duke University Press.

Beer, Gillian. 2000. *Darwin's Plots: Evolutionary Narrative in Darwin, George Eliot and Nineteenth-Century Fiction.* Cambridge: Cambridge University Press.

Bérubé, Michael. 1996. *Life as We Know It: A Father, a Family, and an Exceptional Child.* New York: Pantheon.

Berrios, E. G. and N. Kennedy. (2002). "Erotomania: A Conceptual History." History of Psychiatry 13: 381–400.

Browne, Janet. 2011. *Charles Darwin: The Power of Place.* New York: Knopf.

Buckley, Jerome. 1974. *Season of Youth: The Bildungsroman from Dickens to Golding.* Cambridge, MA: Harvard University Press.

Butler, Judith. 2004. *Undoing Gender.* New York: Routledge

Cecil, Evelyn. 1895. *Primogeniture: A Short History if its Development in Various Countries and Its Practical Effects.* London: J. Murray.

Cleere, Eileen. 2014. *The Sanitary Arts: Aesthetic Culture and the Victorian Cleanliness Campaigns.* Columbus: Ohio State University Press.

Davis, Lennard. 1995. *Enforcing Normalcy: Disability, Deafness and the Body.* New York: Verso.

———. 2012. "An Excess of Sex: Sex Addiction as Disability." In *Sex and Disability* edited by Robert McRuer and Anna Mollow. 313–330. Durham, NC: Duke University Press.

Delyfer, Catherine. 2010. "Lucas Malet's Subversive Late-Gothic: Humanizing the Monster in The History of Sir Richard Calmady." In *Demons of the Body and Mind: Essays on Disability in Gothic Culture*, edited by Ruth Anolik, 80–96. Jefferson: McFarland.

Ellis, Lorna. 1999. *Appearing to Diminish: Female Development and the British Bildungsroman*. Lewisburg, PA: Bucknell University Press.

Eng, David. 2010. *The Feeling of Kinship: Queer Liberalism and the Racialization of Intimacy*. Durham, NC: Duke University Press.

Ferguson, Christine. 2012. *Determined Spirits: Eugenics, Heredity and Racial Regeneration in Anglo-American Spiritualist Writing, 1848–1930*. Edinburgh: Edinburgh University Press.

Garland Thomson, Rosemarie. 1997. *Extraordinary Bodies: Figuring Physical Disability in American Culture and Literature*. New York: Columbia University Press.

Giordano, Frank Jr. 1972. "*Jude the Obscure* and the *Bildungsroman*." *Studies in the Novel* 4(4): 580–91.

———. 1984. *I'd Have My Life Unbe: Thomas Hardy's Self-Destructive Characters*. Tuscaloosa: University of Alabama Press.

Goodman, Helen. 2012. "Madness in Marriage: Erotomania and Marital Rape in *He Knew He Was Right* and *The Forsyte Saga*. *Victorian Networks* 4.2.

Goetz, William. (1983). "The Felicity and Infelicity of Marriage in Jude the Obscure." Nineteenth Century Fiction 38.2: 189–213.

Green, Laura. (1995). '"Strange [in]difference of sex': Hardy, the Victorian Man of Letters, and The Temptation of Androgyny." Victorian Studies 38.4: 532–49.

Hardy, Thomas. 2008 [1895]. *Jude the Obscure*, edited by Patricia Ingham. Oxford: Oxford University Press.

Holmes, Martha Stoddard. 2004. *Fictions of Affliction: Physical Disability in Victorian Culture*. Ann Arbor: University of Michigan Press.

Jamoussi, Zouheir. 2011. *Primogeniture and Entail in England*. Cambridge: Cambridge Scholars Press.

Kafer, Alison. 2013. *Feminist, Queer, Crip*. Bloomington: Indiana University Press.

Krebs, Paula. 2004. *Gender, Race and the Writing of Empire: Public Discourse and the Boer War*. Cambridge: Cambridge University Press.

Lennartz, Norbert. 2014. "Legends of Infernal Drinkers: Representations of Alcohol in Thomas Hardy and Nineteenth-Century British Fiction." In *Drink in the Eighteenth and Nineteenth Centuries*. edited by Susanne Schmid, Barbara Schmidt-Haberkamp. 115–126. London: Pickering and Chatto.

Lundberg, Patricia Lorimer. 2003. *"An Inward Necessity": The Writer's Life of Lucas Malet*. New York: Peter Lang.

Malet, Lucas. 2003 [1901]. *The History of Sir Richard Calmady*, edited by Talia Schaffer. Birmingham: University of Birmingham Press.

Maltz, Diana. 2005. *British Aestheticism and the Urban Working Classes, 1870–1900*. Basingstoke: Palgrave.

McCandless, Peter. 1984. "Curses of Civilization: Insanity and Drunkenness in Victorian Britain." *British Journal of Addiction* 79.1: 49–58.

Merleau-Ponty, Maurice. 1964. *The Primacy of Perception*. Evanston, IL: Northwestern University Press.

Miller, Kathleen. 2012. "'Your loving is unlike any other': Romance and the Disabled Body in the Gothic Fiction of Edith Nesbit and Lucas Malet." In

Writing Women of the Fin-de-siècle: Authors of Change, edited by Adrienne Gavin and Carolyn de la Oulton, 193–203. London: Palgrave.

Mitchell, David and Sharon Snyder. 1997. "Narrative Prosthesis and the Materiality of Metaphor." In *The Disability Studies Reader*, edited by Lennard J. Davis. New York: Routledge.

———. 2006. *Cultural Locations of Disability*. Chicago: University of Chicago Press.

Moretti, Franco. 1987. *The Way of the World: the Bildungsroman and European Culture*. New York: Verso.

Nordau, Max. 1895. *Degeneration*. London: Heinman.

O'Connell, Rachel. 2012. "'That Cruel Spectacle': The Extraordinary Body Eroticized in Lucas Malet's *The History of Sir Richard Calmady*." In *Sex and Disability*, edited by Robert McRuer and Anna Mollow, 108–22. Durham, NC: Duke University Press.

Robb, George. 1996. "The Way of All Flesh: Degeneration, Eugenics, and the Gospel of Free Love." *Journal of the History of Sexuality*. 6.4: 589–603

Schaffer, Talia. 1996. "Malet the Obscure: Thomas Hardy, 'Lucas Malet' and the Literary Politics of Early Modernism." *Women's Writing* 3(3): 261–85.

Srebrnik, Patricia. 1994. "The re-subjection of 'Lucas Malet': Charles Kingsley's daughter and the response to Muscular Christianity." In *Muscular Christianity Embodying the Victorian Age,* edited by Donald Hall, 194–214. Cambridge: Cambridge University Press.

Stockton, Kathryn Bond. 2009. *The Queer Child, or, Growing Sideways in the Twentieth Century*. Durham, NC: Duke University Press.

Summerfield, Giovanna and Lisa Downward. 2010. *New Perspectives on the European Bildungsroman*. London: Continuum.

Valverde, Mariana. 1998. *Diseases of the Will: Alcohol and the Dilemmas of Freedom*. Cambridge: Cambridge University Press.

8 Some Chapter of Some Other Story

Henry James, Lucas Malet, and the Real Past of *The Sense of the Past*

Talia Schaffer

Lucas Malet published a novella called *The Gateless Barrier* in 1900. Sixteen years later, Henry James's rather similar story, *The Sense of the Past*, was posthumously published. While no direct evidence of influence has survived, the stories are comparable enough that we can read them as parallel ways of working out the same dynamic. What does it mean, these authors ask, if a woman haunts what James famously called "the house of fiction"? (James 1986, 45–46). For James, the ghostly woman might be a rival—but for Malet, she might be a role model, or a sobering case study of a predecessor silenced, walled up alive, in a fate that we might be excused for taking as a grim omen of Malet's own history.

Malet, like James, had a strong interest in aesthetic culture, artefacts, and characters. The dilettante collector who appears in so many of James's stories, from Gilbert Osmond and Ned Rosier in *The Portrait of a Lady* (1881) to Adam Verver in *The Golden Bowl* (1904), was also a stock character in Malet's novels, appearing in *A Counsel of Perfection* (1888), *The Wages of Sin* (1890), *The Carissima* (1893), *The Gateless Barrier* (1900), *The History of Sir Richard Calmady* (1901), and *The Score* (1909). The difficulty of late James novels resides in James's insistence that in his characters' endless conversations we read what is only implied or unwritten, the participants' silences or circumlocutions. A similar interest in unspokenness governs Malet's novels too. She uses aesthetic diction as a strategy for depicting the forbidden, an oblique reference to the unrepresentable which it both revealed and concealed.

Malet's work was frequently compared to James's—and not always to James's benefit. In 1885 *The Athenaeum* wrote that some of Malet's prose

> might have been written by Mr. James or Mr. Howells. ... At the same time, we have little hesitation in saying that upon a favourite ground of those ingenious authors, that of international contrasts, they have been fairly beaten by Lucas Malet.
>
> ("Colonel Enderby's Wife" 1885, 723)

Critics sometimes also preferred her psychological insight. *The Wages of Sin* was, in one critic's opinion, "a work which, in my humble judgment, surpasses in psychological insight any English novel published since the death of George Eliot" (MacColl 1891, 252). Another critic writing in 1901 felt that no "living writer could succeed in so profound and vivid a realization of mental history as she has done" ("Sir Richard Calmady" 1901, 260). "None of our later writers of fiction takes higher rank than that which has been won by Lucas Malet," wrote the critic Justin McCarthy (2: 236).

Malet published *The Gateless Barrier* at the end of July 1900. By 14 August 1900, Henry James put down his pen, giving up his ghost story *The Sense of the Past.*[1] James would return to this novel periodically, leaving it unfinished when he died in 1916. Malet's novella and James's manuscript both describe a turn-of-the-century man who travelled back to the Regency to become his own ancestor, replaying that ancestor's passion for his cousin, while risking becoming trapped in the past himself.

It is tempting to imagine that James stopped writing his story because Malet had published her version of the tale, but no records survive that allow us to verify whether James had read *The Gateless Barrier* in July/August 1900. Malet and James were friends, so it is possible that she sent him a copy or asked him to read it in manuscript (Lundberg 2003, 172). James often read and edited other female friends' manuscripts before their publication, as he did for Malet's rival Mrs Humphry Ward and Malet's friend Elizabeth Robins. We know that Malet admired James's work, since she names a painting after James's story "The Madonna of the Future" in her later novel *Adrian Savage.* Both James and Malet made bonfires of their personal papers, so whatever documentation of their possible mutual influence might have existed was almost certainly destroyed (Srebrnik 1994, 199).

Both Malet and James were worried about authorial originality in connection with this story—not unsurprisingly, since, as we shall see, the story itself asks about our debt to past writers. When Malet was working on *The Gateless Barrier* in 1898, she was uncharacteristically anxious to conceal her work. According to one interviewer, "she will divulge neither the title nor a hint as to plot, and does not even trust the typewriter, but is having the necessary copying for the printer done by a member of her immediate family" ("Lucas Malet" 1898, 18).[2]

During the years that James was playing with the unfinished manuscript of *The Sense of the Past*, the idea of rewriting others' work was much on his mind. Adeline Tintner and Isobel Waters have both found several other potential sources for *The Sense of the Past.*[3] On 29 January 1900—during the first weeks of writing *The Sense of the Past*—James told H.G. Wells that "I re-write you, much, as I read—which is the highest tribute my damned impertinence can pay an author" (James 1982, 133).

According to Elizabeth Robins, by 1895 James "positively could not, he said, read anything now, for sake [*sic*] of the story. He had 'lost his innocence.' If a book interested him he wanted to rewrite it" (Robins 1932, 176). In the first several years of the twentieth century, while James was working on *The Sense of the Past,* he was also producing the New York editions. Perhaps that involvement in revisiting and revising his early work accounts for the intense desire to relive history, and the anxiety about swerving from the historical record, in *The Sense of the Past.*[4]

Whether or not *The Gateless Barrier* did in fact influence *The Sense of the Past*, however, it is valuable to read them together. We have a case study of how differently a male and female author treated the same material, when writing at the same time, with comparable careers and reputations. The two stories begin with similarities so uncanny it is hard to imagine they were accidental, but afterwards *The Sense of the Past* and *The Gateless Barrier* diverge markedly. Each wrote a story in which a ghostly woman haunts the house of fiction—but one saw her as a threat, and one as a delight.

Overall, *The Sense of the Past* and *The Gateless Barrier* are so similar that one summary can suffice for both. Each describes a young male amateur writer from New York whose distant English relative dies and bequeaths him the family's ancestral home in England. In Malet's novel, the writer is called Laurence Rivers; James names him Ralph Pendrel. This man immediately travels to see his new house and finds himself fascinated by its aura of history. He neglects his social calls to stare at a portrait, which depicts a young English gentleman who fought against Napoleon. When he views this portrait in an inner chamber during a storm, he realises that, strangely enough, this ancestor looks exactly like him. Laurence is shocked by what he sees:

> [It] was a portrait of whom? Well, of himself—himself, Laurence Rivers. ... He had been a sailor apparently, for he wore the dark-blue, naval uniform of the early years of the century, his brown hair being tied back into a queue. But for these details the resemblance to himself was absolute.
>
> (Malet 1900, 148–9)[5]

James's Ralph has the same eerie recognition: "The young man brown-haired, pale, erect, with the high-collared dark blue coat ... but the face—miracle of miracles, yes—confounded him as his own" (James 1917, 87–88).[6]

Malet's Laurence, like James's Ralph, eventually finds a way to travel back to the earliest years of the nineteenth century and re-enact his ancestor's love story. The Napoleonic sailor had fallen in love with, and proposed to, his charming, sprightly, sweet cousin. The woman plays music and embroiders. She has a pink-and-white complexion, thick curly brown hair, and she wears a gown of sprigged muslin with short sleeves that reveal her lovely arms (*GB* 221, 50; *SP* 123, 120). Similarly, in a discarded passage from *The Sense of the Past*, James writes that "[the] thickness of loose brown hair, helped the dress of sprigged muslin that kept as clear of her neck as it did of her elbows" ("Unpublished" 152–3). The cousins adore one another. They exchange painted miniatures (*GB* 149; *SP* 134). The woman keeps her cousin's love letters tied with pink ribbon, and the man knows his beloved's letters by heart (*GB* 152–3; *SP* 185–9).

In this otherworldly love affair, the hero deliberately ignores the claims of the modern woman to whom he has proposed, a sophisticated New York socialite. But the ancestor had died in the war against Napoleon before he could finish the love affair with his cousin (*GB* 172; *SP* 77). Thus the time traveller also finds himself forced to abandon his affair, and he eventually returns to his modern era and the New York socialite who awaits him. The ghostly lover sweetly fades into self-chosen oblivion.

Both novels focus on the house, a symbolic space whose antique artefacts represent not only the characters' family history but also the cumulative history of English culture and letters. In both novels, the relative who bequeathed the house to the protagonist was a prototypical English man of letters—but Malet and James define that individual rather differently. In James's *The Sense of the Past*, the elderly Mr. Pendrel is a refined critic and gentlemanly reader. His library is formed by his taste and appreciation for fine sentences, and his young relative's *Essay in Aid of the Reading of History* "moved him to gratitude" (*SP* 42). Literary critics are appreciative, hospitable, intelligent interlocutors. The kindly (if intimidating) family friend Sir Cantopher Bland prizes superb china, explaining, "Yes, I've collections, treasures, and all as pretty things of their kind as you can hope anywhere to see" (*SP* 234).

By contrast, however, in *The Gateless Barrier*, the house's dying owner, Montagu Rivers, is a misogynist, vicious decadent. The Rivers men have always read the most subversive literature available; an earlier ancestor had half-crazed himself with the writings of Paine and Rousseau. Their tradition is one of marginalised and dangerous texts. Whereas the elder man in James's story admired his American relative's essay, Montagu has nothing but cynical revulsion for his relation's writing. He is a skeletal decadent who sees women as mere bestial breeding machines:

> I admit, of course, the necessity of the existence of women, since the perpetuation of the race appears at present desirable. It would be childish to argue the matter. She must be kept and cared for by qualified persons, as are the other higher, domestic animals.
>
> (*GB* 43)

This dehumanising misogyny is in the classic dandy tradition, echoing Baudelaire's announcement:

> Woman is the opposite of the dandy. Thus she must inspire horror. Woman is hungry and she wants to eat. Thirsty, and she wants to drink. She is in heat and wants to be fucked. What fine merit! Woman is natural, that is to say, abominable.
>
> (qtd. in Feldman 1993, 6)

Montagu's costume reveals that his sartorial models are Wilde and Beerbohm, who had made violet a permissible colour for male attire. He sports a violet skullcap and fur-lined dressing gown, wearing purple velvet and gold rings even on his deathbed. Like Wilde, Montagu indulges in accessories like jewellery and flowers and fabrics like velvet and satin. In each case, however, he differentiates his choices from women's wear. His preference for soft flowing fabrics is excused by his invalidism. His jewellery and flowers signify exotic learning, not decoration. Montagu's rings are Egyptian scarabs and amethysts carved with Arabic, resembling Wilde's own rings: emeralds engraved with cabalistic signs (Ellmann 1988, 540). His chosen flowers are aesthetic icons tinged with danger: poisonous orchids and "carmine-stained Japanese lilies" (*GB* 160).

Montagu's artefacts refer to death or sex, sometimes both. A leering tapestry depicting a rape covers one door; his bedposts are carved with dark, straining women who seem to writhe in agonised invitation in the firelight (*GB* 194, 199). His table is covered by a "cloth of gold and crimson embroidery—evidently fashioned from some priestly vestment—upon which rested a [skull], about four inches in height, cut out of a solid block of rock crystal" (*GB* 11). The house is panelled in black oak and hung with dark blue damask; this sombre backdrop allows Montagu to display his eccentric but valuable art collections, including some rather demonic marble busts of some of the more unpopular Roman emperors. "The blind, sculptured faces deepened the general sense of oppression by their rigidity, their unalterable and somewhat scornful repose" (*GB* 24–25). As Montagu's doctor tells Laurence, art collections are a sign of nervous degeneration:

> These delicacies of art are, after all, the refuge of those who have outlived or injured their digestion of, and appetite for, simpler and more wholesome diet. Such dyspeptics are to be commiserated rather than commended ... leave the consolations offered by gems, and ivories, and such like sweepings from the ruins of departed civilisations, to the physically and emotionally decrepit.
>
> (*GB* 242–3)

The doctor would have agreed with one female aesthete, Rosamund Marriott Watson, who complained that "modern decoration" resembled "the monster in Mrs. Shelley's story, compacted mainly from fragmentary relics of the dead, and endowed with artificial and unnatural vitality" (Watson 1897, 85).[7]

Montagu collects rather than creates, like Ned Rosier and Gilbert Osmond in *The Portrait of a Lady* (1881), Jean des Esseintes in *A Rebours* (1884), and Dorian Gray in *The Picture of Dorian Gray* (1890/91). Though he is a remarkable scholar, he refuses to use his information to communicate with vulgar souls. His scholarship is as sterile as his life. His house is a hermetically sealed atmosphere, filled with artificial heat and the musky scent of poisonous flowers. Montagu allows no windows to be opened, no visitors, and no women to enter at all; the decoration of his house reflects this male decadent exclusivity. Like Gilbert Osmond, Montagu Rivers represents the worst aspects of male aestheticism—but whereas Isabel claims "I've no [decorating] ideas," Montagu has a female rival (James 1986, 338).

For at the heart of his moribund manor is a secret "yellow drawing room," decorated with fresh eighteenth-century gaiety, filled with women's work and inhabited by the charming ghost of a young woman, Agnes Rivers. Montagu's decadent bitterness actually comes from his inability to confront this haunting feminine presence. And Agnes's garb and room embody a female aesthetic alternative to the house of the decadents.

Agnes wears the romantic fashions of 1805:

> She wore a high-waisted, clinging, rose-pink, silken gown. Her dark hair was gathered up in soft, yet elaborate bows and curls high on her small head, after the fashion prevalent in the early years of the century. A cape of transparent muslin and lace veiled her bare shoulders.
>
> (*GB* 48)

Agnes also wears a string of pearls and small rose-pink satin slippers set with brilliants (*GB* 53). For an 1890s viewer like Laurence, Agnes's costume would mingle signifiers of seductiveness and innocence. The clinging, uncorseted silken gown reveals her body, and displaying bare shoulders in the daytime had become very daring by the 1890s. On the other hand, pearls were reserved for young girls' wear, and pink was also associated with girls making their first public appearance. Agnes is both sexual and virginal to Laurence's eyes.

This outfit fits into the female aesthetes' preference for eighteenth century and Regency style, as I have explained in *The Forgotten Female Aesthetes*. Writers like Mary Eliza Haweis, 'Roy Devereux' (Margaret Pember-Devereux), and Rosamund Marriott Watson endorsed gowns of flowing muslin, with high Empire waists and puffed sleeves, as well as the slender, simple, light-coloured, painted furniture of the period. Agnes's room could hardly be more different from the dark Jacobean oak and dignified blue damask in the rest of the house:

> The furniture of the room was of satinwood, highly polished and painted with garlands of roses, true-lovers' knots of blue ribbon, dainty landscapes, ladies and lovers, after the manner of Boucher. The chairs and sofas were upholstered in brocade, the predominating colors of which were white, pale yellow, and pale pink.
>
> (*GB* 29)

The hand-painted furniture conveys a message of graceful and courtly love, very much opposed to the skulls and writhing nudes in Montagu's collections. Its pale pastel colours are associated with girlishness. The eighteenth-century drawing room is open to a charming garden outside, and it is well-lit and full of pure fresh air. Nothing in it is financially valuable, but everything has a priceless sentimental value. When Laurence opens the escritoire, he finds mementoes of a love affair: a man's shoe buckles, an embroidered waist ribbon, a store of delicate shells, trinkets from India and Italy, a preserved bouquet of posies, a watch, love letters, portraits. The room contains evidence of Agnes's creative production: an escritoire filled with her letters, a piano with her music on it, a harp, a violin, and a workbasket from which her delicate lace spills. Montagu's fear of Agnes makes him "hopelessly lowered in [his own] self-esteem," but even if there was no ghost haunting the yellow drawing room, its violation of all the canons of decadent taste would have probably been enough to repulse Montagu (*GB* 91). The clash between the yellow drawing room and the dark mansion neatly encapsulates two of the main strains of aestheticism, decadent taste and female aesthetic style.

Malet makes Laurence Rivers quite literally the heir of male decadence, but Laurence pities Montagu and instead chooses to attach himself to the ghostly representative of a female literary tradition—a tradition that is very carefully described in Malet's account, although it is absent in James's version. Where Laurence inherits avant-garde prose essays, from Paine and Rousseau to Baudelaire and Wilde, Agnes enacts the history of women's popular fiction. Agnes embodies this tradition quite literally, for during her mock funeral, her empty coffin was stuffed with books to give it the weight of her body. Her real body gets concealed behind the escritoire which contains her letters.

Through the century during which she haunts her drawing room, Agnes moves through the major roles in the canon of women's novels. The events of Agnes's decline and death in 1805 appropriately fit into two of the major narrative genres of the period. Agnes's life makes her the heroine of a novel of sensibility. When Agnes's fiancé was killed just before their wedding, Agnes went mad and finally died of grief. "Though altogether gentle and docile, she studied nothing but to turn over her dead lover's letters, and play with the various gifts he had bestowed upon her," the old family agent reminisces. "It was the pitifulest spectacle under the dome of the sky, that of her affliction" (*GB* 174). But Agnes's death and the subsequent concealment of her corpse in the unhallowed site of a secret room transform her into a gothic heroine. This embedded tale includes a typical gothic villain, a leering, semi-mad father-substitute who imprisons the dead body of the woman he desires, a crime which produces the very gothic episode of the supernatural visitation.

Agnes haunts her yellow drawing room throughout the entire nineteenth century. No wonder that when Laurence first sees her, she has become the ideal Victorian woman. A ghost is an almost satirically perfect Angel in the House. She has no body, no physical desires, no weight, and she cannot speak until spoken to. She depends wholly on her lover's visits, for she can only live through him: "I see with your eyes, I speak with your voice, I comprehend with your mind when you are present. When you are absent, I become as the echo unevoked by any sound" (*GB* 257). Agnes is nothing but a beautiful image. As the Victorian heroine, Agnes enacts a Victorian maiden's role: pining without her lover, she is restored to health and happiness upon his return and their subsequent engagement. But she is unable to face the consequence of acquiring a real body: the prospect of marital relations. Thus she abdicates at her first stirrings of independence. She decides to die and leave her lover and "the desire of [her] heart" (*GB* 305). At the end of the novel, she fades away, represented and remembered only by a spray of pink roses. She has become one of the sentimental mementos of her own drawing room. Agnes is a lovely lady, associated with an idealised past, with a positively angelic capacity for self-annihilation.

But we can also read Agnes's suicide as a consolidation of her power. When Laurence reawakens her in the 1890s, Agnes immediately adapts to the most recent genre of women's fiction: the New Woman novel. She grows more corporeal, acquiring weight, a body, speech, and mental independence. Montagu's decadence and Laurence's amateurism recede as the novel increasingly focuses on Agnes's powerful art. She quite literally occupies a room of her own. Although Montagu seals his house shut, the walls cannot restrain Agnes, for she floats through walls and paces the garden at night. As Montagu slowly dies, Agnes slowly enters into life, turning from a ghost into a living woman. And Laurence Rivers falls in love with her, symbolically transferring his allegiance from the decadent connoisseur to the vital woman writer. When Laurence reads her love letters, he discovers that he is trapped in a repetition of this powerful narrative generated by the force of Agnes's longing. In that sense,

Laurence is nothing but a character in a story told by a woman—as he himself recognises:

> had the gracious spectre ... lived, as he had fondly supposed, through his life, regained reason and glad, human sympathy through the influence of his will, or had the case, in very truth, been precisely the reverse? Had not she been the active, he the merely passive principle? Had he not reached a higher development, and gloried—for a little space—in conscious possession of genius, had he not lived, in short, through her?
>
> (*GB* 186)

In the most literal sense, she has become a new woman. "She grew in womanhood, and she grew in the charm of ... a fine equality" (*GB* 272). Indeed, it is Laurence who is the real ghost, walking mindlessly through the routines of the day and coming to life only at night when near her; she infuses energy and mind into him. Eventually she uses her independence to leave Laurence and break their engagement. Agnes's refusal to enter a conventional marriage is a spiritualistic version of the New Woman's revolt against traditional marital life. Paradoxically enough, her suicide asserts her refusal to disappear: "I will ... go forward—reaching a fairer world than yours. ... There I shall await your coming; and we shall be one at last," she vows (*GB* 307).

The title of *The Gateless Barrier* refers to many barriers: the difference between life and death, the tapestry separating the yellow drawing room from the decadent house, the sea between America and England, the gulf between the old century and the new, and, perhaps most immediately, the gap between decadent men and aesthetic women.[8] Throughout the novel Laurence broaches all these barriers. He speaks with the dead, enters the yellow drawing room, crosses the Atlantic, moves into the past, and becomes Agnes's follower rather than Montagu's. Laurence Rivers represents the writer of the future, and his future is determined by Agnes. Montagu had tried to teach Laurence that 'woman' was only a higher domestic animal, but Laurence concludes, "since you [Agnes] once were woman, no woman shall ever suffer at my hands—all womanhood being sacred thenceforth since you once were woman" (*GB* 353).

Agnes's and Laurence's union represents the union of the two literary traditions they each enact. This mystic marriage would, Malet imagined, give birth to twentieth-century literature. At the end of the novel, Laurence makes the yellow drawing room into his study, thereby producing joint occupancy of the house of fiction. Malet symbolically foresaw a twentieth-century literary school, a version of modernism, born from the union of female culture and male studies. It is, perhaps, significant that Malet considered *The Gateless Barrier* her most autobiographical novel (Lundberg 2003, 210–4).

James, however, took the parable in another direction. In *The Sense of the Past,* the young author rejects the ghostly woman whose flashing wit and powerful art might entrap him. Instead, Ralph Pendrel selects another sort of woman altogether. In *The Sense of the Past*, the future writer learns to bury the creative woman, not to praise her. And *The Sense of the Past* foresaw a male-dominated twentieth-century literary establishment that used and then forgot the ghostly, shrinking, self-sacrificing figure of the woman writer of the past. *The Sense of the Past,* then, takes the same raw materials as *The Gateless Barrier,* but works them into a very different end.

The Sense of the Past does have a strong female figure, although it is unclear what James intended to do with her. Aurora Coyne, Ralph's American beloved, sometimes seems unreasonable but sometimes seems wiser than Pendrel himself. Her initial requirement that Pendrel win her love by leaving her permanently seems to Pendrel to be perversely unfair. But at the end of the novel Aurora travels to England, in violation of her own principles, to rescue Pendrel. We cannot know whether James would have written this scene as Aurora surrendering and acquiescing at long last in Ralph's English affiliation, or whether he would have depicted Aurora triumphantly rescuing a helpless Ralph and towing him home where he belonged. By contrast, in Malet's version, Laurence is absolutely furious when his socialite wife tells him to return. Balanced precariously between success and failure, the modern figure of Aurora Coyne, with its unresolved fate, means that we cannot know how James predicted women's role in the future; we can only read the gender politics James delineated for the past.

Whereas Malet's time traveller adores his ghostly cousin, James's time traveller is only briefly enchanted by *his* long-dead cousin Molly Midmore. Molly exhibits a constant play of banter, judgments, and ideas, with which Ralph finds himself in an exhilarating yet frightening race to "keep up." But Molly's art is not ideal; she misspells words and says things so daring, so irreverent, as to leave Ralph breathless. She is "splendidly shameless," as she makes play with her "bold eyes" (*SP* 188, 184). Conversation with Molly gives Ralph "the impression of something almost deadly in her force" (*SP* 208). Physically, Molly is almost forbiddingly splendid, healthy and tall, with rounded arms and a pink-and-white complexion (*SP* 121, 123). Nor is she particularly modest. When she first sees Ralph, she is "quite as inspired and inflamed as himself" (*SP* 123). This is a threateningly embodied, sexual woman.

Like Agnes, Molly writes love letters to her cousin—but whereas Agnes's letters are eloquent, Molly misspells words. Like Agnes, Molly inhabits a large wainscoted room with a fresh, fair, light atmosphere (*SP* 120). Like Agnes, Molly's room contains evidence of her creativity: an embroidery frame. But Molly's room is furnished with several portraits, which makes it part of the same aesthetic in which the rest of the house is decorated. Similarly, Molly's outfit is identical to Agnes's, but James has excluded both the details and the significance of this gown. Molly, too, wears a sprigged muslin dress which reveals her shoulder and arm (*SP* 121, 123). The prettiness of Molly's attire only suggests to Ralph that he has a right to kiss her; it carries none of the conflicting signs of innocence and sexuality seen in Agnes's dress. Molly's dress is less important because this novel is not trying to explore a model of femininity, but rather to delineate an appropriate male response to a strong woman.

Eventually Ralph decides that Molly is too assertive to understand him, and instead finds himself powerfully attracted to her pale sister Nan. By contrast, Nan is notoriously silent and safely shy (*SP* 277). She is a "slight, fine, concentrated little person ... [a] contrast to her splendid sister." Ralph sees her as "the plainer and weaker and more thankless daughter ... as sober-hued as any nun, and might well, so far as the material side of her presence went, have been trained to fasts and vigils" (*SP* 280–1). Here Nan contrasts not only with her "splendid sister" but also with her fictional predecessor. In *The Gateless Barrier*, Agnes comes to life as she triumphantly gains weight. Laurence begs her to eat so that she can be solid enough to consummate their love (*GB* 298). But in *The Sense of the Past*, Nan's emaciation is supposed to be attractive, and there is no sign that Ralph ever intends to rectify it. Ralph welcomes Nan as the 'modern' sister precisely because of her silence, self-suppression, and nervous maladies (*SP* 280). This identification safely relegates the creative woman to the past, transforming a potential rival into a historical oddity. If Malet's female character was strong and vocal, James's 'modern' woman is more like Hardy's Sue Bridehead, a nervous, sensitive creature.[9] Whereas Malet saw female weakness as a historical stage in a progression towards modern strength, James makes the weak and strong women into sisters, foreclosing any possibility that one might develop into the other: they are static rivals.

When Ralph first sees Nan, he thinks that she resembles one of the "sacrificed creatures he had read in records of the old Catholic world, the oblation made of the plainer and weaker and more thankless daughter to the cloistered life" (*GB* 281). He notices faint signs that she refuses to concur with her self-sacrifice. Readers might hope that Ralph will try to 'save' Nan. Indeed, Ralph tells Nan about the marvels of his own time, firing Nan with an intense desire to see it herself. Laurence had encouraged Agnes's voyage into the future. But James decided to make Ralph leave Nan behind, as she destroys herself to facilitate his journey home to his own time:

> She stands dazzled before [the future] and can only be shut up in the heartbreak of remaining so far back behind it, so dismally and excludedly out of it, while he, with her assistance, shaking her off after he has, as it were, used her, wins his way back to it and out of her sight and sense for ever.
>
> (*SP* 338)

Ralph makes himself the instrument of Nan's self-effacement, not of her salvation. Not only does Nan make an "indispensible, unspeakable sacrifice," but Ralph consigns her to precisely that nun-like spinsterhood he foresaw in her face when he, her lover, elects to leave her (*SP* 348). In other words, although the female ghost makes herself disappear in both stories, Malet writes it as a strong woman's decision, while James writes it as female self-sacrifice.

Nan's robust sister Molly looks, at first glance, like a collectible. Ralph first sees Molly's face in a miniature portrait and next when symbolically framed by her embroidery stand, "a piece of fine tense canvas framed and mounted" (*SP* 120).[10] He is certainly there in order to 'buy' her, since their arranged marriage is meant to rescue the family finances. But after prolonged sparring with Molly, Ralph realises that Molly's verbal facility makes her too powerful. Ralph admits, in his final description of Molly, "she's splendid ... beyond any power of mine to show her off" (*SP* 286). She has become irrelevant to Ralph's desires because he cannot place her on display.

By comparison, Nan is a visual artefact from the start, for when Ralph meets Nan he immediately notices her resemblance to "some mothering Virgin by Van Eyck or Memling" (*SP* 281). Sir Cantopher explains that Nan has perfect taste and that he wants to marry her because he is "such a fancier of every mode of the exquisite," while Molly good-humoredly complains about Nan's interest in *objets d'art*, for Molly herself is ignorant of the value of china (*SP* 238, 244, 248). Sir Cantopher similarly (and flirtatiously) tells Ralph, "you're very fine porcelain indeed" (*SP* 261). The two figures associated with fine china, Ralph and Nan, clearly belong together. In Malet's version, Agnes slowly comes to life, gaining flesh, warmth, weight, but in James's version, Nan remains a delicate piece of porcelain, easily shattered.

In some respects, *The Sense of the Past* records the difficulty of distinguishing oneself from a previous story. The character, Ralph, must fight against his ancestor's fate, but the author, James, must also struggle against the difficulty of falling into the pattern set by *The Gateless Barrier.* The past is a dangerous place against which the protagonist has to work desperately to maintain his own individuality. Ralph feels "unspeakable homesickness for his own time and place" (*SP* 335). At the same time, however, the insistence on one's own contemporaneous difference can feel like a betrayal of the past. James noted that Ralph has committed "deviation, violation, practical treachery, in fact" by choosing Nan, for whom his ancestor "wouldn't have cared a jot" (*SP* 322). As Tintner notes, the crossing of the century divide at 1900 invited writers to think about a divide between the past and the future (Tintner 2000, 155).

Ralph himself notices that he is not an original character: "The first flush of his impression was that of stepping straight into some chapter of some other story" (*SP* 119). Alan W. Bellringer has pointed out that Ralph resembles the novelist, constantly having to figure out characters' motivations and probable actions (Bellringer 1981, 205). Pendrel finds himself caught in someone else's story, with whom he is in intimate, ongoing dialogue, changing important pieces, looking at characters with different eyes. Might this also describe James's own ambivalent entanglement with a precursor text? In reconstructing the history of *The Gateless Barrier* and *The Sense of the Past*, we have to try to recover a past whose records are missing and whose characters are hard to understand. In other words, we find ourselves like Ralph Pendrel and Laurence Rivers, literary readers who discover ourselves to be detectives in someone else's narrative, guests in another time, reading chapters in "some other story."

Thus Ralph's task of controlling and rejecting the witty female rival may be James's own task in writing *The Sense of the Past*. For just as Molly haunts Ralph Pendrel, Malet might have haunted Henry James. The strong woman in *The Sense of the Past* is Mary, nicknamed Molly—and Lucas Malet's real name was also Mary, with the family nickname Polly. Is it a coincidence that in *The Sense of the Past*, the uneasy male writer worries about "keeping up" with a text produced by a witty creative woman named Mary/Molly/Polly? Moreover, in both the real history of James's critical reception and the fictional story of Ralph's growth as a writer, the female rival gets suppressed. Malet prophesied the fate of her own reputation through the figure of Agnes locked for a century in a forgotten room, regardless of her own strength. No matter how strong, how witty, how lovely she was, the woman writer might still be immured. By comparison, the male writer—Laurence Rivers, Ralph Pendrel, or Henry James—achieves the glow of public acclaim, often at the expense of a woman writer.[11]

Susan M. Griffin captures Ralph's first entrance into the house in *The Sense of the Past*: "The doorway, then, is a mirror, but not an everyday solid one. Instead, Ralph is faced with transparent looking glasses like Alice's; indeed, like Alice he eventually steps through one into a world that is the same yet different" (Griffin 1984, 56).[12] Ralph and his ancestor confront each other across a 'gateless barrier,' a doorway that offers a kind of impalpable resistance and sense of otherness. When Ralph enters the door of the house into the past, he feels "an increasingly thick other medium ... like an extraordinarily strong odour inhaled—an inward and inward warm reach" (*SP* 115). This sensation originates in Laurence Rivers's strange feeling of breathless warmth when he fumbles anxiously for the door into the yellow drawing room: "to his surprise, he turned faint and broke into a sweat" (*GB* 28).

Interestingly enough, James broke off his manuscript in 1900 just at the point when Ralph crosses that gateless barrier, as if James feared he was coming too close to a perilous threshold of his own. *The Sense of the Past* is a meditation on authorial originality; can one write one's own story, and if so, would it do damage? By contrast, *The Gateless Barrier* is a fantasy about escaping an oppressively misogynist, decadent, claustrophobic present into a happier, female-identified alternative temporal zone.

If the two novels have different feelings about history, they also offer divergent allegories of gender relations in the literary marketplace. Malet's "house of fiction" is haunted by a woman so powerful that she replaces the male inhabitants. James's "house of fiction," on the other hand, is occupied by women who must be effaced to preserve the elite male writer. At the same time, Malet and James both offer instructions for training the new author of the twentieth century. At the beginning of *The Sense of the Past*, Aurora Coyne rejects Ralph because he is "the mere leader, of the intellectual life, the mere liver in a cultivated corner" (*SP* 351). By the end, however, his sojourn in the past constitutes a "prodigious adventure" which now befits him to be a real writer, worthy of her hand (*SP* 352). In *The Gateless Barrier*, Laurence also becomes a serious writer through his voyage in the past, although ironically he becomes a more Jamesian writer than his Jamesian counterpart. He realises that high art demands a different market:

> He was haunted by the conviction that he had never yet given his best, the highest and strongest of his nature, either in thought, or art, or adventure. ... The demand had been for a thoroughly presentable and immediately marketable article; and the Best is usually far from marketable, often but doubtfully presentable either.
>
> (*GB* 3)

Both James and Malet make their writer characters search for a mode of art that is not "thoroughly presentable and immediately marketable"—that deals with unsavoury topics and appeals to a small readership.

If James constructed an elite readership with the determination to understand his increasingly difficult language, Malet constructed an elite readership with the education to divine the sources of her narrative patterns. *The Gateless Barrier,* like all of Malet's work, is undergirded with a complex structure of other narratives, so that the reader has to be acquainted with *The Pilgrim's Progress*, Genesis, the Mass, the story of the crucifixion, *Paradise Lost*, *The Mysteries of Udolpho*, and even contemporary literature like Oliphant's "The Library Window" and *Lady Audley's Secret* to appreciate the story's highly referential plot.[13]

At the same time, however, it is possible to read *The Gateless Barrier* without access to any of these allusions. Its language is simple; it has very few characters; it is very short. A modern reader can scarcely miss its allegorical significance, but the reviewers of 1900 assumed it was simply an entertaining tale and were puzzled by its mystical story.[14] *The Academy* and *Blackwood's Magazine* both complained that the story was scientifically improbable. They judged the tale according to the standard of domestic realism, in spite of the fact that this standard is not exactly appropriate for a ghost story. These attempts to determine *The Gateless Barrier*'s probability demonstrates that they were unwilling to offer Malet the kind of specialised, high-culture reading that Jamesian novels seemed to demand. While many women may have written anti-realist, rebellious, experimental fiction at the turn of the century, critics found it harder to credit women writers with such intentions. Because women writers' experiments often looked quite different from men's, they could easily be overlooked in accounts of the emergence of modernism. In *The Twentieth-Century World of Henry James,* Adeline R. Tintner claims that "what is absolutely lacking in the novel by Malet is anything indicating 'a sense of the past.'" (Tintner 2000, 156). If one sees James's sense of the past as a powerful, preordained story as the standard, then Malet's joyful, empowering escapist past will simply fail to register. If James's version of history is the sole measure, then Malet's version is not an alternative but simply a blank spot, something "absolutely lacking."

Early examples of this double standard can be found in the reviews that the same newspaper gave to Malet and James. On 19 September 1900, *The Times* complained that, although Malet's story was written with great style and dramatic vigour, its plot was unconvincing and its subject unworthy. "A story with a ghost for heroine must be a thin-blooded business at best" ("Recent Novels" 1900, 2). Seventeen years later, *The Times Literary Supplement* praised the same tale in the hands of Henry James. Enough of the novel appears "to make us sadly aware of our loss of a complete masterpiece. It would surely have been, we feel, the greatest of ghost stories, with a thrill, a frisson, entirely new to literature" ("The Great Henry James Question" 1917, 427). The unintentional irony of declaring *The Sense of the Past* "entirely new" is evident. But what is perhaps not so evident, is the interesting fact that a woman writer in 1900 was being judged according to realist standards that were waived for a male writer in 1917. In 1917 James could win praise for producing a thrill of terror, but in 1900 'terror' was an inappropriate achievement for a woman writer, who was expected to write a convincing, pleasant, love story.[15]

It would be easy to say that *The Gateless Barrier* was neglected because it was ahead of its time, because it attempted a level of sophistication neither expected nor desired from women writing in 1900. The sad fact is that *The Gateless Barrier* was very typical of its time—typical not only in its ambitious complexity and its espousal of alternative female models, but also in its swift decline into obscurity during the twentieth century. *The Gateless Barrier* emerged from the strong movement of female aestheticism, a period when, as Richard Le Gallienne remarked, "man for the present seems to be at a standstill, if not actually retrograde, and the onward movement of the world to be embodied in woman" (qtd. in Sykes 1895, 398–9). Certainly, women's work was seen as more popular than men's. As Ann Ardis notes:

> The common perception in the 1890s was that women were taking over the literary world. New publishing houses, new audiences for fiction, new publication formats: all were seen to give women writers, particularly previously unpublished women writers, a distinct advantage in the literary marketplace.
>
> (Ardis 1990, 43)

No wonder that Agnes is striding towards life, gaining new confidence and new powers by the day; no wonder that she announces, "I will ... go forward—reaching a fairer world than yours" (*GB* 307). The novel's very optimism about women's writing, unfortunately, places it inescapably in the premodernist era.

By contrast, *The Sense of the Past* is a document obsessed with loss and failure and danger, a story about a writer who is literally stuck in his own scenes, an unfinished tale that warns against the past. Yet its very difficulty and indeterminability makes it a paradigmatic modernist text. The modernist canon is full of failed, blocked, suppressed, unhappy, or aimless men: Leopold Bloom, Stephen Dedalus, Septimus Smith, Mrs Dalloway, John Dowell, Merton Densher, Colonel Kurtz, and Lord Jim. Add to that list Ralph Pendrel, who feared he could never escape the past in which he was trapped, and Henry James, who fought to finish a tale he could never quite claim as his own. Perhaps the last gift of *The Gateless Barrier* and *The Sense of the Past* is to make us rethink our own sense of our own past, and the alternative stories we might have had.

Notes

1 Patricia Lorimer Lundberg has found a letter to Malet about *The Gateless Barrier* dated July 22 and 23. James's letter to W.D. Howells explains, in a postscript dated August 14, that he has given up the novel (James 1982, 157–58).
2 Lundberg, however, points out that the manuscript is in Malet's handwriting (Lundberg 2003, 192–93).
3 Tintner believes that James drew on Henry Newbolt's *The Old Country* (1906), another story of a male time traveller moving through an ancient house to find a ghostly woman, although Newbolt sets his story much earlier (Tintner 2000, 157–61). Waters connects it to Gertrude Atherton's "The Bell in the Fog" and James's own "A Passionate Pilgrim" (Waters 2009, 192–193).
4 Oliver Herford traces a fascination with referencing his personal past throughout James's late writings (Herford 2016).
5 Future references to this novel will be marked as *GB* and noted parenthetically in the text.
6 Future references to this novel will be marked as *SP* and noted parenthetically in the text.
7 For more information on Marriott Watson see Schaffer (2000).

8 It is also, as Malet herself points out in her preface, a major Zen koan collection. She borrows this for her own cultural interests.

9 Malet's later novels provide interesting examples of modernist experimentation. *The Far Horizon* (1906) is Malet's experiment with the new naturalism favoured by Moore and Gissing. It shows a humble bank clerk's lonely life enriched by friendship with a rather tawdry actress. *Adrian Savage* (1911) keeps the frame narrative of the Victorian love story, but within that frame explores madness, suicide, hallucinations, and sexual repression in new forms, including stream-of-consciousness perspective. *The Survivors* (1923) describes the erotics of sadism through shifting points of view.

10 This reading of Molly's embroidery comes from Williams (1993, 77). Williams places *The Sense of the Past* in the context of James's other descriptions of portraits and points out that the novel explores a number of concerns finding their way into James's shorter fiction of the same period. James used the theme of a ghost from another time in "The Third Person" (1900) and the American moving to an English estate in "Flickerbridge" (1902).

11 This was a common concern in women's writing of the 1890s; a particularly memorable example is Mabel E. Wotton's story "The Fifth Edition."

12 See Waters (2009, 187) for a discussion of the importance of thresholds, gates, and doors in *The Sense of the Past.*

13 Laurence's journey represents a kind of Pilgrim's Progress through various sorts of temptation. Agnes's forbidden fruit, the bread and wine she is tempted to eat, resonate with Adam and Eve's story and also allude to the Mass. Her self-sacrifice is supposed to be Christlike, since it redeems Laurence, yet the idea of her long wandering out of God's sight is also like Milton's Satan. Malet took some of the specific gothic effects of the novel from Radcliffe and Oliphant. From *Lady Audley's Secret*, Malet borrowed the idea of a locked central room which is feminine and charming but hides an awful secret. This kind of synthesis of multiple sources is characteristic of much nineteenth-century women's writing, particularly popular fiction.

14 On the baffled reviewers, see Lundberg (2003, 206–8).

15 The critic W.L. Courtney declared that all women's fiction amounted to glorified diary entries – a position that would certainly make it hard to know how to read a ghost story (xiii).

Works Cited

The Academy. 59 (1900): 211.

Ardis, Ann L. 1990. *New Women, New Novels: Feminism and Early Modernism.* New Brunswick: Rutgers University Press.

Bellringer, Alan W. 1981. "Henry James's The Sense of the Past: The Backward Vision." *Forum for Modern Language Studies* 17(3): 201–16.

Blackwood's Magazine. 168 (November 1900): 732.

"Colonel Enderby's Wife." 1885. *The Athenaeum* 6: 723.

Courtney, William Leonard. 1904. *The Feminine Note in Fiction.* London: Chapman & Hall, Ltd.

'Devereux, Roy' [Margaret Pember-Devereux]. 1896. *The Ascent of Women.* Boston: Roberts Brothers.

Ellmann, Richard. 1988. *Oscar Wilde*. New York: Vintage Books.

Feldman, Jessica R. 1993. *Gender on the Divide: The Dandy in Modernist Literature*. Ithaca: Cornell University Press.

"The Great Henry James Question." 1917. *The Times Literary* Supplement, 6 September 7, 427.

Griffin, Susan M. 1984. "Seeing Doubles: Reflections of the Self in James's *The Sense of the Past.*" *Modern Language Quarterly* 45(1): 48–60.
Haweis, Mary Eliza. 1978 [1878]. *The Art of* Beauty *and the Art of Dress.* New York: Garland Publishing Inc.
Herford, Oliver. 2016. *Henry James's Style of Retrospect: Late Personal Writings, 1890–1915.* Oxford: Oxford University Press.
James, Henry. 1982. *Henry James: Letters vol. IV: 1895–1916*, edited by Leon Edel. Cambridge: Harvard University Press.
———. "Preface." 1986 [1881]. *The Portrait of a Lady.* New York: Penguin Classics.
———. 1917. *The Sense of the Past.* New York: Charles Scribner's Sons.
———. "Unpublished Papers": TS, bMS Am 1237.8, box 2: 152–53. Houghton Library, Harvard University, Cambridge.
"Lucas Malet: An American Visitor's Portrait of the Novelist." 1898. *New-York Daily Tribune*, 27 February, 18.
"Sir Richard Calmady." 1901. *Literature*, 14 September (vol. 9), 260.
Lundberg, Patricia Lorimer. 2003. *An Inward Necessity: The Writer's Life of Lucas Malet.* New York: Peter Lang.
McCarthy, Justin. 1899. *Reminiscences.* 2 vols. New York: Harper & Brothers.
MacColl, Canon Malcolm. 1891. "Morality in Fiction." *Contemporary Review* 60: 234–52.
Malet, Lucas. 1890. *The Wages of Sin.* Leipzig: Bernhard Tauchnitz.
———. 1900. *The Gateless Barrier.* New York: Dodd, Mead, & Company.
———. 1906. *The Far Horizon.* Leipzig: Bernhard Tauchnitz.
———. 1911. *Adrian Savage.* Leipzig: Bernhard Tauchnitz.
———. 1923. *The Survivors.* London: Cassell and Company, Ltd.
"Recent Novels." 1900. *The Times*, 19 September, 2.
Schaffer, Talia. 2000. *The Forgotten Female Aesthetes: Literary Culture in Late-Victorian England.* Charlottesville: University Press of Virginia.
Srebrnik, Patricia. 1994. "The Re-subjection of 'Lucas Malet': Charles Kingsley's Daughter and the Response to Muscular Christianity." In *Muscular Christianity: Embodying the Victorian Age*, edited by Donald E. Hall, 194–214. Cambridge: Cambridge University Press.
Sykes, A.G.P. 1895. "The Evolution of the Sex." *Westminster Review* 143: 398–99.
Tintner, Adeline R. 2000. *The Twentieth-Century World of Henry James: Changes in His Work After 1900.* Baton Rouge: Louisiana State University Press.
Waters, Isobel. 2009. "'Still and Still Moving': The House as Time Machine in Henry James's *The Sense of the Past.*" *Henry James Review* 30(2): 180–95.
Watson, Rosamund Marriott. 1897. *The Art of the House*, edited by Gleeson White. London: George Bell and Sons.
Williams, Susan S. 1993. "Tell-Tale Representation: James and *The Sense of the Past.*" *The Henry James Review* 14: 72–86.

Part 4

Catholic (Proto-) Modernism

9 Against the English Nation

The Ideological Proto-Modernism of *The Far Horizon*

Holly A. Laird

From multiply marginalised positions, the protagonist of Lucas Malet's novel *The Far Horizon* (1916) delivers a critique of English nationalism. In paternity, ethnicity, occupation, age, religion, and even gender, Dominic Iglesias is positioned at a critical distance from the metanarratives of the Englishman, and his observations become the reader's guide to the narrowness of the English perspective at the turn of the twentieth century. But while the targets of critique are tightly aligned—English, classist, patriarchal, imperialist, and Protestant—the resistant factors operate unevenly, reflecting English norms. *The Far Horizon* does not represent Malet's most radical vision of human possibility. It invokes a return to England's pre-Anglican past—to Roman Catholicism. With unworldly beauties of architecture, music, and ritual; its rich, ancient symbolism; its narratives of extremity in suffering and bliss; and its mystic promise of paradisiac certainty, Roman Catholicism appealed deeply to aesthetes, like poets Lionel Johnson and 'Michael Field', and catered to their sense of themselves and their art as things apart. In *The Far Horizon*, aesthetic methods advance a religiously inflected proto-modernism. This text exemplifies the formal as well as ideological cross currents of its moment, as writers wrestled with what the dawn of the twentieth century might mean, when the ancient had never seemed so distant, the new so ambivalent.

With a Spanish father and partly Irish mother, Dominic repeatedly encounters suspicion among the English. Although he has managed to acquire employment as a bank clerk, he suffers rejection by his sole friend as soon as he confesses to belief in Roman Catholicism. As a man of partly ethnic, partly "aristocratic" features and dignified demeanour, he becomes an exotic object of attraction to women, a fact which he finds repellent (Malet 1906, 86–87). Ordered to retire early at the age of fifty-five, when the bank director's nephew is introducing modern methods, Dominic abruptly faces life as a bachelor in late middle age. Far from imagining marriage as a goal at this ripe time of life, his mind is seized by a crisis of aging. When he befriends a mysterious woman nearly as lonely as he, she dictates the terms of their meetings. He becomes her puppy-like sidekick, obligingly subject to her whims. Through this charismatic woman—a former actress and rich man's mistress—Dominic visits the borders of respectable society. As Patricia Lorimer Lundberg has explained, Malet

> transitioned from novels and essays about female or male renunciation of self—with secular saints and celibate ascetics seeking to transcend life's temptations—to novels focusing on thwarted artistic ambitions and illicit love, stultifying marriages, and sexually bold or erratic characters.
>
> (Lundberg 2003, 134)

In *The Far Horizon* Malet does all these things, using the latter to emphasise the former: a secular saint finds himself in a Platonic relationship with the "sexually bold and erratic" actress Poppy St. John.

Dominic has internalised some British norms, particularly a Protestant work ethic, cleanliness and chaste living, polite reticence, utilitarian "common sense," and (not least) racialism and ageism. Malet does not distance or satirise these assumptions. Still, owing to Dominic's layered marginalisation, he watches without being seen by mainstream middle-class England. As he observes England's misplaced arrogance and foundational prejudices, the narrative turns into an explicit critique of Anglo-centric nationalism.

Set at the turn of the century, the novel records the onset of the Second Boer War. Through Dominic's informed perspective, Malet details the jingoistic complacency with which the British people mistakenly anticipate an easy victory over the Dutch. Extending this critique of Anglo-centrism to the imperial front, the novel registers the effectiveness of Dutch guerrilla methods and the tenacity of a distant land's inhabitants (181). Later, when queen-and-empress, Victoria, dies (398), her name is not mentioned (nor her successor's) as the mid-winter funeral procession becomes mere background for Malet's narrative. A month or so later, with springtime birds and flowers rising, Dominic's own death arrives. In a conclusion unlike the conventional endings of many English novels, *The Far Horizon* upends the social hierarchy to place Dominic, the foreigner, at its centre.

As Talia Schaffer has argued,

> Aestheticism let Malet write proto-modernist novels that post-Victorian readers adored. And her later novels, particularly *The Far Horizon*, *Adrian Savage*, and *The Survivors*, are modernist inasmuch as they explore the consciousnesses of heretofore marginalized figures: the lower-middle-class clerk, the actress/prostitute, the madman, the suicidally repressed spinster.
>
> (Schaffer 2000, 199)

In fact, all these forms of marginalisation appear in *The Far Horizon*, jostling against White Anglo-Saxon Protestant norms. Like both the aesthetes and the modernists, Dominic contests the complacent and bourgeois, yet simultaneously restive and insecure, "horribly prolific" (Malet 1906, 13) and aggressive presumptions of modern England. The novel reached a popular audience nonetheless because, like other pre-modernist novels (for example, Forster's *A Room with A View* or Lawrence's *Sons and Lovers*), it merged turn-of-the-century realism and satire with modernist anti-conventionalism and aesthetic symbolism.

A feature of *The Far Horizon* not commonly associated with either aestheticism or modernism, however, is this novel's embrace of a didactic conversion narrative and an explicit ideological position. While resembling New Woman and suffrage fiction in this respect, the novel advocates neither women's nor labour rights, instead taking a stance against those in favour of a pre-modern past. This too is a modernist strategy increasingly common among the best-known modern writers, who disliked modernity's (necessarily incomplete) results of democratisation and who fretted impatiently for something wholly different. For example, Dominic explains how

> the younger generation pays the debts contracted by the generation immediately preceding it. Justice, indeed, reigns already, always has done so—justice of a rather tremendous sort. But peace? —Peace is still very much to seek, both for the individual and the race.
>
> (82)

Foremost among *The Far Horizon's* aesthetic methods are its rhetoric of the ugly versus the beautiful, the live and energetic versus the dull and entrapped. It engages with the entrapped and subdued versus the prolifically reproductive and restlessly noisy, coupled with oxymoronic assertions of wholeness amid fragmentation and of a pristine pastness dwelling within the chaotic present. Malet deploys the strategies both of aestheticism and proto-modernism to an ideological end.

§

With its first words, *The Far Horizon* heralds its Roman Catholic theme: "DOMINIC IGLESIAS" (1). In contrast to the thoroughly English "Sir Richard Calmady" of Malet's previous novel, "Dominic" derives from the Latin "Dominicus," meaning "of the Lord," while "Iglesias" is a common Spanish name, derived from the word for "churches." His name translates, in other words, as "Holy Church." Set all in capital letters (a convention of novels of this time), these words evoke a Christian invocation, as in "Domine Deus," such that the emphasis falls, not directly on "Deus," or God, but on the Church. Yet Malet endows Dominic also with an earthly beauty that is at once foreign to the English and innately regal. Dominic is a tall man, with "his spare young figure, his thin shapely hands and feet, his blue-black Irish eyes and black hair, his energetic colourless face, his ready yet reticent speech—all these mark [...] him as exotic" (14). Another character describes him as like "a beautiful innocent uncrowned king" (59), and his co-workers nickname him a species of Spanish nobility, "the old Hidalgo" (24). An ethnically mixed character—his Spanish father is mostly absent and his lonely part-Irish mother formed the cornerstone of his youth—Dominic encounters discrimination by English society. "The British employer," in particular, "is half afraid, half contemptuous of the unusual and exotic," "instinctively disliking anything more alert and alive than his own most stolid self" (14).

Dominic enjoys "racial" identification, however, with the European past, as "his mind refuse[s] the limits" of his situation (1). For example, the remnants of the eighteenth century in the architecture of Dominic's lodging house offer "A touch of old-world stateliness in its aspect [that] satisfied his latent pride of race" (5). "Race" exceeds Englishness in this aesthetic context. The English are distinguished instead by "pretentious vulgarity" since, "[t]o certain natures," i.e. Dominic's, not by "obscurity or slender means, but the pretentious vulgarity which, in English-speaking countries, too often goes along with these constitutes the burden and the offence" (5). This text does not question the racialised science—or eugenics—of turn-of-the-century socio-biology. It merely recasts racial hierarchy, thus anticipating the autocratic (ultimately, fascistic) politics of Eliot, Pound, and Yeats's later modernisms.

As the first chapter ends, Malet rewrites and demystifies the impressionistic London of Conrad's *Heart of Darkness*. As she re-enters Conrad's vision, Malet drops in the explanatory detail of "coal smoke." As

> London began to reveal herself to him in her solidarity, under the cloud of dun-blue coal smoke—it was winter-time—which, at once hanging over and penetrating her immensity, adds the majesty of mystery to the majesty of mere size.
>
> (12–13)

The 'revelation,' for Malet, is not London's relation to a pre-civilised savagery but its modernity: the "strange" reality of a "feverishly alive" city with an "angry glare ... along the sky-line" (12). Urban London becomes a spectre of the unnatural, where opposites collapse and indecency thrives:

> When night comes in the country ... the land sinks into peaceful repose. But in cities it is otherwise. There the light leaves heaven for earth; and walks the streets, with much else far from celestial, until the small hours move towards the dawn and usher in the decencies of day.
>
> (12–13)

This ghastly scene proves illuminating for Dominic, who re-expresses its message, ironically, through the neo-romantic ideal of "multeity in unity" (Coleridge 1971, 464): "Never before had he seen London thus and understood it in all its enormous variety, yet as a unit, a whole" (13). Marlow's vision of imperialist Europe in *Heart of Darkness* is echoed in another passage of *The Far Horizon*: "His dreams of power and speculative activity directed themselves, consequently, to the British Colonies, and to those as yet unappropriated spaces of the earth's surface where British influence is still only tentatively present" (159).

Grounded as impressionist methods are in a philosophy of subjectivity and perception, such narrative is also psychological. Malet lends credibility to this moment by offering a caveat: "How much [Dominic] actually beheld with his bodily eyes, how much through the working of a rather exalted condition of imagination induced by loneliness and bodily fatigue, he could never subsequently determine" (13). Regardless of whether "real" or "imagined," this vision constitutes an authentic perception of the city and a valid reading of its symbolic significance: "the great city presented herself to him in the guise of some prodigious living creature, breathing, feeding, suffering, triumphing." Malet's sentence genders the vision female, continuing, "above all mating and breeding, terrible in her power and vitality, age old, yet still unspent" (13). The city presents itself as a grotesque, savage mother, which, again, resembles Conrad's London in spewing forth its people, commodities, and armies across the earth. London

> [p]resented herself to him as horribly prolific, ever out-passing her own unwieldy limits, sending forth her children, year after year, all the wide world over by shipping or by rail; receiving some tithe of them back, proud with accomplished fortune to enhance her glory ...
>
> (13)

But, while still mid-sentence (13), Malet departs from Conrad to emphasise not the adventurous travellers but the masses of unsung people, forced to return to fruitless, impoverished, and diseased lives "or, disgraced and broken, slinking homeward to the cover of her fog and darkness merely to swell the numbers of the nameless who rot and die." Malet emphasises not only those forgotten, failed returnees, but those who never left. Theirs is the worst fate of all:

> He thought of those others, too—and this touched his young ardour with a quick shudder of personal fear—whom she never sends forth at all; but holds in bondage all their lives long, enslaved to her countless and tyrant activities by their own poverty, or by their fellow-creatures' misfortunes, cruelties, and sins.
>
> (12–13)

Unlike Marlow, the seemingly detached, Buddha-like narrator of Conrad's tale, Dominic's perspective shifts London's peripheries to centre-stage and turns its scrutiny away from the slave trade inward, to its own enslaved middle and lower classes. Using both free indirect discourse and emancipatory rhetoric, Malet places her protagonist at the heart of this vast scene of abject beings, as he wonders, "Was it thus she was going to deal with him, Dominic Iglesias?" (13). Six chapters later, he concludes, "London, very evidently, having got him did not mean to let him go" (79).

Malet also describes a portrait of Dominic's former employer that recalls the famous aesthete, Oscar Wilde's, picture of Dorian Gray. Abel Barking's picture captures his degraded inner self from within its statuesque exterior since it is "painted by a well-known artist whose appreciation of the outward as a revelation of the inward man is slightly diabolic in its completeness" (18).

Malet's picture foregrounds both the outward trappings and the inner pretentiousness of the Englishman:

> The portrait was very clever, it was also very like. Looking upon it no sane observer could stand in doubt of Sir Abel's eminent respectability or eminent wealth ... Unluckily nature had been niggardly in the bestowal of those more delicate marks of breeding which, both in man and beast, denote distinction of personality and antiquity of race. Pursy, prolific, Protestant, a commonness pervaded the worthy gentleman's aspect.
>
> (18)

Malet concludes by contrasting this "common," "prolific," modern gentleman with the aesthetic and racially superior figure of Dominic, "as is a cheap oleograph to a fine sketch in pen and ink" (18). Sir Abel Barking remains "sublimely ignorant" (19) of any such revelation by his portrait, instead referring to it as to a vanity mirror, to reassure himself of his worth. On the advice of Reginald Barking, eager to apply modern banking methods, Sir Abel forces Dominic (whose extra diligence and intelligence have raised him by now to head clerk) into retirement. The narrator captures the aggressive imperialism of this gesture by tagging Sir Abel with an Egyptian stereotype: "it is ever a question whether to spoil the Egyptians, or to fling back even the best-earned wages, payable by Egyptians, full in the said Egyptians' face" (21). In the end, Dominic quietly accepts a pension to survive being flung back into unemployment.

While presenting the choice forced upon Dominic in modern capitalist terms of labour versus leisure, the narrator turns this event into an opportunity for proto-modernist defamiliarisation (a concept developed by the twentieth-century Russian formalist Viktor Shklovsky), such that the ordinary seems strange and can be seen afresh. Catherine Delyfer notes that Dominic "matures into a modern version of Marius the Epicurean," yearning, like Marius, for "a lifting of the actual horizon." For Delyfer, Walter Pater's words, "all is new" and even "enhanced ... by the thought of its brevity," resonate with Dominic's own experience, and Pater's "[l]ife in [modern] London" triggers Marius's moment of vision as it does Dominic's (qtd. in Delyfer 2016a, 122, 130).

Dominic's subjection is to the "exigencies of business demand ... that the hours of his journeying should be early and late," but this dulling repetition yields, thanks to his daily trip home occurring at a different time of day. As Malet's narrator remarks, "it came about that the aspect of these actually so-familiar thoroughfares was novel, as beheld in the height of the season at three o'clock in the afternoon" (23).

Malet adds a satiric note when she next defamiliarises the English leisure sport of polo through Dominic's eyes. Dominic asks an omnibus driver why a "stream of carriages and hansoms" causes traffic to slow, to which the driver responds, "Polo at Ranelagh ... Club team plays 'undred and first Lancers" (24). The narrator notes Dominic's amusing ignorance, writing, "The words had been to the inquirer pretty much as phrases from the liturgy of an unknown cult," so he asks, "Pardon me, polo, as I understand, is a species of game?" (27). In the next chapter, Dominic decides to educate himself on the subject, only to suffer exclusion from the club grounds for lack of a ticket (42). We later learn that this incident has not deterred Dominic from informing himself about leisurely pleasures, but unlike his precursor Dorian Gray, he rapidly exhausts that option:

> During the last ten days Mr. Iglesias had striven, with rather pathetic diligence, to cultivate amusement ... [which], as practised in great cities, is merely a matter of cash. Therefore he had dined at smart restaurants; had sampled theatres and music halls; had sat in the Park and watched the world and—in their more decent manifestations—the flesh and the devil drive by ...
>
> (86)

but "all of this left him cold, had bored rather than entertained him" (86). Not that Dominic feels self-righteous: he accounts for this boredom as an effect of old age, of being too old for new tricks. From his earliest youth, Malet adds, his alienating differences from his peers, his reverence for his mother, and his temperamental diffidence had shielded him from the habituating "influences of vice" (15).

The shock of retirement brings more distress than revival, as Dominic faces a spectre enlarged by allegorisation: "Its name was Old Age"

(26–27). Worse than foreign parentage, an ethnic visage, or a second-class career, Dominic is beset by ageism:

> For it gives to drink of the cup not of pleasure, but merely of patience, of physical loss and intellectual humiliation; and, once it has laid its spell upon you, you are past all remedy save the supreme remedy of death.
>
> (27)

Since Malet reached the same age as Dominic one year after this novel's publication, she may have been articulating her own perspective (though she lived another fifteen years, until 1931). Much as she treats race she treats age, as a matter of "the relentless logic of fact" (27). Still, Dominic does not know his remaining time is short and turns his last years into new opportunity. Malet finds new life for him in both a Paterian impressionism and aesthetic experience of the present moment and in a Roman Catholic reframing of death.

Initially, however, Dominic sees his plight as no better than that of a quintessentially anti-aesthetic, rusty machine: "I am a machine now, not a man. To the machine, work is life. Work over, life is over" (31). Having internalised the utilitarian ideal at the heart of the English middle-class work ethic, he mourns:

> Of all kinds of uselessness, that of we godlike human beings is the most utterly obvious when our working day is past … a few years of increasing degradation, a mere senseless killing of time until the very unpleasing goal is reached—along with a growing selfishness, and narrowness of outlook; along, possibly, with some development of senile sensuality, the more detestable because it lacks the provocation of hot blood. Oh! Dominic Iglesias, Dominic Iglesias, is that the ugly road you are doomed to travel—toothless greed for filling your belly with fly-blown dainties off the refuse-heap?
>
> (31)

In this graphic articulation of fears of aging, Malet connects Dominic to London: "through the open window, in sinister accompaniment … came the voice of the great city herself in answer—low, multitudinous, raucous, without emphasis but without briefest relief of interval or of pause" (32). While Dominic had "changed, so he believed, to the point of nullity and final ineptitude," London "remained strong, active, relentless … monstrous," and "from her there was no escape" (32). The word repeated here is not "whole," but the socialist term "solidarity," as "London revealed herself to him in her solidarity, revealed herself as a prodigious living creature, awful in her mysterious vigour, ever big with impending birth, merciless with impending death" (32). As Jane Ford and Delyfer have shown, *The Far Horizon* delivers a sophisticated critique not only of modern capitalism and consumerism but of its primary economic alternatives in the socialisms of Dominic's (and Malet's) father (Ford 2015; Delyfer 2016a).

At this difficult early stage in Dominic's misery, Malet briefly introduces the alternative she privileges, religiously and aesthetically, through a hint of the Miltonic "Uncreated Light":[1]

> Dominic dwelt, consciously and sensibly, in the horror of the Outer Darkness—which horror is known only to that small and somewhat suspect minority of human beings who are also capable, by the operation of the divine mercy, of dwelling in the glory of the Uncreated Light. The swing of the pendulum is equal to right as to left.
>
> (33)

Later, Malet links "the far horizon" to "the Uncreated Light" when she writes that Dominic "had lost sight of the far horizon which is touched by the glory of the Uncreated Light" (201).

Given the minoritisation of the "somewhat suspect" people who embrace God, Dominic's first impulse (distinguishable here from the narrator's) is "self-preservation," and he buoys himself by "directing his thought" like the average Englishman, "to things practical and average" (33). Malet does not let this moment pass in her conversion narrative without reinforcing how culturally marginalised Dominic is, "as he suddenly realised, by temperament and ideals as well as by race!" (33). She draws a further racial distinction in his favour with the following generalisation: "It is characteristic of the Latin to see things written in fire and blood, which the slower-brained Anglo-Saxon only sees written in red paint—if, indeed, he ever arrives at seeing them written at all" (34). Attacking the English stereotype of Latin peoples as irrationally emotional, Malet paradoxically grants Dominic, heretofore a paragon of restraint, the gift of quick-brained passion. "To-night," writes Malet, "the Latin held absolute sway in Dominic Iglesias. With freedom had come a curious reversion to type" (34–35). Dominic's paradoxical "type" anticipates modernist formulations, such as Yeats's "passionate thought" (255) or Lawrence's "blood-consciousness" (470).[2] When Malet reiterates this racial distinction, in the context of Dominic's friendship with George Lovegrove, she anticipates Forster's novels as well as Lawrence's:

> The Latin, unlike the Anglo-Saxon, does not consider it necessary as soon as adolescence is past to extirpate his heart; or, failing successful performance of that heroic operation, strictly to limit

> the activities of it to his amours, legitimate or otherwise. Hence Dominic Iglesias felt no shame that the sight of his old plaything, or of his old school-fellow … should provoke in him a great tenderness. (370)

At first, the alternative plot of friendship (as opposed to the dominant, courtship plot) offers Dominic harbour from within the English nation, but not for long.

The motif heralded by Malet's title, "the far horizon," is first observed—tucked more discreetly into her prose than the "Uncreated Light,"—in a heightened aesthetic context, when Dominic recalls his mother's needlework artistry in "very fine Irish lace." She had "poured forth her soul, as another might pour it forth in music, finding there an imaginative language far surpassing, in its subtlety of suggestion, articulate speech" (82–83). Not only beautiful in design, her tapestries exhibit mastery of narrative description and plot:

> There were deserts of net, of spider's web fineness, to be laboriously traversed; hills of difficulty to be climbed, whence far horizons disclosed themselves; dainty flower-gardens, crossed by open paths, and hedged about with curves, sinuous and full of pretty impediments. (83)

As if in reaction to the decadent implications of the "sinuous" and "pretty impediments," her design withdraws into abstraction. It becomes modernist in its capacity to visualise

> agitating and even fearful things … confusions of outline, broken purposes, multiplicity of opposing intentions, struggle of good and evil powers in the intricacies of some rich arabesque; or monotonous repetitions of design which distressed her as with the terrors of imprisonment and of unescapable fate. (83)

As casually as the "far horizon" is dropped into this description between "hills of difficulty" and "dainty flower-gardens," so too the "struggle of good and evil powers" peeks unobtrusively between "opposing intentions" and "monotonous repetitions"—as if the divine melodrama were a mere detail in this magisterial evocation of a woman's art. This multifaceted vision becomes Dominic's guiding narrative, his Romanised 'pilgrim's progress.' He patiently counted his years as his mother's caretaker, while she grew "mad," and this work became the sole sacred purpose of his young manhood. Her agency resurfaces in his choices in "old age." He adjures himself, "Let him [Dominic] have patience, as she, his mother, had had when traversing deserts and climbing Difficulty

Hill in her lacework; and to him, also, should far horizons be disclosed," the "hunger of his heart and spirit" answered (87).

In stark contrast to Dominic's mother's art, the single writer in the novel's cast of characters is presented caustically, in the next chapter, prey to the worst faults of the self-preoccupied aesthete. While entertaining gentlemen in her apartments, Poppy St. John has separated from her ne'er-do-well husband, a failed playwright, de Courcy Smyth. Smyth's story overturns prior Victorian narratives of the neglected, impoverished hack (94), such as George Gissing's in *New Grub Street* (1891). As clichéd as that story may have been by 1902, Malet goes well beyond stereotype to villainise this character. He becomes tediously hideous, outwardly and inwardly, under her pen. Abusive towards his wife, financially improvident, egregiously vain, endlessly resentful, and irredeemably cynical, he derives not from the margins but from the English upper-class heritage signalled by his name (92, 143). Like Dominic Iglesias, he has lost his last paying job and his youth, but he has saved nothing and leeches onto Dominic.

Unaware as yet of the beckoning "Uncreated Light," Dominic turns from the leisure afforded by consumer culture to the rewards, first, of altruism, referred to only as "his idea" (113), and, second, of friendship. Malet has been compared unfavourably to E. M. Forster (she claimed not to have heard of him prior to a 1922 review of her story collection *Da Silva's Widow*[3]). Nevertheless, in a foretaste of Forster's famous dictum, "only connect," Dominic rediscovers a childhood friendship with Lovegrove and love with Poppy St. John. Easily falling in with her own need for friendship with no strings attached, he embodies that transitional figure of the English gentleman, the "bachelor," who, at the turn of the century, as Katherine V. Snyder has shown, was revalued as a New Man, paralleling the independent New Woman (Snyder 1999). Poppy suggests that Dominic strikes the figure of a dandy (without using that term): "Your tailor's a gem!" (343). But altruism and friendship mark just the first steps in his conversion story's "dark night of the soul" as circumstances push him into depression. By turns, disappointed and bluntly rejected—in altruism with de Courcy Smyth, in friendship with Lovegrove, and in love with Poppy St. John—ultimately, a humbled submission to the Church and relationship with Christ present the only solutions.

In the "depression" that follows Poppy's "dismissal" (199, 200), coinciding with England's "Black Week" of defeats by the Dutch, Dominic's despair is broken by a carved oak panel left to him by his mother. Associated earlier in his life with childhood comforts, then with aesthetic pleasure, the carving now becomes visionary—as its depiction of Calvary transforms "Flesh" into "Word" and "Word" into "Flesh" (205)—fulfilling not only the Baudelairean aesthetic ideal of *correspondances* but religious doctrine. Five chapters later, Malet records Dominic's assiduous study of the various religious creeds and congregations of London, thus producing, though more superficially, this novel's most Daniel Deronda-like interior monologue of metaphysical meditation. Dominic rejects the available Protestant options, from the evangelical outdoor preacher to the recent pseudoscience of spiritualism, in favour of Roman Catholicism. Malet reserves her single evocation of the physical beauty of church and ritual for Chapter XXII's ending, where they become aesthetic vehicles (or "Word") for Dominic's ecstatic submission to the Church (in the "Flesh").

In a twist on the traditional conversion story that enhances the psychological realism of the experience, Dominic's worldly struggles and temptations increase after his conversion—though his depressions become a thing of the past. Each trial exhibits the 'organic' way in which a Christ-like man might live with and through humanity. As Dominic believes, the Roman Catholic Church "is not an organisation, but an organism; a Living Being" (249). Dominic seems as realistic and human a character as ever in the next episodes' threatening plot complications: in the intensifying of relationships with Poppy, de Courcy Smyth, his former employers (Barking Brothers & Barking), and George Lovegrove. It is only at the novel's end that Malet shocks the reader with the full impact of Dominic's conversion to Roman Catholicism in a finale as different from the conventional happy ending of the Victorian novel as it is from the modern open ending.

§

The Far Horizon introduces its critique of the English church early in the novel, in the character of Dominic's neighbourhood Anglican minister, Dr. Nevington. He embodies the muscular Christianity against which Malet had rebelled, as Patricia Srebrnik explains, in the figure of her famous father (Srebrnik 1994, 194, 208). Dr Nevington, with a "studied effect of geniality and benevolence about him, slightly tempered perhaps, by cold and watchful blue-grey eyes" fixes "with unswerving determination upon the shovel-hat, apron, and gaiters of the Anglican episcopate" (62). He is, however, not too busy in this performative role to notice non-Anglicans and apply some missionary zeal. Both "liberal" and "wide-minded" Nevington's 'broad church' thinking receives implicit critique by Malet in his sermonising:

> we should always guard against any appearance of harshness or illiberality in dealing with Christians from whom we have reason to differ in minor questions or practice ... I could wish that certain parties within the Church were animated by the same manly and intelligent intolerance of idolatry and superstition as the majority of the dissenters whom I meet.
>
> (63)

His female audience greets his sermons with enthusiastic idolatry: "The feminine members of his congregation found this most beautiful; having, indeed, been known to declare that did he preach in Chinese, they would still receive edification and spiritual benefit" (63). That Anglicanism is central to British nationalism becomes clear when he says, "Truly the prosperity of the nation ... of this dear old England of ours that we so love, is wholly bound up with the prosperity of her national Church" (69). Dr. Nevington is not shy about politics. He advocates specifically for higher salaries for "many members of my cloth," whose "poverty ... is now a crying scandal—" (69). He envisages churchmen linking church to state, as modern pragmatists: "We have no place in these days for visionaries and dreamers. We want men who march with the times, who are interested in politics, and can make themselves felt" (70). The degree to which he speaks for the times is underlined when Nevington is promoted by the Archbishop to the office of a suffragan bishop (400).

Malet's critique of Englishness reaches its peak in her descriptions of the Second Boer War. She writes, sarcastically,

> Now war is, unquestionably, not a little staggering to the modern civilized conscience; and this particular war possessed the additional unpleasantness of having in it, at first sight, an element of the grotesque ... it struck the majority of the British public as being of the nature of a very bad joke.
>
> (155)

What makes it "grotesque" and "a very bad joke" is its offense against British superiority since "it was as though a very small and very cheeky boy, after making offensive signs, had spat in the nation's face." Attesting to the short memory native to imperialist complacency, Malet notes, "A few persons, it is true remembered Majuba Hill"—England's terrible defeat ending the First Boer War and the worst since the American revolution (55). Malet equates political complacency with financial "wealth apoplexy" (156). After the British are defeated by the Dutch Africans during "Black Week," Dominic thinks this of the English:

> It has been universally assumed that the English are a serious nation. This is an error. They are not serious but indifferent, a nation of individualists, each mainly, not to say exclusively occupied with his own private affairs. With the vast majority unity of sentiment is suspect, and patriotism a passive rather than an active virtue.
>
> (206)

English "individualism," then, is coextensive not with "serious" nationhood, but with a general "indifference" to sentiment even of the patriotic kind.

Yet this narrative is nearly as nationalist as it is anti-English and as aligned with racialism as it is anti-conventional. We see this when Malet writes that "Next to the Jew the Dutchman is the most stubbornly tenacious of human creatures ... [and] is a fighting man into the bargain" (156). Malet's novel is Euro-centric: Black Week is thus "a sorry tale, and one over which Europe at large chuckled" (206). The deliberately unspecific "Egyptian" and "Chinese" references (noted above) echo in similarly abstract references to the "Oriental" (41, 184, 348). "America" too comes in for caricature (159–60). Malet is at her most international in her epigraphs, where she makes the modernist gesture of context-free citation of great texts, eastern and western, ancient and contemporary. The first derives from the book of Jeremiah in the Old Testament; the second "From the Sayings of Lao-Tzu"; and the third from an important modernist precursor, Gustave Flaubert. In these epigraphic texts, the aesthetic creed parallels the biblical, and both become manifestations, through Lao-Tzu, of "universal" truths.

Malet does tweak orthodox relations, but as Srebnik has shown, she also reinforces gender norms for most of the men and women in this novel (Srebnik 1994, 208, 210). Stereotypes of women, their superficiality, petty jealousy, natural maternity, vapidity, vulgarity, and conventional looks, are numerous; they texture Malet's descriptions without qualification or rejoinder. Juxtaposed with Dominic's narrative, in particular with the financial plot, these women's invented romances with him become ludicrous. Yet, as Lundberg emphasises, quoting a reviewer's remarks, this novel seemed "nothing if not up to date" in 1906 (qtd. in Lundberg 2003, 297), and in *The New York Times Saturday Review of Books,* the poet Madison Cawein called it "a book for the future" (Cawain 1907, 202). Its women were modern: the highly satiric Serena's self-preoccupied questioning of social assumptions might have made for a fascinating study of the self-reflective modern woman in another author's hands; Serena's vaguely satiric sister, an influential Christian public speaker and activist, has no voice in the text; Peachie Porcher, a widowed, self-reliant property owner who lets her rooms to bachelors, becomes a poster child for a comedy of the middle-aged marriage market. The only admirable woman in this narrative (a cross between Ellen Terry and Lillie Langtry) is the decorative, Dickensian character whom Dominic thinks of as "The Lady of the Wind-swept Dust." Poppy St. John's story of working-class struggle and her intelligent capacity for engaging conversation with educated men all raise her above her peers but do little to diminish her reaffirmation of the stereotype of the actress-mistress.

Women remain women, while men remain men. A glimpse of conversation between an aristocratic man and woman demonstrates this. Probed by his sister-in-law about the moral character of her daughter's fiancé, Lord Fallowfeild reminds her of the world's ways and justifies them as a matter of Hardyesque blind chance:

> I don't want to seem a brute, but she must just take her chance along with the rest of you. Marriage always has been a confounded uncertain business, ... The sort of remedies excited persons suggest to mitigate the dangers of it are a good deal worse than the disease, in my opinion. Every woman has to take her chance. Every man has to take his, too, you know.
>
> (106)

Falling into a seemingly democratising language—everyone "has to take" his or her chance—and creed of self-reliance, Lord Fallowfeild dismisses all actual modern proposals for remedies. Though not the typical Englishman, then, Dominic is carefully marked as masculine. His response to Dr. Nevington's sermonising is, inwardly, "to trample," while outwardly he preserves the stiffest of (British) upper lips (71). When trapped, Dominic identifies with a "majestical" tree, whose branches creaked "not weakly, but rather with virility, as of a strong man chained and groaning against his fetters" (145).

Dominic evinces distaste for marriage and avoids the company of socially suitable women, but he advocates the "institution" for others, and Malet assures us of his reproductive "normal[cy]": "Be under no misapprehension, dear friend," he tells Poppy (who otherwise plays the male, aggressive role in their relationship), "I am a perfectly normal piece of flesh and blood, with a man's normal passions, and his natural craving for wife, and child, home, family, and the like" (352). What constrained him when young was being "bound" to serve his mother, and what binds him now is old age. Fifty-five, he says, is not "a due and proper time," as there is for "everything, as the Preacher testifies," but rather an "objectionabl[e]" "spectacle of amorous uxorious efflorescence" (352).

In situating her novel in a specifically 'modern' setting, Malet indicates that progress and, with it, a century of democratic, social, and religious reforms, has failed. The failure of social reform may be inferred also from the social history she gives Dominic Iglesias. His father's extensive absences from the household are explained (in letters he sees after his mother's death—from Paris, Naples, Prague, and Petersburg) by socialist revolutionary activities, especially in Spain. Dominic's father had a

> far from ignoble nature, but of narrow outlook and undying hatreds, ... deeply involved in revolutionary intrigue of the most advanced type ... [his] self-confidence was colossal; all rule being abominable to him—save his own—all rulers hideous, save himself ... The anarchist, rightly understood, is merely the autocrat, the tyrant, turned

> inside out ... this man ... [Dominic's] mother had loved, with all the faithfulness and pure passion of her Irish blood.
>
> (8–9)

A family friend, Pascal Pelletier (probably French), served as an occasional surrogate father for Dominic. Pelletier—"an angel-faced long-haired hysteric creature, inspired by an impassioned enthusiasm for infernal machines and wholesale slaughter in theory," if also "gentle," "devot[ed]," and "tender-hearted" towards Dominic and his mother—held "unlimited" belief and optimistic hope in the elder Iglesias, "in his demonic power and fertility of resource" (9–10). The absent father and the enthusiastic Pelletier, the latter broken by illness and poverty, are Dominic's living symbols of socialism, revolution, and anarchism. Together with women's seemingly meaningless rise in the public and private spheres of modernity, these men exhaust the novel's representation of the fruits of democratic change. When first confronting his retirement, Dominic allegorises "Freedom" and "Loneliness," equating them as oppressive spectres, before proclaiming the worst of the three "Old Age."

§

With its complex tragi-comic plotting, satiric accents, frequently orthodox social constructions, and explicit religious position, this novel might have reached any number of conventional endings. But though Dominic falls in love, he successfully resists both sexual temptation and marriage. The 'fallen woman' whom he loves, Poppy St. John, does not have to die, and his friend George Lovegrove is not lost to him, after all. A lonely and repentant George is welcomed back; Poppy St. John achieves fame for her art, fulfilling her 'genius' (396); and Dominic achieves certainty as a practicing believer in Roman Catholicism. 'Happy'" as all this is, the ending is not saccharine or sentimental. It possesses the abruptness of the ending of Nella Larsen's 1929 *Passing*—in which the protagonist falls from a window—though neither its ambiguity nor its tragedy. It is as absolute as Penelope's "Yes" with which Joyce's 1922 *Ulysses* ends, though Malet's novel ends with Poppy's "painted face," quietly weeping, as she kneels (Malet 1906, 424). What elides sentimentality is this chapter's leavening by Poppy's characteristic humour and irony shortly before the conclusion; Malet's consistency in characterisation of Dominic's restraint and calm; and the assiduous realism, alternating with lyricism, of Dominic 's final hours. Diagnosed with heart disease, Dominic coolly refuses treatment, and Malet enacts the "very fine art" of dying (415), with which he lets himself drift into sleep, dream, and death. Malet grants Dominic and Poppy a credible final conversation, builds suspense, and uses Poppy's thrilled theatre audience to delay her return—she misses Dominic's actual death.

The death scene confronts Poppy, and the reader, jarringly in the following paragraph, producing a spectacle unlike anything in the ordinary Protestant experience of death. Writing at the end of the previous paragraph, "[I]n the door-way [Poppy] faltered, set her teeth, bowed her head and paused," the narrator next describes this scene:

> For in the centre of the room a bier was dressed, and on either side of it stood lighted tapers of browning wax, in tall black and gold candlesticks. At the foot, some distance apart, two low-seated rush-bottomed high-backed prie-dieu had been placed. Upon the one on the left a little nun knelt, her loose black habit concealing all the outline of her figure. The white linen pall was turned back, across the chest of the corpse, to where the shapely long-fingered hands were folded upon an ebony and silver crucifix. ... Beautiful in death as in life, serene, proud, austere, but young now with the eternal youth of those who have believed, and attained, the Land of the Far Horizon, Dominic Iglesias lay before her.
>
> (423–4)

In presenting the actual trappings of a Roman Catholic death scene, Malet suggests oneness of Word with flesh: Dominic is royal in death, as he was regal in life, having reached the crowning glory of a dedicated Christian life. During its composition, this novel's first title was "The Paradise of Dominic Iglesias" (Lundberg 2003, 266), to be replaced and distanced by "the far horizon." But Dominic has tutored the reader to understand the symbol as the thing itself. As Delyfer explains:

> the novel constructs Iglesias as ... hanker[ing] after the lost unity of signifier and signified ... something of "a poet" himself [140], yearning for the "language of symbol" [79], "the language of the spirit," the "adjustment between the exterior and interior life" [89], [and] he is particularly alert to the problematic of representation in general, that is to say, to the gap that separates the sign from its referent, from its ground of value or meaning.
>
> (Delyfer 2016b, 170–1)

In Dominic's Roman Catholicism, the symbol becomes the thing, the value, and the significance. For Malet's novel, aesthetic method becomes precisely suited for a literal enactment of religious conversion, for her own affirmation of belief through Dominic, and for her reader's potential enlightenment.

Ironically, only a year would elapse after the publication of this novel in 1906 before Pope Pius X condemned theological speculation along with any deviation from church doctrine, and Dominic 's version, with its intense aestheticism, its hint of transcendentalism, its sensual interludes of the erotic, might well have struck him as heretical—a pernicious "modernism." At the end, Dominic lies dead with his hands laced around an ebony and silver crucifix, four great candles at the corners of his bier, and kneelers at his feet, one for a small nun, the other for a visitor. The visitor is the Lady of the Wind-swept Dust, who will kneel through a night of spiritual vigil. For Malet's mostly Protestant audience, this memorable scene brings the shock of recognition of this novel's religious difference.

Notes

1 This phrase is usually associated with Milton's *Paradise Lost*, where he writes, "HAil [*sic*] holy light, ofspring of Heav'n first-born, / Of th'Eternal Coeternal beam /... since God is light, / And never but in unapproached light/ Dwelt from Eternitie, dwelt then in thee, / Bright effluence of bright increate! (Book III, ll. 1–6), and it is based on 1 Timothy 6:16 in the Bible—"dwelling in light which no man can approach unto" —in the New Testament of the Bible. The precise phrase appears to have been coined by James Thomson, who writes of God as "Light Himself, in uncreated light," (line 176), in the "Summer" section of his long poem *The Seasons*.

2 Dominic's implicitly "quicker-brained" capacity "'to see things written in fire and blood'" anticipates the more famous paradoxes of Yeats and Lawrence: respectively, of "'thought'" engrained with "'passion'" and of a mental "'consciousness'" within the "'blood.'"

3 See "Pale Souls" (1922, 4). Malet responded to *The Times* declaring that she had never heard of Forster. For an account of the exchange see Goldstein (2017, 169–71).

Works Cited

Cawein, Madison. 1907. "Lucas Malet's Book for the Future." *The New York Times Saturday Review of Books*, 6 April, 202.

Coleridge, Samuel Taylor. 1971 [1814]. "On the Principles of Genial Criticism." *Critical Theory Since Plato*, edited by Hazard Adams, 463–7. New York: Harcourt Brace Jovanovich.

Delyfer, Catherine. 2016a. "The Aesthete, the Banker, and the Saint: Economies of Gift and Desire in Lucas Malet's *The Far Horizon* (1906)." In *Economies of Desire at the Victorian Fin de Siècle: Libidinal Lives*, edited by Jane Ford, Kim Edwards Keates, and Patricia Pulham, 122–42. New York: Routledge.

———. 2016b. "Speculating on Art in *Fin-de-Siècle* Fiction." In *Reconnecting Aestheticism and Modernism: Continuities, Revisions, Speculations*, edited by Bénédicte Coste, Catherine Delyfer, and Christine Reynier, 165–74. London: Routledge.

Ford, Jane. 2015. "Socialism, Capitalism, and the Fiction of Lucas Malet: 'The Spirit of the Hive.'" *English Literature in Transition* 58(4): 551–7.

Goldstein, Bill. 2017. *The World Broke in Two: Virginia Woolf, T.S. Eliot, D.H. Lawrence, E.M. Forster and the Year that Changed Literature*. London: Bloomsbury.

Lawrence, D. H. 1981. *The Letters of D. H. Lawrence, Volume II: June 1913-October 1916*, edited by George J. Zytaruk and James T. Boulton. Cambridge: Cambridge University Press.

Lorimer Lundberg, Patricia. 2003. *An Inward Necessity: The Writer's Life of Lucas Malet*. New York: Peter Lang.

Malet, Lucas. 1888. "The Progress of Woman: In Literature." *The Universal Review* 2(7): 295–301.

———. 1905. "The Threated Re-Subjection of Woman." *Fortnightly Review* 77: 806–19.

———. 1906. *The Far Horizon*. London: Hutchinson.

Milton, John. 1667. *Paradise Lost. The John Milton Reading Room,* edited by Thomas J. Luxton (Trustees of Dartmouth College, 1977–2017). Available at www.dartmouth.edu/~milton/reading_room/contents/text.shtml#paradiseLost, (accessed 10 January 2017).

"Pale Souls: Lucas Malet's New Stories." 1922. *The Times*, 6 June, 14.

———. 2000. *The Forgotten Female Aesthetes: Literary Culture in Late-Victorian England*. Charlottesville: University Press of Virginia.

Snyder, Katherine V. 1999. *Bachelors, Manhood, and the Novel 1850–1925*. Cambridge: Cambridge University Press.

Srebrnik, Patricia. 1994. "The Re-Subjection of 'Lucas Malet': Charles Kingsley's Daughter and the Response to Muscular Christianity." In *Muscular Christianity: Embodying the Victorian Age*, edited Donald E. Hall, 194–214. Cambridge: Cambridge University Press.

Thomas, James. 1727. *The Seasons*, edited by Percivale Stockdale. Printed for A. Hamilton Gray's Inn at Holborn, 56. In *Full Text of … Archive. org*. Available at https://archive.org/stream/seasonsbyjamest00thomgoog/seasonsbyjamest00thomgoog_djvu.txt, (accessed 10 January 2017).

Yeats, William Butler. 2007. "Art and Ideas." In *The Collected Works of W. B. Yeats, Volume IV: Early Essays*, edited by Richard J. Finneran and George Bornstein, 250–6. New York: Simon and Schuster.

10 "[U]ndecode-able wireless signals"

Telepathy and Contamination in *The Survivors*

Jane Ford

In "still weather" the "drumming" sound of gunfire travelled over the Channel to Maidsworthy Hall, the Hampstead estate of Rupert Secker, protagonist of Lucas Malet's 1923 novel, *The Survivors* (30, 20). This "roll of ghostly drums" is like white noise or electromagnetic interference, sometimes impeding the "wireless calls" that travel between individuals of the "ultra-receptive" sort (29, 12, 9). Secker, who is a Foreign Office official and darling of his extended family-set, is just such a creature. In the opening scenes of the novel, at a Maidsworthy gathering—a "spasm of repose," he calls it—Secker finds his attention "oddly switched aside by some telepathic call upon it from without" (1, 9). The transmitter of these "wireless calls which had so perplexed him," it is later revealed, is the enigmatic Lydia Alywin, Secker's "adopted niece" (12, 4). In a kind of Marxian adherence to the linguistic conventions of his occupation, Secker conceptualises psychic experience as communications intelligence; he considers, for instance, whether "those uncoded and, so far, undecode-able wireless messages had actually been sent, or were they no more than projections of his own morbidly active imagination?" (16). In psychoanalytic terms, it is clear that the *thing* encoded in this psychic experience is the civil servant's erotic desire for the distant cousin he calls niece—later that evening he tries, unsuccessfully, to kiss Lydia's "pouting lips" and imagines her "stiffen[ing] under his hands" (37). But while Secker is unable to decipher these encrypted messages, his self-scrutiny implies that telepathic communication and human cognition/subjectivity (themselves volatile and ambiguous) are, for him, structurally similar.

Existing scholarship has often read telepathic communication as a psychical counterpart to modernist narrative. Helen Sword notably argues that phenomena such as automatic writing or telepathic transference "engage with all the major tropes of literary modernism": "linguistic playfulness, decentrings of consciousness, fracturing of conventional gender roles" (Sword 1999, 87). Likewise, Roger Luckhurst remarks that the "conjuncture[s], where telepathy, mystical communion, supernatural 'possession', and sexual transference overlay each other, become nodal points for Modernist investigations of the limits of consciousness" (Luckhurst 2002, 262). Certainly, telepathy is one of the hallmarks of the modernist development of Malet's style—a way she achieves the disorienting psychological effects characteristic to modernist narrative. Catherine Delyfer points out that *The Survivors* "alternatively dilates and skips, and the focus keeps shifting, thus destabilizing the reader's horizon of expectation" (Delyfer 2011, 117). For Delyfer, there are clear parallels between the novel's "narrative directionlessness" and the disorientation of the battlefield (117). Indeed, Malet reimagines the Maidsworthy dining room as a battle-line, the principal artillery of which is social intercourse. Reminiscent of Wilfred Owen's "shrill, demented choirs of wailing shells" Buckton Puce, the irascible son of Rosemond—Secker's cousin and former love-interest—"burst out" in condemnation of Lydia's failure to observe correct dining etiquette, the "shrillness of his speech" leaving Francis, Secker's nephew and private secretary, "shocked" and in "shattered wits" (Malet 1923, 11–12; Owen 1997, 25). Meanwhile, Lydia's "wireless calls," "attacked [Secker] with an increased force and urgency" (12, 9).

My argument is not, however, that Malet deploys telepathic motifs to bolster her modernist credentials; rather, I will suggest that the narrative instability which Sword argues is common to modernist poetics and psychical phenomena, allows Malet to renegotiate a much older, theological preoccupation. That is to say, obscure networks of telepathic communication are subject to the same doubts and epistemological challenges that beset the Word (itself muddied in theological conflicts and ambiguities). A converted Catholic, Malet plays on this structural equivalence, joining telepathy's stylistic and psychological opportunities with her own theological awareness of embodiment, divine revelation, and the worldliness of the church. The cast of *The Survivors* perpetually strive to transcend the somatic frontier of the physical body—a yearning Malet often rehearses—using variants on the idea of telepathic transmission to circumvent the linguistic constraints of human discourse.[1] But the 'sinful' body of man, unlike the body of Christ, is a contaminant, an imperfect aerial, vulnerable to (erotically inflected) communicative infelicities. Malet shows us this and with the First World War setting foregrounds the impossibility of this particular brand of transcendence. In this way, this chapter significantly reshapes the perception of Malet's writing following her conversion, demonstrating that far from enshrining more conservative values, her religious beliefs are a driving force behind what is an unfairly neglected and formally adventurous exploration of (post-)war subjectivity.

§

Following his fruitless attempts to decode Lydia's "wireless calls," Rupert "Secker became unpleasantly conscious of his own fatigue," "the psychic strain of the evening productive not of "the kindly tiredness which presages sleep" but a "moral" and "intellectual" tiredness (12, 16). Malet writes:

> [P]resently, sitting thus alone in the luminous half-dark, Night stretched out her arms to him, enclosing, embracing him, holding him, a not unwilling captive, against her breast … Thought ceased, transmuted into a wordless yearning towards Nature and the mystery that—for whoso is gifted with vision—stands back of Nature, penetrating which, the travel-stained soul of man, his vesture of flesh discarded, will, as we fondly trust, find rest at last in the presence of God.
>
> (16–17)

Secker's retreat from this obscure network of communication is articulated in strikingly Romantic terms. Like the rendering and receiving mind of Shelley's "Mont Blanc"—conducting "unremitting interchange" with the "universe of things around"—Secker's "ultra-perceptive condition" is a corollary of his "ultra-receptive one" (Malet 1923, 9; Shelley 2012, 1105). His repose upon the "breast" of Night and "wordless yearning towards Nature" reads like a Coleridgean lapse into a preverbal milieu of Romantic infancy. In fact, Secker's regression from "intellectual" weariness to "wordless" nativity relies on the same binaries that define Romantic representations of adulthood and childhood: instinct versus reason, emotion versus intellect, and so on.

For contemporary readers, telepathic communication belongs to the same ontological category as ghost-writing or, mediumship. For Malet's protagonist, though, it assumes the complexion of his own *terrestrial* conditions—of code, intelligence, and war-work. What Secker desires is to discard "his vesture of flesh" (and with it corporeal communication) in favour of a form of intercourse that does not just short circuit, but actually *precedes* the linguistic encumbrances of embodied adulthood. As I have intimated, Malet uses the trope of telepathy to rework themes that have long featured in her writing. In her 1901 bestseller, *The History of Sir Richard Calmady*, Sir Richard is born with a deformity—his lower legs are entirely absent but his feet, which are of "normal size," are "embedded in the stump[s]" (Malet 2003, 42). Richard imagines himself as "human wreckage" in a "world peopled by beings maimed as he was himself, but after a more subtle and intimate fashion—a fashion intellectual or moral rather than merely physical" (405, 310) (note that Secker himself was not *physically* tired but "morally, intellectually" so). Richard attempts to achieve wholeness first, through an (unsuccessful) attempt to marry and have children and later, through the creation of a care home for people similarly maimed or disfigured (Ford 2015, 553). He eventually comes to believe that his bodily incompleteness provides a partial release from the fallenness of his terrestrial condition. A Christ-like figure, Richard was, "by the fact of his deformity," "emancipated from the delusions of his class, was made one, in right of the suffering and humiliation of it" (371). Pertinent to the present discussion, in one episode Richard contemplates a Velasquez painting of a "hideous and misshapen dwarf," sensing a "tragic freemasonry between himself and this outcasted being, begotten of a common knowledge, a common experience" (364).[2] As I point out elsewhere "[o]pening up a channel of communication or "freemasonry" between himself and his inanimate double, Richard's disfigurement indicates a disintegration of the individual body and external world ..." (Ford 2015, 559).

As the fulfilment of a curse which, several generations before, had been placed on the Calmady family, Richard—a kind of messiah—is accorded a special status in Malet's oeuvre. Other characters, try as they might to bypass the "vesture of flesh" which inhibits intercourse, engage in less edifying forms of communicative activity (Malet 1923, 16). In *The Survivors* Sybella Alywin (note the correspondence between Sybella and a sybil, a prophetess) the widowed mother of Lydia and matron of a private war hospital, imagines herself empathetically wired to her patients. A "tremulous, large-eyed, ultra-feminine being" Sybella forms bonds with many of her "stricken young warriors," but one Captain Braybrooke, who is thirteen years her junior and an amputee, becomes the locus of her romantic attentions (32, 35). To secure the Captain's continued dependence and devotion at a time when young men were at "such a tremendous premium," Sybella lobbies for (and secures) an operation to remove his one remaining leg (26). Prior to the surgery Sybella "became possessed with the idea that Braybrooke called to her. That his spirit, leaving his maimed body, struggled to force a passage, reach and cling to her, at once protecting and protected from that dancing rout of emanations" (162). Addressing Braybrooke, she explains:

> you know ... you called to me ... That kept me listening, ready to answer your call and come to you. But the difficulties were considerable. I lost hope. Then by an apparent accident my way was made plain. It would have distressed me infinitely to fail you when you called, because these demands and correspondences between mind and mind are sacred, mystic.
>
> (169)

Once again, the physical body is imagined as a frontier impeding total identification between individuals. Unlike Secker, who doubts the authenticity of these mind-created messages, Sybella interprets the "telepathic" episode as a momentary release from the encumbrance of the human body—actually believes that Braybrooke shook off his "maimed body" to send out an S.O.S call (162). Through Sybella, Malet dramatises the psychology of self-deception; not only does Sybella define the "correspondences between mind and mind [as] sacred, mystic" but regards herself as the "appointed vehicle of [the high gods'] intention" (160); the intention, that is, to expand Braybrooke's mutilation. Malet writes, "was she not yielding herself obediently to the 'great spiritual influences'?—a phrase she favoured, attaching to it conveniently elastic meanings" (160). In her reading of the novel's iconography, Catherine Delyfer reveals some striking similarities between a scene in which Braybrooke reclines upon Sybella's breast and "Our Lady of Good Counsel," a fresco painting of the Madonna and the child at a Genazzano Church ("Lady of Good Counsel" is, as Delyfer points out, an epithet Braybrooke uses in relation to Sybella). Delyfer argues that "Lady Aylwin becomes enamoured not so much with the young officer per se, but rather with her own performance as Holy mother" (130). Indeed, if Sybella's self-styled apotheosis does not entirely negate the purity of their psychic communion, then the erotic tenor of her therapeutic involvement certainly does. After serving, for a period, in Sybella's war hospital, Lydia complains that the philanthropic atmosphere of the place is a "good deal over-charged with the smirched business of sex," and McNaughten, the hospital's principal physician, complains, "[t]hese philanthropic side-shows [are] forcing houses for sexual neurosis" (217). Invoking the dual images of sexual penetration and vibrating sperm cells, Braybrooke's "spirit" "struggled to force a passage" amidst a "dancing rout of emanations" (162). These 'emanations' are something like post-traumatic phantoms but the verb 'emanate' also implies ejaculation/ejaculate. Given Sybella's Marian complex, the fact that Braybrooke's spirit psychically *forces* a passage to her maternal body, might be productively read as an imagined form of immaculate conception.

It may be that the character of Sybella is, in part, inspired by Malet's cousin, the African explorer, Mary Henrietta Kingsley. The author of *Travels in West Africa* (1897) and *West African Studies* (1899), Kingsley made three trips to Africa in her lifetime. In 1900, on her third visit, Kingsley died of fever nursing Boer prisoners. Like Sybella, Kingsley was an experienced nurse and Malet summoned her cousin to Brighton when William Harrison, her (estranged) husband, suffered his final illness in 1897—the same year that *Travels in West Africa* was published (Lundberg 2003, 188). Given that *Travels* was, by the time of Harrison's death, a huge commercial success, it seems likely that, during their time at Brighton, the cousins discussed Kingsley's book. Certainly, Malet was conversant with Kingsley's ideas and had given feedback on the manuscript (Frank 2005, 229). In *Travels*, Kingsley characterises the African point of view as a kind of pathogen from which the more rational European mind must protect itself; she writes "your own mind requires protection when you send it stalking ... through the tangled forests, the dark caves, the swamps and fogs of the Ethiopian intellect"

(440). Then later: "the fascination with the African point of view is as sure to linger in your mind as the malaria in your body" (441). As a woman with, as she saw it, a more highly developed empathetic faculty, Kingsley regarded herself as particularly susceptible to the kind of 'contagion' she believed fetish belief to be. In *The Invention of Telepathy*, Roger Luckhurst points out that Kingsley located

> her empathetic powers in her femininity. Writing to someone taking up a colonial posting in Sierra Leone, she said of the African: 'He is a woman. ... I know these things because I am a woman, a woman of the masculine race but a woman still.'
>
> (Luckhurst 2002, 170)

Exploiting associations between femininity and superstition, Kingsley claims a kind of telepathic connection with the African native, who she regards as an evolutionary equivalent to the European woman. In an 1896 letter, Kingsley admits "I seem to have a mind so nearly akin to that of the savage that I can enter into his thoughts and follow them" (qtd. in Luckhurst 2002, 169).

In *The Survivors*, the surgeon McNaughten experiences Sybella's "feminine nerves" in the same manner that Mary Kingsley experienced the "swamps and fogs of the African intellect." Their quarrel over the fate of Braybrooke's damaged limb is set against the "stifling sense and smell" of the "dank" London fog, which, as a counterpart to the "tangled forests" of the African mind, externalises Sybella's "clinging, melting" feminine logic (139, 131). Indeed, Sybella states her case, "rapidly, even somewhat breathlessly—the fog to blame, no doubt—as one driven by compassion, by the commendable anxiety of the nurse for the well-being of the patient entrusted to her care" (139–40). McNaughten's usually "steel-plated" masculine nerves were "touched by her words" and he "winced now and then" at the "hysterical threatening" of her discourse (137). McNaughton contemplates the "hereditary weapon of the [female] sex in its eternal warfare with the male" (132). Imagining Sybella as a kind of Medusa, he judged it "safer, perhaps, not to look [at her] overlong," fixing his gaze instead "upon the blank surface of the wall opposite" (137–8). Nonetheless he becomes infected with Sybella's feminine mode of "imaginative sympathy," eventually admitting an "uncommon weakness for the lad" (140, 138). Malet writes that Sybella "did care, violently, *almost savagely* [for] the attainment of her purpose: possession, namely, of a certain human life, a certain human body ... in perpetuity" [emphasis added] (134). Like Kingsley, who draws analogues between the mind of woman and native, Malet schematises Sybella, the "large-eyed, ultra-feminine being" as a kind of savage, lusting after the ritual dismemberment of her much-desired lover (32). Interestingly, as a contest over the removal of Braybrooke's leg, the scene also invokes

Pope's *The Rape of the Lock* which likewise depicts a gendered battle, enacted over the excision of bodily matter (though, of course, Malet's own skirmish lacks Pope's inflationary wit). At the same time that it resonates with Kingsley's geography of the African intellect, the "acrid" fog, together with Sybella's rising hysteria, recall Pope's cave of spleen where "A constant *Vapour* o'er the Palace flies; / Strange Phantoms rising as the Mists arise" (Pope 2006, 92).

Sybella's telepathic fantasy depends on the divisibility of spirit and matter (or, substance dualism) which, given Malet's Catholicism would seem to have a Christological root. Using the trope of clothing, Secker's own desire to discard his "vesture of flesh," recollects Revelation 19:13: "*his cloak was soaked in blood.* He is known by the name, The Word of God." However, Malet's sartorial depiction of the jointure between spirit and body, equally recalls elements of Kingsley's African field-work. In "The Forms of Apparitions in West Africa," an 1898 address to the Society for Psychical Research, Kingsley attempts to sketch out the basics of the African belief system. She explains that the African "is endowed with a super-sensitive nervous organisation" speculating that long "acclimatization to malarial districts" has left the native in a "chronic state of … delirium"; otherwise, the "African mind may be a more perfect photographic plate on which the spirit world can imprint itself" (331). According to Kingsley, "an African can conceive a powerful spirit wearing … a rock, a fierce river rapid, or the everlasting, booming, man-killing surf itself, as a garment" (333). The African, she notes, displays "absolute carelessness as to what becomes of the garment of the spirit" for, once the "spirit has thrown [the garment] off, itself be thrown away, or left to rot, it does not matter" (333). The scene during which Braybrooke's spirit supposedly "leav[es] his maimed body," is populated with phantoms (162). Sybella asks, "were such nightmare shapes circling about him at this moment joined in a *Danse Macabre* of grisly significance? Would they suck his strength, unseat his reason, steal him away through the black magic of pain …?" (162). Then later, "she lost her self-control and beat with her hands on the mantleshelf in a frenzy of nervous excitement" (162). Highly ambivalent about their own terrestrial "garments" characters like Secker, Braybrooke, and Malet's earlier creation, Richard Calmady, share traits with the native, but it is Sybella, beating her fists with primal intemperance, who, to borrow a phrase from Kingsley, has the ability to "think in black." Of a similar "super-sensitive" constitution to Kingsley's African, Sybella is psychically attuned to the "phantoms of war scenes" which, in fetish-dance formation, circle the "beds where sick men slept" (Malet 162). She, moreover, attributes Braybrooke's suffering to supernatural agency or, "black magic" (162).

How Malet felt about Kingsley's claim to have psychic insight into the mind of the African is unclear but she certainly punctures a similar conceit in the character of Sybella. When Sybella's thoughts turn to the subject of her daughter—who she casts in the unlikely role of romantic rival—the channel of her psychic union with Braybrooke closes up; he complains "I can't reach you, can't get at you." Moments later "[t] he circuit was restored; mind played upon mind; emotion reached to emotion—with limitations ... This [was] fortunate, since at the back of her mind was that best, perhaps, unread by whoso would love her" (178). Malet's critique of Sybella's telepathic conceit here operates at the level of her syntax. Consecutive use of epanadiplosis—"mind played upon mind; emotion reached to emotion"—creates a sense of twinning or, equilibrium: the mapping of one mind onto its kindred. The illusion of total identification is then undercut with the abrupt, one might say bathetic, "—with limitations" (178). Malet's next statement—that it was "fortunate" the "back of [Sybella's] mind" remained "unread" by her lover—is essentially ironic since the imposition of limitations on their communion implies that Sybella is more in control of the interaction than one could reasonably expect given its psychic nature (178). Elsewhere, too, Sybella imagines herself psychically wired to victims and sufferers. Earlier in the novel, she pays a visit to her cousin, Amanda Levipoulos, who had recently lost her unfaithful husband, a corrupt Greek financier. Though Sybella experienced Amanda's welcome like a "frost" to her brimming sympathy, she nonetheless declares that:

> Some telepathic correspondence must have taken place between us. ... These unspoken, almost involuntary linkings-up of mind with mind, the silent give and take of them, are so inspiring, so comforting! I've come across convincingly many instances of them recently. (54)

The great human cost of the First World War may be counted amongst the factors which sustained the Victorian preoccupation with psychical phenomena well into the twentieth century: a fact to which Sybella alludes when she remarks, "I've come across ... many instances of [telepathic correspondence] recently." Practices such as automatic writing as well as experiments in telepathy provided hoped-for "evidence" of the post-mortem survival of the spirit. Notably, in 1916, the physicist, Oliver Lodge, published *Raymond or, Life after Death*—a book which controversially documented the spiritual communications of the son he lost at Ypres in 1915. In "Psycho-analysis and Telepathy" (1921) Freud remarks that the interest in occult phenomena is

> an expression of the loss of value by which everything has been affected since the world catastrophe of the Great War [and also] an attempt at compensation, at making up in another ... sphere for the attractions which have been lost by life on this earth. (177)

In the emotional economy of war Sybella is not a sufferer, but an exploiter. Like a rogue spiritual medium, Sybella scopes around for affective vulnerabilities:

> But from Amanda's tears appeal and invitation were singularly absent. They asked no help, they told no story: and thus offered with witness no foothold, not so much as the veriest chink or crevice in which to hit [Sybella's] ready little grappling-irons. They left her outside ... and to be left and kept outside, whatever drama might be going, was a thing she sincerely abominated. It rendered her impotent, the personal medium being the only one in which she could function.
>
> (57)

Malet conceptualises Sybella's cognitive space as her "personal medium," phraseology which, alongside Sybella's pursuit of a "story," is consistent with her posturing as clairvoyant. Once again, Malet organises interpersonal relations around the spatial binary of inside-outside. The sexual metaphor, "impotent," is apt since what Sybella strives for is symbolic penetration, her "little grappling-irons" a penile instrument that seeks out some kind of "crevice" in Amanda's emotional armoury (the rock-climbing imagery, too, implies erotic 'mounting'). Though Sybella implores Amanda, "[b]e open with me," the frontier between women remains intact (57). It is not that Amanda is entirely unresponsive to human kindness but that Sybella's brand of ebullient emotion requires a more substantial discursive mooring than Amanda's clipped, ironical vernacular affords.

It is, in fact, Sybella's daughter, Lydia, who gains admittance to Amanda's personal "drama." Meeting first in the parlour of the spinster sisters, Daphne and Diana Leighton, the two women are conscious of a kind of electrical attraction. Malet writes, "And something happened. Some electric current, spontaneously generated, flowed back and forth between the women and the girl, uniting, binding them to they knew not what enterprise, what mutual undertaking" (123). Attraction is figured here, as in Sybella and Braybrooke's union, as electric energy, but without the narrative irony which undercuts this relationship. Where the current of her mother's union with Braybrooke is "limited," unstable, liable to drop out at any moment, Lydia's (electrical) connection with Amanda has bilateral stability which presumably stems from the women's sexual sameness. The eroticism between the women is figured spatially too. At a Maidsworthy New Year celebration, Lydia and Amanda's rooms are connected by "a door of communication" (235). That night Lydia lets herself into Amanda's bedchamber, remarking that "it is a little short of immoral to invade you at this time of night" (235). The two women lie on the bed together; Amanda "wanted to keep Lydia for her own, for herself" (247). She "touched our maiden lovingly on the cheek. Let her hand travel down over the firm delicate swell of the girl's bosom, to find and hold those pointed, stiffly joined finger-tips" (247). At first stroking the girl's voluptuous breasts, then seizing her "stiff" and "pointed" fingers, Amanda draws attention to the hermaphroditic quality of Lydia's "sweet breathing body" (246). Indeed, Malet treats the reader to frequent descriptions of Lydia's phallic fingers variously depicted as "long," "pointed" and "stiffly joined" (37, 247). On one occasion Lydia "laid the tips of her pointed fingers delicately on [Amanda's] bosom" (200). On another, Lydia sits at a "proud height" in the upper-most seat of a pony carriage, while Amanda, who complains of a "wild crick in [her] neck," sits directly in front and beneath her—positioning which is suggestive of fellatio (129). Conscious of an overmastering attraction exercised by Amanda (a "queer craving"), Lydia finds herself "fingering" the older woman's veil (129).

But Amanda's and Lydia's bedroom intimacy does far more than valorise female same-sex eroticism. Punctuated by "church bells … ringing in the New Year" (246), this scene depicts a witching hour, a moment when narrative folds in on itself to reveal the women's, or at least Lydia's, own fictionality:

> "And how about the heading of the new chapter, my lamb?" she asked, unable to control an urgency, almost a pleading in her voice.
> "Are you so desperately anxious it should be entitled Francis?"
> Whereat, feeling somewhat Judus-like: "On the whole," Amanda answered, "I believe I should prefer to have you leave it blank …
> (247)

Aware that her own narrative of failed marriage belongs to a Victorian cultural moment, Amanda reneges on a promise to forward Francis Secker's suit. The terms through which she does this—"my lamb" and "Judas-like"—set up associations between Lydia and Jesus, "lamb of god" (John 1:29). These allusions point to the ominous potential of Lydia's own sacrifice on the altar of matrimony. But Lydia's life becomes a fiction over which she assumes narrative control. In harmony with Amanda's desire to leave the next chapter "blank," Lydia explains that Francis "offers no playing field, still less a battlefield to [her] imagination"; a "*character*" she remarks "must do one or both of those two" [emphasis added] (248). One has the sense that Malet does not quite know how to dispose of Lydia in fiction; like Amanda's lingering gaze, the narrative pauses at this threshold—contemplates how to rewrite the benighted marriage plot for the "Neo-Georgian" woman (240). Like Amanda, Malet experienced her own widowhood as a release from an unhappy Victorian marriage. In fact, there is plenty of Malet in Amanda. Amanda was "jealous for [Lydia's] body, tender of it, strangely desirous it should endure no rough usage, should suffer no violence—however natural—of passion, from the pains and perils of childbirth remain immune" (246). She "gave chastity an exalted place, seeing it not only lovely and precious in itself, but as a vehicle of finer intuitions" (247). According to former Kingsley family literary executor, Angela Covey-Crump, Malet "feared childbirth" and we know that she actively encouraged the celibacy of Gabrielle Vallings, the second cousin she "informally" adopted (later Malet's companion and an occasional opera singer) (Lundberg 2003, 34, 107).

It is possible to read Amanda's desire to protect Lydia from the violence of childbirth (and, by extension, Malet's need to protect Vallings from the same) as a form of repressed homoerotic desire. This is indeed how Patricia Lorimer Lundberg interprets the elevation of celibacy in Malet's fiction; she argues that Malet structures abstinence as "a pathway to a sublimated state if not to sainthood. ... It would become a lifelong preoccupation, one likely enacted in her own life as a way to sublimate her own erotic lesbian desire" (Lundberg 2003, 107–8). In the sense that erotic consummation is one of a number of scripts or, narrative possibilities open to Lydia—a nascent author (of herself)—I would argue that here, at least, there is nothing particularly latent about the women's sexual attraction. When Lydia asks, following some slight application of pressure on her "close-joined finger tips," if Amanda would like her to leave, the older woman responds, "Stay-the longer, the better I shall be pleased" (248). It seems clear it is not just Lydia's physical presence that is under negotiation here. A meaningful pause is followed by a confession or, perhaps, an apology:

> Have I ever told you, Amanda, about the place where—where I had the time of my life? It marked something which remains indelible ... I'd like to tell you about it now at the beginning of this new chapter. It seems to belong, to fit in, somehow.
>
> "Yes," the other murmured, "yes"
>
> ... [It was at a] convent of expulsed French nuns, tucked away in the Austrian Tyrol.
>
> (249)

Lydia's confession gives new meaning to her name since Lydia was the first European convert to Christianity (Acts 16: 11–15). Her tale, moreover, has the "indelibility" of print. Juggling the pieces of her own personal plot, Lydia admits to "indulg[ing] in autobiography," instinctively feels that her spiritual sojourn "fit[s] in" at the "beginning of this new chapter" (251). This is also a rejection of the textual possibilities of sexual union with Amanda. "I loved these holy women" Lydia explains "and they loved me"; "they walked with God, Amanda. That's not a phrase. They did walk with God ... . I never knew such a thing could really be—such closeness, confidence, I mean, of communion." (250). In contrast with the infelicitous, partial, and erotically imbued telepathic messages that appear to link up the members of the novelistic community, Lydia aspires to a form of, to use Amanda's words, "finer intuition" or, spiritual communion.

Her insistence that it was not merely "a phrase" when she claimed the holy women *really did* walk with God is ironic since a phrase is precisely what Lydia's remark *is* (and a well-worn one at that). I suppose the point is that, for Lydia, the fictive spills into the spiritual and this is nowhere more apparent than in Lydia's conception of herself as a kind of creative hermaphrodite:

> The discovery she possessed a gift of putting words and phrases fruitfully together, evoking scenes and characters, coherently, convincingly building up a world deliciously her own, exclusive of the exterior world of sight, sound or sense, was still sufficiently new to cause her ecstasy. Magical solitary ecstasy, since the teller of tales and maker of stories is bi-sexual, hermaphrodite—he who begets, she who conceives, complete in one … . Now, reviewing her handiwork, she pronounced it good.
>
> (277)

Here homoerotic consummation is rejected in favour of autoerotic creation; as Lydia's male and female characteristics fuse together, she experiences an orgasm-like "ecstasy" which culminates in her "embryo" of a book (277). Noting the ways in which *fin-de-siècle* homosexual writers restructure biological reproduction around artistic creation, Martha Vicinus points out that "[m]en and women whose sexual lives were in opposition to biological reproduction did not defy its hegemony but, rather insisted on a superior option—art." She continues, "[i]n story after story the natural reproductive cycle was thwarted, side-stepped, or intentionally avoided. … Yet … the *fin-de-siècle* homosexual tale did not usurp the divine (and maternal) prerogative of generation but instead celebrated the privileged choice of artistic creativity" (Vicinus 1994, 94). Though Malet certainly privileges artistic generation over biological reproduction, the two are conflated here. That is to say, Malet conceptualises art as the offspring of an original autoerotic act. Characteristically, the rhetoric here—"she pronounced it good"—mirrors Genesis 1:31, and this is important because the virtue of artistic reproduction is precisely that it originates from a single author-creator; it is, or has the ability to be, sacrosanct.

But the sanctity of authorship is fragile, as Malet well knows. Over the years Malet's writing was frequently compared to her male contemporaries, particularly Henry James. As Talia Schaffer notes, James and Hardy probably appropriated ideas from Malet and she, in turn, "adopt[ed]

Jamesian phrasing and allud[ed] to James's titles" (Schaffer 1996, 112). Two years prior to the publication of *The Survivors*, a damning review of her short story collection, *Da Silva's Widow, and Other Stories* (1922), appeared in *The Times*. The reviewer complains, "Hardly one of these short stories does not carry a remainder, by its subject, of some other author. Most often the author is Henry James, but once or twice he is … Mr E. M. Forster. …" By contrast, Malet's "handling of [these] reminiscent subjects" "betrays little affinity with Henry James, Mr Forster, or anybody else". The reviewer suggests that Malet "conveys that impression of wordiness which is fatal to a short story, and allows her characters to talk, whether at ease or in crises with an unnatural inflation of phrase." The article concludes, "[w]e prefer [Lucas Malet] when she is writing at large and 'on her own'" ("Pale Souls" 1992, 14). The point seems to be that not only are Malet's stories derivative but that they lack the stylistic verve to pull the imitation off. This appraisal is hardly fair and one might well wonder that the reviewer finds much that is laudable in James given his apparent distaste for elevated dialogue and wordiness. This critique (and others of its kind), may well have weighed heavy on Malet's mind. In *The Survivors* Lydia, still thrilling over her act of creation, declares "I must be careful what I read. Style rubs off, phrases stick in one's mind detestably. … Still it is good. And it belongs to me—absolutely to me" (278). In a sense, Mary Henrietta Kingsley's declaration that "your own mind requires protection when it is stalking through … tangled forests [and] dark caves" might as well apply to the literary scene as the "African intellect." Though Lydia schematises fiction writing as a purer, divine, more exalted form of communicative activity, she, like Malet, is anxious to protect the integrity of the Word.

In its exploration of mediumship, communications technology, and literary influence, *The Survivors* shares characteristics with Rudyard Kipling's 1902 short story, "Wireless": a tale about a consumptive apothecarist's assistant who falls into a drug-induced trance while the building is magnetised for a Marconi telegraphy experiment. The experiment runs awry (picking up warship code instead of the intended missive from Poole), but the assistant (who has no knowledge of literature) mechanically reproduces lines from Keats's "Eve of St. Agnes." Of course, the apothecarist's profession and his tuberculosis imply a spiritual sympathy with Keats, but as with *The Survivors*, mediumship is collapsed into communications technology. Moreover, these wireless signals operate as a metaphor for networks of literary influence. In a diary entry for May 1918, H. Rider Haggard recalls a conservation with Kipling, in which the latter laments the necessarily derivative nature of all literary productions. Haggard records that

> … he went on to show that anything any of us did *well* was no credit to us: that it came from somewhere else: 'we are only telephone lines.' As an example he instanced (I think) 'Recessional' in

> his own case and *She* in mine. 'You didn't write *She* you know,' he said, 'Something wrote it through you!' or some such words.
> (Cohen 1965, 100)

This image of an infinite network of telephone lines, connecting people, speaking *through* people anticipates Barthes's concept of the text as "tissue of quotations drawn from innumerable centres of culture" (Barthes 1977, 146). Indeed, if the industrial transformations of the eighteenth and nineteenth centuries fuelled expressive realist notions of authorship then innovations in communications technology—at least for Kipling and Malet—would seem to symbolise the inverse.

Nonetheless, the desire for textual purity is one which runs through the heart of Malet's religious ideology. In *The Far Horizon* (1906), a novel written just four years after her conversion to Catholicism, the protagonist, Dominic Iglesias, is a lapsed Catholic who reconnects with the faith of his childhood. His "Romanism" sends shock waves through his blinkered London-suburb community and is a particular source of unease to his most loyal friend, George Lovegrove. In conversation with George, Dominic explains his decision in the following terms: "[w]hy hamper yourself with a late, expurgated, and mutilated edition, when the original, in all its splendour and historic completeness, bearing the sign manual of the Author is there ready to your hand?" (264). Ventriloquising Malet, Dominic's distrust of Anglicanism stems from a belief that it is corruption or, "mutilation" of a purer (textual) predecessor. Of course, Malet rides slipshod over the scriptural ambiguities and conflicts which have dogged the holy book since the rise of biblical criticism. Malet regards the Catholic Bible as a "hotline" to God (a "sign manual" no less). It is perhaps surprising that the Catholic Church's provenance or "historical completeness" is articulated through the related motifs of text, authorship, and scripture, given that they themselves were particularly vulnerable to attack, a fact that Pope Leo XIII's *Providentissimus Deus* (1893)—an encyclical letter defending scripture against "rationalist" studies of the Bible—amply demonstrates. Given that Malet is keen to emphasise the parallels between divine revelation and terrestrial authorship, she must certainly have been aware that the criticisms levelled at her own oeuvre bear some resemblance to attacks on biblical scripture, for instance, on the Mosaic authorship of the Pentateuch. Why, then, does Malet insist on the opposition between the "finer" communicative possibilities of (divine) authorship and the degraded forms of human discourse?

Ironically, given the nature of interpretative divisions between Catholics and Anglicans—we make a mistake if we read the motifs of text, scripture, and authorship *literally*. When Dominic bemoans the "mutilation" and "expurgation" of the later "edition" Malet is lamenting not authorised Protestant translations of the Bible but a perceived triangulation (or, phrased differently, a Reformation) of the Christian faith—a religion carved up, nationalised. Indeed, when George Lovegrove asks "why did you not come into our own national English Church," Dominic replies "Very much because it is English and national, I think" (Malet 1906, 264). Like the somatic frontier of the physical body, the National Church is, in her view, responsible for erecting barriers between Christian adherents; it is an impediment to total communion/communication. Moreover, the First World War had opened the door to forms of spiritual performance and charlatanism which, alongside the influence of human sexuality only exacerbated by the diminished stock of male citizens had, as far as Malet was concerned, a debasing influence on human interaction. For Malet, heterosexual attraction is particularly culpable and she deploys the trope of telepathy (an analogue of scriptural revelation) to make the point that intercourse founded on (heterosexual) bodily desire is volatile and, by its very nature, combative. By contrast, Malet inverts the principles of electrical polarity, to structure same-sex eroticism as a more stable electrical current or, telepathic missive. While Malet is relatively sanguine about the communicative possibilities of Lydia's relationship with Amanda, in a scene of potential consummation, Lydia opts for a religiously inspired alternative: artistic creation. That is because, for Malet, authorship is a god-like (or at least, god-inspired) activity which has the capacity to transcend contaminated, imperfect forms of bodily intercourse.

Notes

1 Of course, tensions between embodiment and disembodiment are literalised in the Eucharist in Catholic practice through transubstantiation itself, which turns of the belief in the divine becoming (always momentarily) incarnate.
2 I might also add that the language here—"begotten of a common knowledge, a common experience"—resonates with the Nicene Creed. Emphasising the consubstantial nature of the son of God, the creed reads "begotten, not made, / of one in being with the Father" which is pertinent given this moment of affinity between Richard and his Velasquez double.

Works Cited

Barthes, Roland. 1977. "The Death of the Author." In *Image-Music-Text*, translated by Stephen Heath, 142–8. London: Fontana Press.
Cohen, Morton N. (ed.). 1965. *Rudyard Kipling to Rider Haggard: The Record of a Friendship*. Rutherford: Fairleigh Dickinson University Press.
Delyfer, Catherine. 2011. *Art and Womanhood in Fin-de-Siècle Writing: The Fiction of Lucas Malet, 1880–1931*. London: Pickering & Chatto.
Ford, Jane. 2015. "Socialism, Capitalism and the Fiction of Lucas Malet: 'The Spirit of the Hive.'" *English Literature in Transition, 1880–1920* 58(4): 551–71.
Frank, Katherine. 2005. *A Voyager Out: The Life of Mary Kingsley*. New York: Tauris.

Freud, Sigmund. 1975. "Psycho-analysis and Telepathy." *The Complete Psychological Works of Sigmund Freud*, translated by James Strachey, vol. XVIII (1920–1922), 177–93. London: Hogarth Press.
Kingsley, Mary. 1897. *Travels in West Africa*. London: Macmillan.
———. 1898–99. "The Forms of Apparitions in West Africa." *Proceedings for the Society of Psychical Research* 14: 331–42.
Kipling, Rudyard. 1902. "Wireless." In *Traffics and Discoveries*, 197–223. New York: Doubleday, Page and Company.
Lodge, Oliver J. 1916. *Raymond: or, Life after death, with examples of the evidence for survival of memory and affection after death*. London: Methuen.
Lorimer Lundberg, Patricia. 2003. *An Inward Necessity: The Writer's Life of Lucas Malet*. New York: Peter Lang.
Luckhurst, Roger. 2002. *The Invention of Telepathy, 1870–1901*. Oxford: Oxford University Press.
Malet, Lucas. 1906. *The Far Horizon*. London: Hutchinson.
———. 1923. *The Survivors: A Novel*. Cassell & Company.
———. 2003. *The History of Sir Richard Calmady*, edited by Talia Schaffer. Birmingham: University of Birmingham Press.
Owen, Wilfred. 1997. "Anthem for Doomed Youth." *World War One British Poets: Brooke, Owen, Sassoon, Rosenberg and Others*, edited by Candace Ward, 25. London: Dover.
"Pale Souls: Lucas Malet's New Stories." 1922. *The Times*, 6 June, 14.
Pope, Alexander. 2006. "The Rape of the Lock." In *The Major Works*, edited by Pat Rogers, 79–100. Oxford: Oxford University Press.
Schaffer, Talia. 1996. "Some Chapter of Some Other Story: Henry James, Lucas Malet, and the Real Past of *The Sense of the Past*." *The Henry James Review* 17(2): 109–128
Shelley, Percy Bysshe. 2012. "Mont Blanc. Lines Written in the Vale of Chamouni." *Romanticism: An Anthology*, edited by Duncan Wu, 1104–7. 4th ed. Oxford: Wiley-Blackwell.
Sword, Helen. 1999. "Necrobibliography: Books in the Spirit World." *Modern Language Quarterly* 60(1): 85–112.
Vicinus, Martha. 1994. "The Adolescent Boy: Fin de Siècle Femme Fatale?" *Journal of the History of Sexuality* 5(1): 90–114.

Appendix A
In Memoriam, Ernest D. Chesterfield[1]

Lucas Malet

Friendship, truly considered, is religion. And the older creeds, having served their passing purpose in the development of the race, die out one by one, friendship probably will alone remain the recognised and cherished symbol of that universal and crucial truth which they have all more or less adequately embodied: i.e. that it is by their illusions, and by these alone that men live. Believing this, & believing also that all religions have their pieties and duties, I now feel bound to offer—not to the public as a whole, but the select few, to that little band of waiters and watchers for a clearer morning, when eloquent words and still more eloquent silence is doing so much to recast the faith and the morality of our day, this brief record of one, whose mind and action alike, exemplified so completely and harmoniously, some of their dearest hopes and deepest aspirations. To those who, like myself, had the privilege of knowing Ernest D Chesterfield, I need offer no apology for their memoir. To those who knew him not, yet who have some of his spirit moving within them I need offer no apology either. There is a free-masonry between the elect in every age; conventionalities are borne down by the generous outrush of true heart feeling.

Ernest D Chesterfield was born in 1856. Of his infancy we have unfortunately no record, unless the following sentences may be accepted as relating to him—"it is very red. It cries a great deal. I hope to goodness poor Charlotte is not going to have a large family." Ernest's father was a retired naval officer of moderate fortune. His harsh and antiquated religious views, his unimaginative veracity, above all his insular patriotism, and narrow adherence to that outworn superstition formerly called <u>honour</u>, began very early to alienate the affection of his son. When quite a child Ernest one day cut out a rough figure in paper with his mother's scissors, wrote across it in blue pencil, "This is papa," and burnt it slowly in the nursery fire.

Admiral Chesterfield being determined to give his son every so-called advantage, sent him to a noted and expensive preparatory school in the South of England. But both of this period and of his subsequent career at Eton precise details are unhappily lacking. I have received letters in answer to my enquiries from various school fellows of Ernest's, men now distinguished in politics, in literature, or art, but they agree in informing me that he never appeared to them in any way remarkable. This is easily accounted for. The boy had none of that loud brutality, none of those horribly punitive red Indian tastes and instincts that gain an easy reputation for their possessor in the semi-savage microcosm of the English public school. Yet some few anecdotes of his school life are still extant in which we may, I think, perceive indication of the qualities that were afterwards so conspicuous in him. The beautiful gift of sympathy in the joys and sorrows of others and craving for intimate fellowship, which rendered him in later life, so eminently loveable, were foreshadowed by his caressing attentions to those of his school fellows who had lately received a remittance in money or in kind from home; while his exquisite humility and dread of hurting the feelings of those about him, often induced him to permit younger boys to recite Latin verses or exercises to him, which with delicate self-abnegation he subsequently sent up to his house or form master as his own.

It was at Cambridge that I first became acquainted with him. Many will remember the singular influence exercised by him over the younger members of the university. Not that he distinguished himself on the river, in athletics, in society or even in the schools. He had no vulgar practical ambition. That he told us he was seeking to lead the "Wider Life" and we believed it. Belief runs superior to cold, scientific demonstration. We asked for no proofs of his talents. Faith is the substance, it has been said somewhere of things hoped for. We hoped great things of Ernest. Which of us will dare to admit that he has disappointed us?

At this time he was clean shaven with the expectation of a slight and very fair moustache. I remember the first time I saw him, one side of it was singed and unsightly— the result of an accident in relighting a short cigar-end from a candle, early one morning at the close of a wine party. I can recall the brooding seriousness of his large pale eyes. The lids of them both upper and lower had always a certain redness about them—as he said, referring to it afterwards:—

> the effect is without its antecedent cause. It is a duty fearlessly to face the reason of things yet not to let it deter us from doing them again if we feel inclined to. Physical courage may not be ours. But moral courage we are bound to cultivate.

Ernest always maintained that there is a certain immorality in resisting the dictates of strongly felt inclination. But in this, as in all questions of conduct or morals, he begged us to understand his words in an esoteric sense. We so understand them, and found it made a world of difference—revealing as it does the higher might which almost always lies behind the lower wrong and palliates the commission of the latter. "This is the great emancipation," he would say. "Grasp the idea in its fullness and life bears you to a new meaning and purpose. This is the modern revelation of the doctrine of justification by faith."[2]

He always wore flannel shirts. He continued to wear them, I believe, to the end. I remember meeting him once in Pall Mall—after he had left the University—in the height of the London season. He was then wearing a flannel shirt, an applied turned down white linen collar and a red silk tie confined by a gold ring. In his rooms at college, he often went without his collar, and unbuttoned the neck band of his shirt. He had a deep seated dislike of all restraint. And to this I infer a disregard of authority, a rebellion against all pressure bought to bear on him from the outside, which was very noticeable in him, and which, but for his ready tact would on more than one occasion have bought him into serious collisions with the university officials. This love of liberty, however, had no violent, incendiary, revolutionary element about it. He would never have preached sedition openly or mounted a barricade. His repugnance to restraint and to the insolent usurpations of authority took its rise in no overflowing of passionate youthful enthusiasm. It was, rather a profound life purpose, a self-dedication to the services of a precious idea, a vital and unalienable principle of his being. For there was in Ernest Chesterfield a deep spring of individualism, which chastened even the tenderist friendship, and tempered his speech and action, even in his most intimate relations and expansive moments. And it was just this strong strain of personal character that gave him so much of his influence. We were all sure that though he might appear to be thinking or acting exclusively for the benefit of others, the great, essential, vitalizing idea of himself, the I, the ego, remained distinct and undiminished before him. It gave him a repose, a steadiness and strength of intention which were above all praise.

I have already said he was not athletic. A tall, large-limbed man, whose figure even in the early college days—days, which come back to me, now that he is lost to us forever, with a subtle mingling of sweetness and regret—gave promise of the fullness, the magnificently massive proportions which it eventually attained. His face was pale; and there was a meditative languor in its expression and his slow unstudied gestures which was wonderfully attractive. He was never in a hurry. He carried dignity into all the trivial every day matters of life. At meals, I remember, the quiet self-recollection—if the term may be allowed me—was especially remarkable. This calm concentration of the mind upon the simple duty of assimilating sufficient nutriment, had in it something of an almost religious character. "Every act" as he once said, "may rise into an act of worship, if we conceive it reverently, and perform it with hearty earnestness." Then he would quote, with that raising of the head and slight quivering of the eye-lids that was so characteristic of him, Emerson's saying: "I once knew a man who in an ecstatic moment considered it the highest honour to wash his own face."[3] "There you have it," he would add, in his gentle, playful way "if we would only conduct habitually in that spirit how the old narrow nature would slough off from us, bearing the Wider Nature, to which all things are lawful and pure, radiantly, triumphantly free!"

But it was perhaps in his relation to men younger than himself that the highest function of Ernest's genius manifested itself. He had fearlessly met and solved most of the great moral and spiritual problems himself at a comparatively early age, and in pithy and pregnant sentences, he would give forth as occasion demanded it the garnered wisdom of his own experience. His scholarship and culture was not of the routine-serving cut and dried kind—which may satisfy examiners, and bring a man credit among dreary, machine made "dons" and tutors of the old school. The stamp of modern thought and feeling was upon it; it was at once too catholic in its range, too subtle and delicately ingenious in the intimacy of its knowledge for such persons to appreciate or comprehend it. Many will remember the titles of books, on the wide divan that ran along the side of his sitting room, and under the charming oriel-window, with its delicious view of the lazy river, and that wealth of garden, smooth turf, and noble trees known familiarly as "the Backs."[4] On this divan, strewn with large soft cushions and pillows which he would arrange and rearrange to suit each change of attitude, Ernest would lie half the day reading and thinking, filling his mind with waste stores of knowledge, and cultivating the vaguely emotional mental condition which he believed to be essential to a perception of high truth. Music he found a great assistance in the producing of this emotional condition. Among his friends were several excellent pianists, who were only too glad to repay something of the deep, individual and moral debt they owed to him by playing to him for the hour together. Chopin's nocturnes he said he found peculiarly efficacious.

But to return to his choice of books. Besides certain periods of classic literature, which appealed to him specially from their deep insight and fearless portrayal of its many different manifestations of the passion of love, he was well up in the Italian Renaissance, had studied for instance the novelle of Bandello and Sgr Lascar[5], much of the popular poetry and burlesque and the domestic history of that memorable epoch. Villon[6] he valued highly; and among modern Frenchman, to mention a few names where I might mention many dozen, Baudelaire, Gautier in his earlier manner and Flaubert commanded his admiration. I once spoke to him of Victor Hugo. "Good at times" he said, "but he knows a little too well what he wants. Beware, always, of a direct intention." The play-wrights of the English Restoration he maintained had considerable humanity though his delicate nature shrank painfully from the brutal horse-play into which they too often degenerate. "The English are always vulgar" he would say "because they are always healthy. Strike that word with its old-fashioned acceptation out of your vocabulary. It is an abomination!"

I believe he studied the writing of certain ecclesiastical writers of the 17th century, Lessius, Hurtado de Mendoza, Suárez, Lamy etc[7] finding in them a freedom from prejudice, a nice ingenuity in the appreciation of means to ends, and a width of moral out-look which could not but appeal strongly to his acute and tolerant mind.

I remember well one languorous June evening, when I coming suddenly into his untidy, picturesque sitting room found him lying at full length among the sad coloured cushions of his divan, and laughing softly to himself—that sincere laugh of his, not of this life merely, but up-welling from the heart—over the pages of Madame Bovary. "It is not the book in itself that I care for" he said, turning to me with a swift deepening of purpose in his face "It is the revelation of common temptation, suffering, and trial that I care for. Plato holds there is no real sin save ignorance. I read that I may know; and in knowing learn to help." And so it came about that, secure of his ready and comprehensive sympathy, younger men opened their innocent hearts to him. The simple way in which he would lay one large, soft hand tenderly on the shoulder of some shame-faced lad and say "I understand" had in it the true spirit of absolution. He knew so well the restoration and strength that comes of confession. "Tell me everything, all the details" he would say; and then after a time of patient, absorbed listening, would add "Now you are through with it. Make your penitence brief and bright. And remember, acts in themselves are nothing. It is the motive, the purpose with which the act is done that makes all the difference." On such occasions, he was fond of quoting the final lines of a speech of one of Moliere's famous characters:

......il est une science
D'étendre les liens de notre conscience,
Et de rectifier le mal de l'action
Avec la pureté de notre intention.[8]

He had, I think, got far beyond the stage of religious thought, in which there is a clinging to dogma. I have been told that once, when a heated discussion as to the tenable limits of faith, was going on in his rooms, he waited till there was a little pause, and then said gently:—"why speak."

Notes

1 Given that Ernest D. is set up as a kind of sham aesthetic genius, the name "Ernest" resonates with Wilde and particularly, *The Importance of Being Ernest* (1895)—a play which derives its comedy from the fact that characters are not whom they initially appear to be.

2 The concept of 'justification' (becoming righteous) is a key site of theological conflict between Protestants and Catholics. Put simply, Catholic doctrine holds that salvation can be achieved through the operations of faith and good works. The idea of justification by faith alone meaning salvation

through the belief in Jesus Christ irrespective of good works, is a feature of Protestant (especially Lutheran) thought. It seems that Ernest D abuses the concept of justification by faith to encourage his 'disciples' to pursue their "strongly felt inclinations" with impunity. Of course, as a Catholic (or soon-to-be- Catholic) writer, Malet may also have intended to poke fun at Protestant doctrine.

3 This quotation is from "Works and Days," an essay from Emerson's *Society and Solitude* (1870) and refers to the American poet, Jones Very. While working as a tutor at Harvard, Very came to believe that he was the Second Coming of Christ and was committed, for a period, to an asylum. Emerson was fascinated with Very and helped him to publish a volume of poetry. The quotation actually reads, "I knew a man in a certain religious exhaltation who 'thought it an honor to wash his own face.' He seemed to me more sane than those who hold themselves cheap" (Ralph Waldo Emerson. 1871. *Society and Solitude: Twelve Chapters*. Boston: James R. Osgood and Company, 159).

4 The "backs of the colleges." The area behind the Cambridge colleges which runs down to the River Cam.

5 Matteo Bandello (c.1480–1562), Italian renaissance author and (later) Bishop of Agen. Likened to Bocaccio's *Decameron* Bandello's *Novelle*, were translated into English by John Payne in 1890. Although the handwriting is difficult to read, it seems likely Malet also refers to Janus Lascaris (c.1445–1535), Greek renaissance scholar who studied in Italy and produced first editions of a number of seminal works of classicism, including plays by Euripides. It is difficult to tell from Malet's handwriting whether this is "Signor." Since Ernest D. Chesterfield is said to have been born in 1856, Malet implies here that he read Bandello and Lascaris in the original Italian/Greek.

6 François Villon (c.1431–1463), French poet of the Middle Ages.

7 Leonardus Lessius (1554–1623), Belgian theologian interested in economics; Pedro Hurtado de Mendoza (1578–1651), Spanish Jesuit scholar associated with nominalism; Francisco Suárez (1548–1617), Spanish Jesuit theologian best known for his *Disputationes Metaphysicae* (1597), a book which had a major impact on modern philosophy, influencing Descartes, Spinoza, and others; Dom François Lamy (1636–1711), Benedictine Monk and Cartesian thinker. The range and variety of Ernest's reading imply that he is a dilettante.

8 These lines are spoken by the character of Tartuffe in Act 4, Scene 5 of Molière's 1669 comedy of the same name. In Richard Wilbur's translation the lines read, "There is a science, lately formulated / Whereby one's conscience may be liberated / And any wrongful act you care to mention / May be redeemed by purity of intention" (Molière. 1992. *Tartuffe*, translated by Richard Wilbur. New York: Harcourt Brace & Co, 126). The reference to *Tartuffe* (subtitled "The Impostor") is a clear gesture towards Ernest D's religious and aesthetic hypocrisy.

Appendix B
Retelling the Untold Stories
Lucas Malet's Critique of an Aesthetic Trope

Ruth Robbins

In her very important book on *The Forgotten Female Aesthetes*, Talia Schaffer enumerates the reasons for the absence of women writers from the aesthetic canon. Schaffer's sense is that their invisibility is not determined by the *texts* they wrote, not a matter of what they wrote *about* or the manner in which they did so. It is rather the result of extrinsic causes: a combination of faulty histories constructed by male critics, who were too ready to take at face value some of the views of the 1880s and 1890s taste makers, a misevaluation of women's writings and contributions to the movement, and a self-interested view of what 'counted' as aesthetic which left out the female voices:

> Our exclusive focus on male aesthetes has made us think that Beauty means the admiration of bodies and homes; language experimentation means the careful, condensed language of the little essay or poem or drawing-room comedy; and social circles means acquaintance with Wilde.
>
> (Schaffer 2000, 4)

Using only those (male) figures who are the "acknowledged aesthetes"—Schaffer names Wilde, Dowson, Johnson, Beerbohm, and Yeats as the key male writers (3)—to define what was meant by aestheticism leads to a very partial, in all senses of that word, picture of the networks of production and influence that aestheticism involved. Most seriously, it leaves out the women writers for whom what Schaffer identifies as the fashion for aesthetic matters was a hospitable and productive space.

There is a risk with Schaffer's case, which she herself recognises. In stretching the boundaries of what the term means, there is a danger that it is stretched so far as to mean nothing at all. The boundaries of definition always have to leave someone out of the feast. Her response is to consider aestheticism as a far more elastic term than one that is concerned purely with the high-art productions of a coterie of bohemian men. It is instead, she argues, a fashion which takes place in a material culture, and as a literary and artistic mode, it was open to women to use and to modify. The claim is not that female aesthetes write the exact same things as men and therefore ought to be included in the same canon. It is that the very idea of aestheticism as a canon, rather than as a *repertoire* of tropes, images, ideas, techniques, and responses via which any writer of the period—including women writers—might have performed the art of writing, is mistaken.

This is a compelling and important argument, especially when Schaffer shows it in action in her readings of the individual writers whom she claims for aestheticist femininity: Ouida, Alice Meynell, and Lucas Malet, for example. In the case of the latter,

> Lucas Malet was an aesthete in the same way (and for the same reasons) as Henry James was. ... [her texts display] a shimmering drapery of symbols to distract us from, and yet to represent, the dark body that it cannot reveal. Aestheticism became a strategically deployed semiotic for depicting the forbidden, a language that hid itself by speaking, an oblique reference to the unrepresentatable that is both revealed and concealed. In her mastery of indirection and dissimulation, Malet became one of the pioneers of a new use of aestheticism.
>
> (Schaffer 2000, 199–200)

What I want to show in this essay is that as well as her deployment of the aesthetic sleight of hand that Schaffer notices, Malet was also using some of her short fiction to debate with and to mount a critique of the aestheticism of some of her male contemporaries. In two stories, one published ("The Birth of a Masterpiece") and one not ("In Memoriam, Ernest D. Chesterfield") Malet offers us narrators who are either archly knowing or utterly ingenuous, who write in praise of dead 'geniuses,' and yet who may just be telling us (deliberately or not) about the emptiness of their aesthetic posturing and of the dangers of an unthinking discipleship. If aestheticism is often understood via Gautier's phrase as the valuation above all things of "art for art's sake," Malet's stories use that idea to suggest that is merely a pose and a repellent pose at that.

One of the key tropes of the aesthetic and decadent fictions of the *fin de siècle* and beyond is the story of the artist who fails to produce. It is a story that recurs several times in the shorter fictions of Henry James, for example, in tales such as "The Death of the Lion" (1894) or "The Private Life" (1892), where narrators are heavily invested in the genius of their chosen idols. They are either fooled by (or possibly not fooled) or self-deluded about the resolute nonappearance of the great work, while they also narrate at length the deliberate evasion of anything that looks like the hard labour of writing or painting on the part of the alleged genius. This trope is picked up by New Women writers who use it for far more clearly political purposes. In George Egerton's 1894 *Yellow Book* story "A Lost Masterpiece," for example, a bumptious egocentric male narrator finds his inspiration for a brilliant new work destroyed by the insistent intrusion into his thoughts and line of vision of an assertive New Woman who, in the words of Kate Krueger, "commands" (2014, 118) the city streets despite her gender. Or again, in Sarah Grand's "The Undefinable: A Fantasia" (1908), an artist is stymied in his attempts to capture the essence of a mysterious model who arrives uninvited at his door because of her strongly expressed contempt for his current work. For both of these stories, the point is that the male artist needs to be chastened to a new understanding of the purposes and possibilities of the representation of the female form. They are very clearly political—stories with a purpose.

This is not quite the situation of Malet's two stories, for the point of her satire is not the male artist in particular, but male egotism in general, especially when it has an aestheticist cloak of special value. And if James's plots and serpentine sentences are one of the aesthetic targets of her tales, the presiding genius of both stories bears some very important traces of the life and attitudes of Oscar Wilde.

The first of the untold stories of my title is the narrative that Heber Pogson never writes in "The Birth of a Masterpiece." That a masterpiece should be written or that genius should be possessed by a man with such a resolutely mundane name is of course an early clue to this story's trajectory. The narrative recounts that Pogson is the centre of an aesthetic circle of "ingenuous youth" seeking new artistic sensations, and apparently finding them in Pogson's home and at Pogson's feet. The auguries are not however promising, and the feet are almost bound to be feet of clay:

> He was a large, sleek, pink creature, slow and rare of movement, from much sitting bulky, not to say squashy in figure, mild-eyed, slyly jovial and … resigned. A positive glutton of books, he read as instinctively, almost as unconsciously, as other men breathe. But he not only absorbed. He gave forth; and that copiously.
>
> (Malet 1922, 147)

The accumulation of adjectives is sly and insidious. What appears at first glance to be about praise of the narrator's self-discovered idol becomes more or less abject in emphasis on Pogson's pinkness; sleekness; bulk and squishiness; gluttony (even if that is only for books); and copious conversation, which has about it the disgust attached to vomit. This is retrospective narration, though, and the narrator was, at the time when the story is set, unambiguously attached to Pogson. He is looking back, he tells us, from a distance of time—"it began in the early and ended in the middle-eighties" (147). As well as describing a particular episode, he could also in that phrase suggest that the whole business of aestheticism was over by 1885, a youthful folly with no longevity and no essential meaning.

The plot itself is slight because it is about a story that is not told. The young men sit at Pogson's feet and listen to what they identify (we surmise, wrongly) as his brilliant conversation. They enjoy his hospitality and they ignore his wife. So far, so very Wildean, by the way. As W.B. Yeats recounted in his *Autobiographies*, when he met Wilde he was "astonished"—"I had never before heard a man talking with such perfect sentences, as if he had written them all overnight with labour and yet all spontaneous" (Yeats 1999, 124). And Wilde too surrounded himself with young men, ignored his wife, and was gluttonous (in his case not only for books). Into this regular meeting at Pogson's salon, one of the young men brings his sister, Arabella, and her appearance is disastrous: "For she had received insufficient instruction in ritual, in the suitable forms of approach to so august a presence as our host" (Malet 1922, 152). Again, Yeats provides a touchstone. Writing of Lionel Johnson, he says, "Johnson's favourite phrase, that life is ritual, expressed something that was in some degree in all our thoughts" (Yeats 1999, 234). The repeated acts of homage of Pogson's admirers blind them to his emptiness. Arabella is not so blind. She teases Pogson to read a little from the novel he is supposed to be writing. He refuses but offers instead a passage he has been working on, quoted verbatim from memory.

As the narrator and Arabella's brother walk her home that night, Arabella mischievously identifies the passage as an act of plagiarism:

> Why, it was good to the point of being inevitable. One seemed—I certainly did—to know every phrase, every word, which was coming. None could have been other, or have been placed otherwise than it was—and that's the highest praise one can give to anybody's prose, surely. One jumped to the perfect rightness of the whole—a rightness so perfect as to make the passage sound quite extraordinarily familiar.
>
> (154)

Its familiarity derives from the fact that it is taken wholesale from George Meredith's *The Egoist*, a brilliantly ironic choice given that literary theft from a text with that title speaks to Pogson's utter lack of personality, not to the assertion of personality as genius. Wilde matters here too, for of course, he was accused of plagiarism repeatedly, from his first volume of poems in 1881, via his acrimonious disputes with Whistler in the 1880s (Wilde: I wish I had said that. Whistler: You will, Oscar, you will.[1]), through to the reception of *Salomé* in 1894. For Pogson, though, this demand to share his work, and the suspicion that he has been detected as a fraud, is the beginning of the end. The narrator begins to absent himself from the salon, jumps at the chance to travel abroad, and only returns eighteen months later to the news that Arabella has married someone else and that Pogson has died. The narrative ends with his confrontation with Pogson's unconsidered wife whom he visits to offer his conventional condolences. She rounds on him as someone she hates as the indirect cause of her husband's misery. Her husband, she says, "did not possess the creative faculty." There was never any chance that he would produce a novel, and the expectation that he might made his life a burden to him. Even the hospitality that the young admirers had enjoyed as fraudulent—based on materialism not on art: "'All the money was mine,' she said" (161–2) in the last words of the story. The wife was ignored during her husband's life, but whatever art he possessed was down to her alone.

The narrator of "The Birth of a Masterpiece" never comments on the ending of his aesthetic dream. But the narrator of Malet's unpublished story—which is also therefore an almost untold story—"In Memoriam: Ernest D. Chesterfield" may just be deliberately trashing the posthumous reputation of his subject and of Oscar Wilde too, though this is a crafty story, and it is hard to be sure how 'knowing' the narrative actually is about the real nature of its eponymous (anti-)hero. The reader, though, knows that Chesterfield was an indolent bully (he offers "caressing attentions to those of his school fellows who had lately received a remittance in money or in kind from home" and he permitted younger schoolboys to "recite Latin verses ... to him, which with delicate self-abnegation he subsequently sent up to his house or form master as his own" ("In Memoriam" n.d., 222).[2] We can intuit that he was insincere. And in the bathos provided by the narrator's incongruous juxtaposition of commentary on his clothing and on his morals, we can also see his flagrant, if lazy, disavowal of conventional proprieties:

> He always wore flannel shirts. He continued to wear them, I believe, to the end. I remember meeting him once in Pall Mall ... in the height of the London season. He was then wearing a flannel shirt, an applied turned town white linen collar and a red silk tie confined by a gold ring. He had a deep seated dislike of all restraint.
>
> ("In Memoriam" n.d., 223)

He is also greedy: "At meals, I remember, the quiet self-recollection ... was especially remarkable" (223). He lives in the moment because it suits him in a deeply debased version of Walter Pater's more ascetic aesthetic vision in *The Renaissance*, where living for the moment's sake is the aim of a well-lived life.[3]

Like Pogson, Chesterfield is also the centre of a coterie of young men, but his influence on them is more harmful than Pogson's. He encourages them to indolence to match his own, and he gives them advice: "younger men opened their innocent hearts to him" in rooms, like Basil

Hallward's in *The Picture of Dorian Gray* (though Chesterfield's are more sordid and less pretty), where he lolls around in "his untidy, picturesque sitting-room ... lying at full length among the sad coloured cushions of his divan" (225). He is not, either physically or morally, an upright character, Malet's narrator points out, though this narrator might be saying more than he means to. Chesterfield's life's philosophy, which he passes on to his acolytes, is summed up by a quotation from Molière's *Tartuffe* (the Hypocrite, as if we needed more evidence), which translates roughly as saying that it is useful knowledge to be able to stretch the limits of our consciences and to justify our evil actions with the purity our intentions. Or more shortly, so long as you mean well it does not matter what you do.

Schaffer is right to point out that the décor of aestheticism, its ideas, objects, images, and style, are all part of what makes Malet's literary palette. Her writing is a response to literature à la mode of the late Victorian period. I wonder, though, if that is quite the same as saying that she herself was an aesthete. The sustained hostility to the useless lives of egocentric men, her satirical use of both the trope of the unconsummated artistic endeavour, her pastiche of James's late style, and utter disapproval of false idols and foolish disciples, all point to the possibility that she would have disavowed a label about which she so clearly felt ambivalent. Using the tools of the trade of aestheticism is not quite the same thing as agreeing with their philosophical basis. Malet was perhaps, more of a borrower of the peacock plumes for her own purposes rather than a wholehearted member of the order of the green carnation.

Notes

1 See for example Bristow et al. (2011) for the repeated accusations and repeated evidence of Wilde's borrowings.
2 All references to this story will be given parenthetically and refer to the transcript of the story published in this edition.
3 In Pater's version: "Not the fruit of experience, but experience itself, is the end. A counted number of pulses only is given to us of a variegated dramatic life. How may we see in them all that is to be seen in them by the finest senses?" (Pater 1980, 188).

Works Cited

Bristow, Joseph, and Rebecca N. Mitchell. "On Oscar Wilde and Plagiarism." *The Public Domain Review*. Internet Source. Available at https://publicdomainreview.org/2016/01/13/on-oscar-wilde-and-plagiarism/ (accessed 12 February 2018).

Egerton, George. 1894. "A Lost Masterpiece." *The Yellow Book* 1: 189–96. Reprinted in Kostas Boyiopoulos, Yoonjoung Choi, and Matthew Brinton Tildsley (eds.). 2015. *The Decadent Short Story: An Annotated Anthology*, 98–103. Edinburgh: Edinburgh University Press.

Grand, Sarah. 1894. "The Undefinable: A Fantasia" reprinted in Angelique Richardson (Ed.). 2002. *Women Who Did: Stories by Men and Women 1890–1914*. London: Penguin.

James, Henry. 1962a. "The Private Life" reprinted in *The Complete Tales of Henry James, Volume VIII*, edited by Leon Edel. London: Rupert Hart-Davis.

James, Henry. 1962b. "The Death of a Lion." In *The Complete Tales of Henry James, Volume VIII*, edited by Leon Edel. London: Rupert Hart-Davis.

Krueger, Kate. 2014. *British Women Writers and the Short Story, 1850–1930*. Basingstoke: Palgrave.

Malet, Lucas. 1922. "The Birth of a Masterpiece." In *Da Silva's Widow and Other Stories*, 145–162. London: Hutchinson.

Malet, Lucas. "In Memoriam, Ernest D. Chesterfield." L. Tom Perry Special Collections, Harold B. Lee Library, Brigham Young University, Utah. MSS 8149, n.p.

Pater, Walter. 1980. *The Renaissance: Studies in Art and Poetry, the 1893 Text*, edited by Donald L. Hill. Los Angeles: University of California Press.

Schaffer, Talia. 2000. *The Forgotten Female Aesthetes: Literary Culture in Late Victorian England*. Charlottesville: University of Virginia Press.

Index

Note: Page number followed by "n" denote notes.

www.ingramcontent.com/pod-product-compliance
Lightning Source LLC
Chambersburg PA
CBHW071510110726
47908CB00003B/791

* 9 7 8 0 3 6 7 6 6 1 9 3 9 *